THE LAST NINE INNINGS

Inside the Real Game Fans Never See

Charles C. Euchner

Sourcebooks, Inc.®
Naperville, Illinois

Published by Sourcebooks, Inc.
P.O. Box 4410, Naperville, Illinois 60567–4410
(630) 961-3900
FAX: (630) 961-2168
www.sourcebooks.com

Library of Congress Cataloging-in-Publication Data
Euchner, Charles C.
The last nine innings / Charles C. Euchner.
p. cm.
ISBN 1-4022-0579-1 (alk. paper)
1. World Series (Baseball) (2001) 2. New York Yankees (Baseball team) 3. Arizona Diamondbacks (Baseball team) 4. Baseball. I. Title.

GV878.4.E93 2005
796.357´648—dc22

2005019882

Printed and bound in the United States of America
LB 10 9 8 7 6 5 4 3 2 1

For Isabel

ACKNOWLEDGMENTS

Writing is a lot like pitching. Both writer and pitcher hold the basic responsibility for the job at hand. But no matter what he does, the writer or pitcher needs incredible help from a team to succeed.

Dozens of baseball people made the book possible. Most of them can be found in quotations from interviews. Some others deserve special recognition. The Arizona Diamondbacks, specifically Mike Swanson and Susan Webner, helped arrange interviews, made me feel welcome at the team's spring training facility and ballpark in Phoenix, and provided great photographs. The New York Yankees also offered generous help. Rick Cerrone opened the Bronx Bombers' field and clubhouse and Al Santisiere provided photographs

The statistics companies Tendu, Stats Inc., and Inside Edge provided proprietary data and graphics so that I could understand the game's inner logic. The American Sports Medicine Institute—most particularly Glenn Fleisig and his research team—let me see their studies in action, explained their findings in detail, and provided images used in this book.

My literary agent, the creative Sorche Fairbank, helped develop the idea at its earliest stages and stayed engaged until the very end. My wise editor, Hillel Black of Sourcebooks, kept me focused and provided invaluable advice throughout the project. Other professionals at Sourcebooks helped to shepherd the book from conception to birth—most notably, CEO and publisher Dominique Raccah, editorial director Todd Stocke, editors Jill Amack and Stephanie Frerich, designer Matt Diamond, and publicist Tony Viardo.

Pete Fornatale helped me think through the original idea. John Tierney gave one of the final drafts a thorough and thoughtful reading. Eric Kramer also offered good criticisms. Mark Kramer of Harvard's Nieman Fellowship let me sit in his seminar about nonfiction narrative writing.

My greatest thanks are due to Wayne Coffey and Isabel Chenoweth. Wayne has encouraged me and embraced me for what I am since I was a high-school kid writing for an obscure Long Island newspaper. Isabel has been a dear friend for almost as long. She has believed in me so completely it's almost scary. I dedicate this book to her, with love.

CONTENTS

PREGAME: Prelude to a World Series Classic vii

FIRST INNING

1. Four-Tenths of a Second 1
2. Gambling Early 7

SECOND INNING

3. Bodies in Motion 17
4. Inside the Diamond 33
5. Calling the Game 45
6. *Dramatis Personae* *59*

THIRD INNING

7. Standing at the Plate 69
8. Swinging Styles 75

FOURTH INNING

9. The Philosophy of Pitching .93
10. The Science of Pitching 107

FIFTH INNING

11. Trench Warfare 127
12. Managing the Game 141

SIXTH INNING

13. The Numbers Game 153
14. Strategy of Scoring 163
15. The Next Generation 181

SEVENTH INNING

16. Virtues of Veterans 191
17. Specialization 207

EIGHTH INNING

18. Going Global 217
19. Striving 229
20. Mo 239

NINTH INNING

21. The Big Unit 253
22. Breaks of the Game 265
23. End Game 279

POSTGAME: Ecstasy and Agony 289

Index 297

SPORTS
NOVEMBER 4, 2001
Photo courtesy of Arizona Diamondbacks
Fans at Bank One Ball Park remember September 11
MORE INSIDE

Baseball provided an emotional salve for a nation stunned by the terrorist attacks of September 11. Fans at stadiums across the country—including Bank One Ballpark, the site of the final game of the World Series—expressed a patriotic fervor rarely seen in sports.

PREGAME

In which one of baseball's greatest Fall Classics produces two stunning ninth-inning rallies, historic pitching performances, a parade of the game's most compelling players—and unites a grieving nation

PRELUDE TO A WORLD SERIES CLASSIC

THREE TALL, THIN young men clothed in long undershorts and T-shirts, with reflective markers the size of golf balls taped to twelve joints, took turns pitching off a plywood bank.

The men—top pitching prospects of the Boston Red Sox—threw first casually and then powerfully off the makeshift mound. A crew of researchers recorded every movement with scientific precision. The researchers used six infrared motion analysis cameras positioned on both sides of the pitcher and four video cameras positioned above, in front of, and alongside the pitcher.

Al Nipper and I were sitting on folding chairs in the gym/lab operated by the American Sports Medicine Institute. "If they had this when I was playing, I might have lasted a few more years," Nipper said. "This shows you things that I never really knew happened." Nipper pitched for seven years. Three years older than Roger Clemens, he left the majors fifteen years before Clemens played his twenty-first season in 2005. Nipper played an important role on the Red Sox team that almost won the World Series in 1986, winning ten games in 159 innings, but he never achieved the power or durability of his friend, nicknamed the Rocket.

The American Sports Medicine Institute is a research organization founded by the legendary Dr. James Andrews. Andrews is known best as the pioneer of Tommy John surgery, the procedure in which tendons from a wrist or hamstring are used to reconstruct the ligament in the pitcher's elbow. Once a radical medical treatment, the surgery has come to symbolize a revolution in sports medicine. Injuries once considered unanswerable calls for surrender—shoulder and elbow injuries, knee and hip injuries, back ailments—have been answered by Tommy John and other innovative procedures. If athletes dedicate themselves to their rehabilitation, many injuries that once ended careers early can now be fixed. Some pitchers coming back from Tommy John surgery actually throw harder than they did before their injuries.

Still, Andrews was dismayed by the lengthening parade of injured pitchers and other athletes to his operating room at the University of Alabama in Birmingham. And so he created the ASMI to undertake scientific studies of the movements of athletes to determine how to reduce the incidence of injuries. He logic was simple: If a player can learn how to throw, swing, run, slide, and kick the right way, he will put minimal strain on the vulnerable parts of his body. The injuries that do the most to disable athletes—repetitive-action injuries, sustained by continuous pressure and pounding on body parts—could be minimized and even eliminated.

As they studied ways to prevent injuries, Andrews and his team of researchers also found the motions that enabled athletes to perform expertly. The ASMI has logged video and computer analyses of almost a thousand pitchers and identified a sequence of movements that enable the pitcher to throw safely and effectively. Roger Clemens was one of about fifty pitchers that ASMI concluded had virtually perfect mechanics.

◆ ◆ ◆

I WAS VISITING the American Sports Medicine Institute because I wanted to understand why the pitching motion of Clemens was so superior. Part of me wanted to believe that Clemens was a freak of nature—everyone likes the mythology of the superman, right?—but I thought his dedication and near-perfect mechanics offered a more telling explanation. I wanted to understand the phenomenon of Roger Clemens because I was trying to understand the underlying logic of the seventh game of the 2001 World Series between the New York Yankees and the Arizona Diamondbacks.

I decided to write about the 2001 Fall Classic when, early for a meeting in Boston, I went to a nearby bookstore to pass some time. I picked up John McPhee's *Levels of the Game,* a dramatic rendering of a tennis match in 1968 between Arthur Ashe and Clark Graebner. McPhee's work explains what happened on the court by examining the lives of the players—where they came from, what they believed, how they trained, where they got their passion. McPhee managed to keep a decades-old match exciting and beautiful forever. But McPhee's account did even more. In 150 brief pages, McPhee used that match to say something revealing about sports, families, race, class, business, and psychology. Not everything, but something.

In a flash, I decided that someone should try to do the same thing for baseball. In that same flash, I decided that the seventh game of the 2001 World Series provided a perfect subject for such a work.

The 2001 World Series finale—which the Diamondbacks won in the bottom of the ninth inning to end the Yankees' string of three straight championships—might not have been the most exciting baseball game ever. In the modern era, the game that Carlton Fisk won with a dramatic arm-waving home run, which sent the 1975 series to a seventh game between the Boston Red Sox and Cincinnati Reds, might be the best ever. The Pittsburgh Pirates' seventh-game victory over the Yankees in 1960 was another great one. So was the New York Mets' come-from-behind win over the Red Sox in Game Six of the 1986 series. Jack Morris's ten-inning 1–0 masterpiece for the Minnesota Twins over the Atlanta Braves in 1991 remains one of the all-time classic fall pitching duels.

But the 2001 finale was not just dramatic. In nine taut innings, the game provided telling glimpses of everything that makes baseball a great sport. Four of the game's greatest pitchers—Roger Clemens, Curt Schilling, Randy Johnson, and Mariano Rivera—delivered textbook performances of intelligence and power. One of the game's rising stars,

Alfonso Soriano, displayed the drama of power hitting. Fielders like Steve Finley, Derek Jeter, and Mark Grace made clutch plays that demanded to be deconstructed. Some of the game's old stars, like Matt Williams and Tino Martinez and Paul O'Neill, showed how they could shape a game while making outs. And finally, one of the game's slugging stars, Luis Gonzalez, won the game when he choked up and barely made contact—and, as luck would have it, dropped a soft fly ball into a part of the field recently left untended by the Yankee fielders.

Few games say so much in such a dramatic way as the Diamondbacks' 3–2 win over the Yankees in Phoenix on November 4, 2001.

◆ ◆ ◆

SOMETHING ELSE GAVE the 2001 World Series finale its enduring meaning. The game capped the most emotional six weeks of baseball ever played.

On the warm and clear morning of September 11, Moslem extremists hijacked four airplanes, crashing two planes into the World Trade Center towers in lower Manhattan, one into the Pentagon in suburban Washington, D.C., and one in a field in western Pennsylvania.

Baseball suspended play from September 11 to September 16. When the players returned, they felt awkward about playing a game at a time of national tragedy and danger. But the games provided a salve. The players embodied the nation's fears, but they also embodied a desperate will to do something ordinary.

"The first flight, everybody was real nervous," remembers Shane Spencer, who played outfield for the Yankees. "We flew into Chicago and rough, real bad weather. The plane was bouncing all over the place. We got off the plane and everybody was nervous because we see the Sears Tower. I'm like, 'Oh man, is that going to go next? What's going to happen?' It's freaky, because everybody all saw the towers go down. Next thing you know, a plane just flies right over our head, and I swear, half the bus jumped up. That's how nervous we were."

Once play resumed, stadiums across the nation took on a new mood. Teams honored firefighters and police—the people who risked and gave their lives to rescue victims of the attacks—in ceremonies before games.

Huge American flags unfurled and the fans sang "God Bless America" and "America the Beautiful" before and during games. Fans chanted "USA! USA!" as if exhorting Olympians.

"We didn't play our best ball. But still there was something magical," Spencer told me. "We had to go through some tough times. You come to the field and you want to play baseball. And they're having a special ceremony for the firefighters, and you're out there holding hands with firefighters and policemen, and they're all crying. And then you're crying. And the fans are crying. And you're looking at the people crying in the stands, and you're like, 'Is this really that important?' But to the fans, it was. And we rode that. We just had some magical moments. We hit some big home runs. You know, the Diamondbacks really could have swept us in four games. But there was something about Yankee Stadium that is just magical and we found a way."

Everywhere they went, the Yankees became poignant ambassadors of New York. Players from both New York teams visited Ground Zero, the still-smoldering superblocks of Lower Manhattan where the 110-story Twin Towers stood. Visitors did the same.

"We had serious reservations about going to Ground Zero," Arizona Diamondbacks manager Bob Brenly said, years later, tears in his eyes. "We didn't want to trivialize the efforts that were going on down there at the time. And several of the players chose not to go. But for the guys that wanted to go, it was one of those life-changing experiences. Seeing something that just was so overwhelming that there was no way to safely tuck it away and be done with it.... Once we got there, they were so glad to see Curt Schilling and Randy Johnson and all these guys who took the time to come down there. A lot of the rescue workers were dialing up their family on the cell phone and having Schill and R.J. say hello to the kids at home."

◆ ◆ ◆

I DON'T PUT much stock in elegiac and mythical portrayals of baseball. Contrary to the late Yale scholar and baseball commissioner Bart Giamatti, baseball does not embody mankind's eternal Odyssean struggle to return home. Contrary to poets like Donald Hall, baseball is not an essential source of bonding between fathers and sons. Contrary to essayists like Jacques Barzun and George Will, baseball doesn't provide the most telling lens into the American psyche.

But baseball is a damn good game, and sometimes it unfolds in ways that astonish and please even cynics. Sometimes, because it can astonish and please, the game creates something that *seems* bigger than it really is. And people sometimes need something that seems bigger than it is.

Illusion is okay once in a while, especially when you need a reprieve from pain.

When the Yankees returned to the Bronx, they carried the city's emotions forward into October and November. Even though they weren't baseball's best team in 2001—they won only 95 games, compared with the Seattle Mariners' 116 wins—they seemed to possess a rare karma. They won when they needed, often in dramatic fashion. Derek Jeter made a magical play in the first round of the playoffs against the Oakland A's, and then Jeter and Martinez and Soriano produced two of the most stunning comebacks ever in the last two nights of baseball at Yankee Stadium.

◆ ◆ ◆

WHEN I DECIDED to write about the 2001 finale, I started with videotapes of the game. I looked at the pitching motions of Curt Schilling and the other pitchers and found myself fascinated with the subtle but violent movements of the body.

I watched Derek Jeter catch a relay from the outfield and make a perfect throw to third base, and I was amazed just how much went into that one play. It first looked like Jeter made the play all in one motion, but the play was really an exquisite display of complex coordination. It could—and should—be broken down into a whole series of perfect movements.

I watched Steve Finley glide across the outfield and I wondered how he could be so physically and mentally smart. Finley and other fielders provided astonishing performances of power ballet every night. I wanted to understand how that ballet works.

I watched great hitters like Matt Williams and Derek Jeter, Luis Gonzalez and Mark Grace, and I wanted to separate what was basic from what was unique in their batting styles.

Scientists at ASMI and other research institutions study every aspect of athletes' physical movements. What kinds of force and rotation did pitchers cause when they reared back and threw a ball? What's the best pitching motion for power and control and the health of the pitcher? How did a batter create power to hit a ball? What factors affected the ball's movement before and after it hit the bat? How do fielders perceive the ball's movement into the field, even before the batter hit it?

Even further away from the world of real athletes, statisticians sat in rooms glowing with computer screens and worked to discover the hidden patterns of the game. I wondered: How much can statistics tell? Will the explosion of statistical analysis suck the life out of a game long known for the smarts that come from a lifetime of involvement? And how might a new generation of statistics revolutionize the physical conditioning, training, and care of players?

If statistics are but cold indicators of performance, how can we move inward and understand the psyches of players? What inner traits do winners have? How do players like the Yankees' Paul O'Neill and Bernie Williams and the Diamondbacks' Randy Johnson and Curt Schilling show about the psychology of elite performance?

At a time when so much of the game is reduced to scientific examination and action, I also wondered why the best players seemed to come from Latin America. If we have become a nation of superkids with superparents who hire supercoaches and use videos and stats and scientific research to teach throwing, hitting, running, and sliding to the privileged scions of the American Dream, why do so many great and innovative players come from places where bats need to be carved out of tree trunks?

◆ ◆ ◆

THE 2001 WORLD SERIES provided the ultimate story line for these kinds of questions.

The Diamondbacks took the first two games of the World Series in Phoenix, behind the power pitching of Curt Schilling and Randy

Johnson. When the Series moved to New York's Yankee Stadium for Game Three, Roger Clemens and Mariano Rivera—arguably the best starter and the best reliever in baseball history—pitched the Yankees to a 2–1 victory.

With the Yankees trailing in the Series two games to one, the pitching clinic continued in Game Four. Schilling dominated the Yankees again, yielding just one run and three hits over seven innings while striking out nine batters. But as midnight approached on Halloween, the surreal prevailed. While leading Game Four by a 3–1 score, the Diamondbacks' manager Bob Brenly took Schilling out of the game in the eighth inning. Byung-Hyun Kim, a dynamic reliever from South Korea, came in to close the game. Kim used his baffling submarine motion to strike out three Yankees in the eighth inning. But in the ninth inning, Paul O'Neill dropped a soft single into the outfield and then Tino Martinez got his first hit of the Series—a line drive home run over the short right-field fence. After Kim got the first two Yankees in the tenth inning, Derek Jeter homered over the right-field wall on a 3–2 count to give the Yankees a stunning victory. The Yankees pulled even with the Diamondbacks, two games apiece.

The next night produced an even more dramatic finish. The Diamondbacks' Miguel Batista pitched seven and two-thirds scoreless innings and Greg Swindell quelled a brief Yankee rally in the eighth. The Diamondbacks again asked Kim to protect a two-run lead in the bottom of the ninth. With a runner on second and two outs, the slumping veteran Scott Brosius slammed a flat slider over the left-field wall to tie the game. With the inning over, Kim's teammates rushed to the mound to console him. Alfonso Soriano singled home the game winner in the twelfth inning.

Despite the Diamondbacks' brutal losses in the fourth and fifth games of the series, an eerie calm prevailed in the clubhouse. "As devastating as the losses could have been, I don't think it really made much of a ripple," Bob Brenly remembers. "It was almost as if the players were laughing: 'Can you *believe* it happened again?' I never sensed any desperation or 'Oh my God, we blew our chance to win a World Series.' It was almost like it was out of our hands. Certain aspects of this game are just meant to be. All the preparation in the world and all the effort in the world—sometimes it doesn't make any difference."

Brenly experienced this kind of gods-must-be-crazy atmosphere once before. Back in 1986, playing for the San Francisco Giants against the Atlanta Braves, he matched a baseball record by committing four errors in one inning and later hit the game-winning home run. "When I made that fourth error at third base, it was like I left my body, and I was watching the rest of the stuff happen. It was like I had no control over it. It was just happening. It was meant to be. And there's nothing you can do to change it. That's the way I felt that day, and that's the way I felt for Game Seven."

The Diamondbacks routed the Yankees, 15–2, in the sixth game of the Series. The Yankees' Andy Pettitte tipped off his pitch selection with a hitch in his motion and the Diamondbacks hit him hard. Randy Johnson won his second Series game, yielding two runs over seven innings.

The Fall Classic was already one of the best in history when Curt Schilling trotted out to the mound on a hot November evening in Phoenix.

It was time for the last nine innings of the 2001 season.

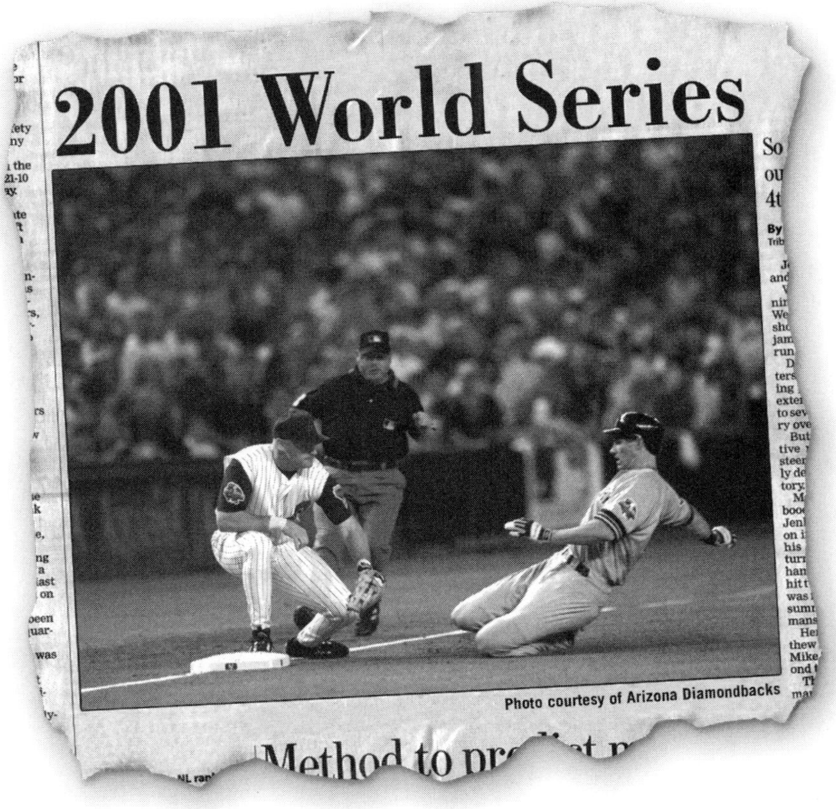

Split-second decisions often determine the shape of the game. When Paul O'Neill failed in his attempt to stretch a double into a triple in the first inning, the Yankees were deprived of a critical scoring opportunity against the power-pitching of Curt Schilling.

FIRST INNING

In which the New York Yankees and the Arizona Diamondbacks take the field one last time in 2001, both stinging from recent humiliating losses and both determined to win the finale of the World Series

Chapter One

FOUR-TENTHS OF A SECOND

EVERYTHING—THE PITCHER'S motion that medical researchers say involves the most violent act in all sports, the hitter's complex calculations about speed and movement of a five-ounce ball traveling upwards of a hundred miles an hour, the swing of the bat that generates about ten horsepower of energy, the eight thousand pounds of force of the bat against the ball—happens so fast.

From the time the pitcher releases the ball to the time the ball arrives near the plate, sixty feet and six inches from the mound, only about four-tenths of one second elapses.

The batter has about half that time—two-tenths of a second—to decide what to do. As the ball comes out of the pitcher's hand, the batter has to make countless complex calculations.

The batter tracks the ball coming out of the hand and notices the arm angle, gets a glimpse of the ball's spin, and assesses the speed of the arm's whipping action. The batter uses these calculations to make a decision about what to do with the bat when the ball is about twenty feet out of the pitcher's hand. Since it takes the batter about two-tenths of a second to swing, he has to decide what to do long before the ball approaches the plate. He has to figure out whether it's a fastball before the ball sizzles anywhere near the plate, a curveball long before the ball bends, a cutter or a splitter long before one of those exotic missiles burns in on the hands or off the plate.

When the batter makes his decision to swing, he needs to mobilize a whole army of muscles to do his bidding. The muscles activate the way troops charge over a hill, with precision and pulsing strength, in wave after wave, each supporting the other.

When the batter's eyes and brain and muscles do their job, they smash the ball in a period lasting roughly one one-thousandth of a second. For that brief interval, the ball gets squashed like a bean bag. The ball momentarily stops. The bat, which had been whipping forward at eighty or eighty-five miles an hour, gets pushed back. The bat and ball burn with the heat generated by the collision. Different sounds vibrate across space—*crack* when the ball is hit well, on the sweet spot of the bat, *clunk* when the ball is hit on other parts of the bat.

Donald Stuss, a neuropsychologist at the Rotman Research Institute in Toronto, has found that different parts of the brain contribute to processing high-speed information. Neurons in the front of the brain—specifically, the top middle area of the brain's frontal lobes—create a state of readiness for responding to high-speed stimuli. To the left of that part of the brain, a different set of nerve cells determines how and when the body should respond. On the opposite side, a different group of nerve cells determines what stimuli to filter out of consciousness. The brain cannot treat all information equally. The brain's "executive function" gathers all of this information and makes and carries out a decision about whether to swing, when, and how.

Baseball is called a "game of inches," but it's really a game of milliseconds and millimeters. Tiny fragments of time and space can make the difference between swinging and missing, fouling the ball to one side of the diamond or the other, hitting the ball on a line to the outfield or in a screaming arc over the outfield fence.

Derek Jeter, the shortstop for the defending world champion Yankees, doesn't analyze hitting much. His attitude is that if he keeps his body strong and flexible and pays attention to what's happening, his brain and body will be able to synthesize what he needs to know and do.

Jeter—the first batter in the seventh game of the 2001 World Series—guesses fastball on virtually every pitch. That way, he has enough time to adjust if he judges that the pitcher is throwing something else. Figuring out what pitch the pitcher throws can be tricky. Hitters look for clues in the speed and angle of the pitcher's arm. The best pitchers—Curt Schilling among them—throw different pitches with indistinguishable arm motions. So hitters need to look for other clues. If the ball's red seams spin to produce the appearance of a pink dot, Jeter knows the pitcher has thrown a slider and has the time to make the necessary adjustment in his swing. If he can see the ball's red stitches turning toward him, from twelve o'clock to six o'clock, he knows he's getting a curveball.

Talking about hitting, Jeter has the nonchalance of a veteran stockbroker explaining the basics of Wall Street to a rookie trader.

"To be perfectly honest, I don't even think about it too much," Jeter says. "I think a lot of times you can think too much and it gets you in trouble. I'm aggressive, swing early. I don't guess pitches. It's just more of a reaction. You just try to pick up the seams on the ball as it comes out of the pitcher's hand, as soon as possible, to tell if it's a fastball, slider, or split [fastball], whatever. Some guys pick it up sooner than others and other guys never pick it up. Seeing it isn't enough. You can see the seams and still not hit it."

◆ ◆ ◆

TO MOVE INTO his pitching motion, the Diamondbacks' Curt Schilling stands with his right leg in front, as if he is in the midst of walking forward. He burns the catcher's target with his eyes. He holds his hands in front of him, as if he is waiting for an egg toss. He lifts his hands above his head. As he turns and lifts his left leg, he leans back slightly.

The pitcher's motion is really a set of discrete jerks away from the body and back toward the body. Jerk out, jerk in. The shoulders jerk, the elbows and the wrist jerk, the back and knees jerk, the thighs and buttocks jerk. Schilling leans back on his right leg, lifting his left knee into the shape of an inverted "V," taut like an open safety pin.

Schilling's catcher, Damian Miller, lifts his glove to make a target. He waits until after Jeter trains his eyes forward. No reason to allow Jeter to look back and see what pitch he's getting.

As Schilling's back leg takes more and more of his body's weight, he brings his front leg down and moves it forward. That front leg falls almost to ground level when Schilling takes the ball from his glove and moves it behind his body. His pitching arm hangs back, waiting to be whipped forward, while his glove hand hangs in front. Then, in a moment of explosion, the right arm lashes around the body, over his shoulder and trunk and down to the other side of the body. After releasing the ball, Schilling's pitching hand almost grazes the ground.

The force of the arm's movement on a pitch can be 125 percent of the pitcher's body weight—meaning that there is a force of about 190 or 200 pounds pulling away from the shoulder socket. To keep the arm in the socket, other muscles have to exert countervailing pressure. Different parts of the body are at war with each other—some trying to pull the body apart, some trying to keep it together.

Schilling's front leg is stiff, almost straight, as he completes his motion. That stiff front leg absorbs the terrible shock that his arm has just experienced throwing the baseball.

The ball is about forty-five feet away when the batter begins to swing.

◆ ◆ ◆

THE FIRST PITCH of the seventh game of the 2001 World Series comes in toward the plate at a speed of 94 miles an hour.

Derek Jeter swings faster than most hitters, so he can take more time to commit himself to swing. The ball is one-third of the way to the plate and the right-handed Jeter has just lifted his front foot. He has not begun to swing but he has decided to do so. His feet about a foot apart, his knees bent, Jeter moves his weight to his back leg. With his arm extended, Jeter's fists slowly pull back in anticipation of a swing.

The wrists act as the swing's hinge, allowing Jeter to direct the greatest force possible to the end of the bat. On the most powerful swings, the acceleration of the bat makes it feel as if the bat's barrel is pulling the hands away from the body—but the hands resist. Centripetal (inward) force is at war with centrifugal (outward) force. As Jeter brings the bat around, his eyes focus on a zone just in front of the plate.

On this pitch, the bat comes around late and extends too far as the ball moves in. Jeter tries to pull his body in so he can get the fat part of the bat on the ball. But he can only hold his body in so far and still take his swing—to which he's already committed. The ball moves too far inside anyway. Even if Jeter had swung for an inside pitch, he could not have gotten the fat part of the bat on the ball unless he had taken a small step back in the box when taking his stance.

If he had done *that,* Schilling and Miller would adjust *their* approach. "I adjust to a batter's approach rather than his stance, unless he's consistently moving up and back in the box," Curt Schilling says. "But one thing I will do is see if he's looking a little uncomfortable in what he's doing."

Schilling has a broad repertoire to use when making his adjustments. "He could go with the 98-mile-an-hour, four-seam fastball up around the letters," Diamondbacks' manager Bob Brenly says. "He could throw the splitter in the dirt. He could drop a curveball on you. It's almost like he never really repeated pitches on the same hitters. He'd get them out one way their first at bat, and then, as they were making the adjustment, coming to the plate for their second at bat, he would do something different. And with the arsenal of pitches that he has and the command that he has, unless he was really having a bad day, the opposing team is at his mercy."

Jeter fouls the pitch toward the first base stands and tumbles forward out of the batter's box. By trying to pull in his body to make a full swing on the inside pitch, Jeter loses his balance. He lets go of his top hand as the bat reaches out to the other side of his body. His whole body twists away from the plate, from the ball, from the pitcher. Soon all his weight is on his back foot—a sure sign that he has been fooled. The bat wraps behind Jeter's body. He hops his way back to a balanced position.

◆ ◆ ◆

On one pitch, Schilling shows that he has the command he needs to play an inside-outside game with the Yankees. Pitch 'em in on the hands, or up by the eyes, and then go away off the plate.

Schilling's goal tonight is to get hitters to strike out or hit weak pop flies. If Schilling's pitches weren't so hard, the flies might go for doubles and triples and homers. But the fly balls come on harmless inside-out swings, on late swings, on checked swings. And Schilling has the best defense in the National League to chase down those fly balls.

The next three pitches veer inside, high and then low. Schilling throws the fourth pitch off the plate, 97 miles per hour. It arcs from several feet off the plate to just off the plate's outside corner. Jeter leans over to look at the pitch. Umpire Steve Rippley pulls an imaginary chainsaw to call strike three. Jeter's out.

Later, Jeter is asked about the pitch. "It was a foot outside," he says. "But Schilling is pitching. He's going to get a foot plus. The strike zone gets bigger when Schilling is pitching."

Jeter wears a look of sarcastic amusement as he stands for a moment at the plate. He slowly walks away, shaking his head.

CHAPTER TWO

GAMBLING EARLY

THE INSTANT THAT a batter puts the ball into play, he becomes a base runner and needs to shift from a narrow focus on hitting the ball to a broad focus on the flow of the game on the whole field. The moment he becomes a base runner, he has the opportunity to put pressure on the defense to make mistakes. In a close game, even between two superior teams, mistakes determine who wins and who loses.

Those thoughts are on Paul O'Neill's mind when he swings like a cricket player at a one-ball pitch from Curt Schilling in the top of the first inning.

With one out, O'Neill stands erect at the plate, wags the bat stiffly, like a reluctant wave across a room. His face twitches, tight in concentration. He looks like the Man in the Yellow Hat, the patient guardian of the children's book character Curious George—square-jawed, angular, strong, focused.

A left-handed hitter, O'Neill takes the first pitch low and inside for a ball. He is window-shopping on that pitch, content to see what kinds of pitches Curt Schilling might be selling tonight. He wants to assess

Schilling, get ahead in the count to set up a pitch over the plate. He barely moves but mutters to himself as he stands in for the second pitch.

The second pitch comes in knee-high on the inside part of the plate, and O'Neill whacks it. As Schilling releases the ball, O'Neill moves his front foot straight out, like he's going to kick a can. He swings sooner than Jeter. He has to, since his bat speed has slowed with age. His eyes track the ball, his head motionless. He holds his bat close to his body. He extends the bat forward rather than taking a full roundhouse swing, as if tossing out a ball on a chain. But he grips the bat with both hands all the way around. O'Neill's front foot anchors his body as he hits the ball.

As he completes his swing, he's already running to first base. The jerk of the bat pulls his legs into motion. Instantly, he changes from hitter to base runner.

The ball floats into right-center field, bouncing twice before hitting the wall. Right fielder Danny Bautista runs hard to get to the ball, waving his hands to slow down. Bautista picks up the ball as it drops off the fence.

"When I saw him get the ball, I'm looking at O'Neill and I'm like, 'Go to third, go to third,'" center fielder Steve Finley remembers. "I wanted O'Neill to run, because I knew when the ball was in flight, he's going to be out. With any kind of throw at all, he's going to be out." Bautista has the same thought: "I always hope the guys go for it. The guy's really hustling up. But if he goes for more than a double, we got more chance to get out of the inning."

Before the play, Finley told Bautista to play in straightaway right field. As he chased the ball, Bautista listened for Finley's instructions. "When you go pick up the ball, you don't know what to do. You don't see the cutoff man. He can see it right away. Fins said, 'Hit the cut-off!'"

Spread-eagle, Bautista throws the ball into short center field, beyond second base, where second baseman Craig Counsell and shortstop Tony Womack wait.

O'Neill considers stopping with an easy double but picks up the pace just as he reaches second base. But his foot lands on the top of the base—*plop!*—rather than cutting the corner the way the textbook teaches. As he motors to third base, O'Neill runs straight up, his midsection steady as he churns his fists. He keeps his eyes on third base.

By the time O'Neill has reached second, Counsell grabs the cutoff throw on one bounce, belt high. Womack drops in front of Counsell to get out of his way. In one motion, Counsell throws a hard rainbow to the outfield side of third base where Matt Williams waits to catch the ball.

Williams takes the throw high and slaps down the tag. He has enough time to check that he's swiping in the right place and that O'Neill has not beaten the throw or hooked around the tag.

"I'm looking where Danny's at and I'm looking where Counsell's lining up and I'm trying to position myself on either side of that bag to receive that ball so it doesn't hit Paul," Williams says. "Regardless of where the ball is coming from—left field, right field, center field—the runner's always in the way. It's not like second base when the runner's stealing and you have a clear path from the catcher to the shortstop or second baseman for that tag. That runner's always conflicting with the flight of the ball. You need to get in a position where you can have a clear view."

As Williams tags O'Neill, he holds his glove up to show umpire Ed Rapuano that he still has the ball. Rapuano calls O'Neill out, punching the air for emphasis.

Tim McCarver, a former star catcher for the St. Louis Cardinals and Philadelphia Phillies, is calling the game for the national Fox TV audience. He tells the audience that O'Neill took a smart gamble with his try for a triple. When you force the other team to execute defensive plays perfectly, you can take an extra base or two—and set up a big inning. *In fact, all other things being equal, baserunning is the most important element of the game on the field.*

"If you have two lineups with the same level of players, and they are just as good as each other on hitting and pitching and fielding, the team that runs the bases aggressively and well will clean their clock every time," McCarver says later. There's an added bonus: "You're going to make fewer mistakes running aggressively and well than running cautiously. O'Neill did exactly the right thing." Just as fielders make more mistakes when they back up on a ball rather than attack the ball, base runners lose quickness and judgment when they hesitate.

Problem is, McCarver says, most players do not understand the need to shift their mindset from that of a hitter to that of a runner once they hit the ball. "I see players hit the ball and they think their job is over, but in reality their job is just beginning," he says, his booming Southern drawl rising to a squeak. "Baserunning determines who wins games more than anything else. Just watch the way they go to first base. You see players—I don't want to name names, but Juan Gonzalez and Ruben Sierra come to mind—who just watch as the ball is going into the gap and they run to the bag. But the right way to run the bases, the only way, is to run through the bag. It's that extra bit of aggressiveness and alertness that matters. It's about being in the game all the time."

Baseball usually requires players to focus their attention on one thing. Pitchers want to put the ball where the hitter can't hit it hard; batters want to hit the ball on the sweet spot. Fielders want to first catch the ball, then throw it to the right player. But baserunning requires a knowledge and awareness of the game's flow similar to that of a basketball or hockey player. Wayne Gretzky was hockey's greatest player because he seemed to see the puck 360 degrees around him, and anticipate plays three, four, or even five plays ahead. Great base runners do the same. They know whether to challenge a fielder's arm before the ball is hit into play, before the ball skips or dies on the grass, before the ball jumps off the bat hard or softly, before the fielder shows whether he can get forward movement on a throw, before other fielders align themselves for cutoff throws.

How much easier would it be for the Yankees to score with a runner on third? Baseball Prospectus, a statistics and analysis Internet site, gathered statistics for every game situation during the 2001 season. Analysts at BP have determined the average number of runs a team could expect to score in an inning under twenty-four different situations. Teams with one out and a runner on third base can expect to score .9790 runs; teams with a runner on second and one out can expect to score .7026 runs. That's a difference of .2764 runs. But getting thrown out at third is costly; teams can expect to score only .1160 runs with two outs and no runners. (See chart on page 165.)

Statistically, O'Neill's gamble might not make much sense. The payoff is not great enough to justify the risk. But O'Neill wanted to force the Diamondbacks to make a mistake. Whatever the risk, he wanted to try to get the Yankees an early lead in the game. An early run against Schilling is worth a lot to the Yankees with their ace, Roger Clemens, on the mound.

The Yankees have struggled to get men into scoring position throughout the World Series. Until Game Six, when they were losing 15–0, the Yankees failed to advance a single runner to third base with fewer than two outs. O'Neill was trying to give the Yankees an early scoring possibility.

"Any kink in that chain and he's safe," Matt Williams says. Getting the runner requires perfect execution of actions at three points on an imaginary line from the outfield wall to third base. "Counsell's job is to get it there as quickly as he can get it there, on a line, whether it's on a line or on one hop or two hops or whatever—get it there before the runner. His job is to throw it to the base, not to avoid the runner. My job is to position myself so that I can come around the runner and catch it and swipe him as he's coming around."

A couple years ago, O'Neill would have been safe. He's still a supreme physical specimen, but baseball's actuarial tables say O'Neill is now an old man. His success depends more and more on judgment and will, less and less on physical prowess.

On this play, the Diamondbacks' physical skills and execution beat O'Neill's daring.

◆ ◆ ◆

THE CROWD EXPLODES.

"That play right there got our fans into the game," left fielder Luis Gonzalez says. "We're feeling pretty good then...when that play happened, after we're walking back to our positions, people are going nuts. So you knew it was going to be an emotional game. During that play, I was constantly telling myself to calm down. You're just so hyper. It's the game you've been waiting your whole life for. Seven games is great for the fans and for the national audiences. But for players, you're an emotional wreck when you go to Game Seven."

◆ ◆ ◆

As Curt Schilling and then Roger Clemens settle into their pitching grooves, the rest of the first inning takes the slow, steady beat of the first movement of Ravel's *Bolero*.

The Yankees' cool-jazz center fielder, Bernie Williams, lifts an outside fastball to center field to end the visitors' half of the first inning.

Roger Clemens has no trouble dispatching the Diamondbacks in the bottom of the first inning. After Tony Womack pops out, Craig Counsell reaches when Tino Martinez fumbles a ground ball and Clemens fumbles his toss at first base. But no matter. Clemens gets Luis Gonzalez on a groundout and Matt Williams on a strikeout.

Two minor moments of drama—hints of a quickening pace to come—occur after the Martinez-Clemens error. Counsell dances off first base, distracting Clemens and prompting him to make two pickoff throws. Clemens picked off Counsell in the opening frame of Game Three, but the Diamondbacks' infielder controls the cat-and-mouse game now. Later, with two strikes on Matt Williams, catcher Jorge Posada drops a foul tip, giving the slugger an extra swing.

But it doesn't matter. The next pitch, a forkball over the plate, gets Williams swinging.

Williams is rueful about Clemens's masterful alternation of down-and-away and up-and-in pitches. "You want the ball up but he throws that riding fastball that you have to lay off," Williams says. "And his split-finger [pitch] is one of the most difficult pitches to hit because it looks—as its coming out of his hand—like a fastball. Those were the pitches I was fouling off. It looks like a fastball so you go commit yourself to swing. He throws hard so you have to commit. And then the ball just falls out of the strike zone. So at that point, you're just trying to get your bat to it somehow."

Not always successfully, even with an extra swing.

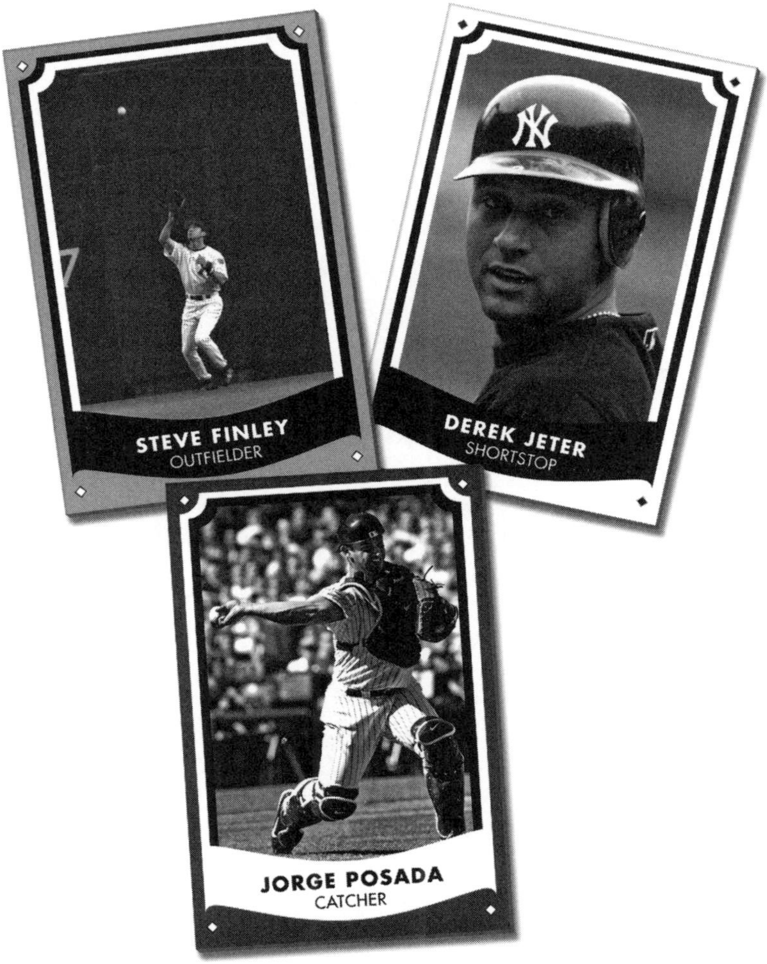

Defense is the invisible dimension in baseball. Good fielding improves pitching dramatically, but assessing fielding skills can be a tricky proposition. Steve Finley has long been acknowledged as a superb center fielder. Derek Jeter's skills at shortstop provoke great debate. After early struggles, Jorge Posada has become a strong receiver.

Photos courtesy of New York Yankees and Arizona Diamondbacks

SECOND INNING

In which the art of fielding—
the game's power ballet—and
a new approach to training
take center stage

Chapter Three

BODIES IN MOTION

As the Yankees' left fielder Shane Spencer walks to home plate in the top of the second inning, Curt Schilling turns to remind his fielders where to position themselves. Schilling spent the previous day reviewing video clips of the Yankees' hitters. How did he retire Bernie Williams in Game One? How about Derek Jeter? Where did the Yankees hit the ball and how hard? How did umpire Steve Rippley call balls and strikes in his previous game? Schilling knows what has happened with every hitter he has faced, and he has an idea of how to pitch every batter on every pitch.

Positioning the fielders would not do much good if Schilling didn't have dartlike control. "He can put the ball where he wants to," says Craig Colbrunn, a utility infielder for the Diamondbacks. "If he's going to pitch a hitter away, we're going to play him away and the guy's not going to yank it."

Steve Finley moves to the shallow part of center field. Luis Gonzalez takes a couple steps forward in left field and Danny Bautista stands in straightaway right field. Bautista is happy to yield to Finley's direction. "He's one of the greatest center fielders. He knows the hitters more than me, he's been so long in this league." The trio of outfielders expects Spencer to come around a microsecond late on Schilling's 95-mile-an-hour fastball or his biting split-fastball.

◆ ◆ ◆

STEVE FINLEY SWAYS, waiting for the pitch. Every muscle is awake to the brain's commands to run this way and twist that way and leap that way.

Finley might be the fittest player in baseball. Beginning when he studied physiology at Southern Illinois University, Finley has searched for new training techniques to improve his strength and flexibility and lengthen his playing career. "Everyone is used to saying that when you get into your thirties you're on the way down. That's always been the mindset," says the thirty-six-year-old. "It doesn't have to be that way. I feel like I can play for as long as I want. I haven't lost a step...what we are trying to do is get the body working more efficiently. We are trying to take the nervous system to a higher level."

The human body contains 640 muscles, fed by about 60,000 miles of blood vessels, but most people—even athletes—use only one-third to one-half of the muscles. Many of the muscles are small and located in places where it is hard to engage them in weight lifting and other workouts. When dormant, those do not provide adequate support, putting undue strain on the working muscles and neglecting key sources of strength and flexibility.

"You have muscles in your body that shut down, that just quit working," Finley says. "And the body's a brilliant machine and it will make the adjustment for that lack of work from that muscle. Other muscles will take over for its functions. Over the course of time, that's going to cause an injury because those other muscles are pulling an overload."

Since 1998, Finley has worked with a chiropractor named Edythe Heus to train and maintain his body. His regimen uses equipment and routines that throw his body out of balance, which forces all of his muscles and nerves to become active, moving the body. Most high-level workouts isolate muscle groups for intensive training, but Finley's workout is designed to make sure that the power muscles are supported by the legions of smaller muscles. Finley exerts greater power and flexibility with less effort and less stress and strain. "You're performing at a high intensity," Finley says, "but your body's not working as hard to get there."

Finley's workout includes big rubber balls, balance disks (a board with a softball-sized fulcrum), slant boards (a platform with an inverted V-shaped fulcrum), small weights, and medicine balls.

When he lifts weights or does other exercises on a wobble board—the weights themselves are unstable, with water or sand sloshing around inside—dormant muscles become activated to balance the body. It's as if the body sends emergency alerts to the body's secondary muscles: *Get in the game! You're needed to stabilize the body!* All the muscles begin to work together. The muscles also make the joints stronger, by strengthening the ligaments (the tissues that connect bones with cartilage) and tendons (tissues that connect muscles and bones).

The workout does not just improve power and flexibility. With the nerves in the joints more active—and quicker—they send stronger and more precise information to the brain.

"Sensors throughout our body have to work at peak efficiency to send the right messages to the brain," Heus says. "The brain takes the information it is gathering from the environment and says, 'Oh, I have to get that muscle working with a certain degree of contraction and relaxation.'"

Humans evolved to encounter an uneven, rough world, which required the use of all the body's muscles and nerves and senses. Without thinking about it, children use uneven terrains to train their growing bodies. "Kids walking along a stream will want to walk on the rocks, the round rocks and the jagged rocks, and jump on logs and climb trees and hang from them," Heus says. "Children are always looking for ways to challenge their own balance.... The nervous system likes [physical] surprises and challenges. We need to take advantage of that." Finley's routine amounts to a concerted effort to recover the rock-climbing playfulness of children, which was hardwired into our system but often lost in the modern age.

The spine is the center of Finley's workout—and movement on the field. "You have all these little muscles up and down your spine," Finley says. "They're little short muscles that have about 20 percent more nerve endings than the rest of the muscles in your body. They're kind of initiators, the movement on the spine. People don't usually train those. By putting your body out of balance, you're forcing those to always correct. They're having to work and move. The first time I did the workout, two days later I called Edythe. I said, 'You messed up my spine, what the hell did you do to me?' I was so sore, just right up and down my spine. I was like, 'What the hell's going on here?' And she's like, '*Yes!* That's what I want you to feel!'" Activate the neglected spine muscles—and hundreds of other muscles, too—and the whole body becomes more alert and coordinated.

When Finley started working with Heus in 1997, he had underused muscles all over his body—his feet, lower abdominals, hip rotators, and back muscles—and the strength of some muscles was way out of balance with others. His biggest problem was his feet. "When I first saw Steve, he had these bunions. His feet were awful. It was shocking to see how long it took for his feet to really work well. The feet are key. The power that comes from the big toe is critical for power in the lower extremities. And that's critical for carrying the upper body and for allowing both the upper and lower bodies to do what they can do."

Exercises take place barefoot. The feet provide critical receptors for environmental information—and thereby help to activate the whole body. The advantage of athletic shoes such as those made by Nike, from the streets of the inner city to the floors of the NBA, turns out to be illusory. All the arch support, all the springboard action, all the ankle and foot support actually deaden the body's most useful receptors.

The surprising part of Heus's regimen—at least to athletes raised on the Charles Atlas ideal—is that it rarely involves heavy weights. When Finley started his balance workouts, he never lifted weights heavier than twenty-five pounds. "I kept asking her all winter, 'When am I going to start lifting heavy weights?' She goes, 'Just trust me.' I didn't know. I felt normal. I didn't feel super-strong. I felt great, though. My body felt great."

"You're not Superman, stronger than you were before," Finley says. "You're just working more efficiently than you were before. Therefore, you are stronger, and you're able to maintain your high level with so much less effort, which in turn makes your body feel a lot better. Your endurance is much better."

◆ ◆ ◆

EDYTHE HEUS WORKS with clients ranging from Olympian Amy Acuff to Ashrita Furman, an athlete and showman who has set eighty-seven records in the *Guinness Book of World Records.* She developed her approach over years of experimentation.

The process began when Heus, a Wisconsin native who had never played in the ocean, strained her spine while bodysurfing on the south shore of Long Island. She sought treatment from chiropractors but never got any satisfaction. "I did everything I could to learn about the body," she says. "I took movement classes, exercise classes, dance classes."

Working with elderly patients, she discovered the importance of the feet. "It seemed that the elderly were most impacted by their feet. The discomfort had an immediate and pervasive effect. People who wore shoes that were too small screwed up their body from the waist down."

Once, while attending the Cirque du Soleil in the 1980s, she watched contortionists with amazement. "They have this capability to lengthen their spine and twist it. It tells me that the spine can do way more than we think." That's when she started paying attention to the micromuscles along the spine, part of the axis running from the pelvic floor through the top of the head.

Over time, Heus put together the pieces of a new/old approach to fitness. The approach challenges her clients to move in old ways, the ways that men and women have moved for most of history.

◆ ◆ ◆

THE EDYTHE HEUS routine provides a workout that is the antithesis of the dominant training strategy of professional sports. Players like Barry Bonds, Mark McGwire, and Sammy Sosa lift heavy weights to increase the upper and lower body muscle mass. Those giants focus on building the muscles in the triceps (the area below the shoulder and above the elbow) and forearms that produce power hitting, building overwhelming power in isolated parts of the body rather than balanced power.

The allure of big muscles has produced one of the greatest scandals and tragedies in modern sports—the illicit use of performance-enhancing drugs. As many as two-thirds of all major league players are rumored to have tried using illegal drugs to bulk up. Once-svelte players have reported to spring training carrying as much as thirty pounds more weight in muscles. Ken Caminiti, whose steroid use helped him become the most valuable player in the National League in 1996, says half of all big-leaguers take illicit drugs to bulk up.

Until the 1980s, the average big league slugger stood around six feet tall and weighed about 185 pounds. Today sluggers are three or four inches taller and weigh forty or fifty more pounds. Over his career, Barry Bonds transformed himself from a skinny 200-pound singles and doubles hitter to a 228-pound block of a home run hitter. Bonds denies using drugs to build muscle mass, although he was called to testify before a grand jury investigating a notorious San Francisco fitness guru. McGwire went from 210 to 250 pounds later in his career; he acknowledges using androstenedione, a legal supplement concocted to increase testosterone.

Public health experts, like Charles Yesalis of Pennsylvania State University, state—*definitively*—that the last generation's bulking up would have been impossible without the use of steroids and other illegal drugs. "Three or four pounds would be a hell of a success if you're talking about an athlete who has already reached the top of his profession—like Major League Baseball players," he declares. "You don't get to that level [the major leagues] without heavy strength training from high school on." Adding much bulk afterwards requires extraordinary means, like steroids.

Steroids and other drugs allow players to push themselves harder and harder, so they can lift heavier weights and recover from workouts quicker. Muscles grow when the athlete lifts enough weight to produce infinitesimal tears in the muscles. When these tears heal, the muscles get bigger.

An enduring myth about steroids is that they help only hitters, not pitchers. But steroids can help any athlete that wants greater strength. If the most important part of a pitcher's body is his legs—which create the power that propels the body forward and acts like a shock absorber for the body as it completes its violent motion forward—then improving the strength of the legs can improve the pitcher's power. Steroids also reduce the recovery time for injuries. But maybe more important, performance drugs could give pitchers the stamina they need to survive the season of 162 games and 19 more postseason games. In fact, when baseball adopted its first drug-testing program in 2005, pitchers were as likely to test positive as position players.

Performance-enhancing drugs are designed to improve a player's execution of isolated tasks—like hitting a baseball—not in performing a wide range of acrobatic movements. Every steroid a player injects moves the game away from fielding and other intricacies and toward power hitting and power pitching.

The cost of those bulky bodies is huge. *The American Journal of Sports Medicine* found that the number of days lost to injuries increased 60 percent from 1989 to 2001, and 30 percent just since 1996. Major league teams paid $317 million for players on the disabled list in 2001—and $1 billion since 1997. Baseball injuries have become more like football injuries—tears and ruptures. Heavier muscles performing more put strain on the tendons and ligaments holding the muscles and the rest of the body together. And the hands, wrists, rib cages, and lower backs all suffer with the extra torque powered by the bulging muscles.

Questions of morality and money aside, the steroids scandal raises questions about the best way to condition a body to play baseball.

Which, in turn, raises the question of a balanced training regimen. Finley's workout is designed to get all of the body's 640 muscles working together, taking pressure off all muscles to do too much, and creating a better sense of time and space.

So far, few players have adopted Finley's approach. "You can't make somebody do a [training] program," he says. "The unfortunate part about this program is that a lot of people don't get into it until after they've been injured and they really get desperate: 'I've got to find something.' But it's hard, just like it was hard for me, to take [out] the traditional bench pressing."

◆ ◆ ◆

SINCE HE DEBUTED with the Baltimore Orioles in 1989, Finley has been one of the best and most aggressive defensive outfielders in the game. On his first play as a major leaguer, he crashed into the right-center field wall making a diving catch. Since then he has won three Gold Glove Awards. In 2001, he was the best fielder on the best fielding team in baseball. Finley saved two runs in Game Three when he raced down a drive by Yankees' slugger Tino Martinez in the first inning. Finley leapt to catch Martinez's drive at the dirt just before the right-center field fence to end a Yankees' rally.

Finley's training has produced a new level of energy, flexibility, quickness, and endurance—unusual among even elite athletes—which he uses every day when he tracks down a fly ball, runs the bases, or swings the bat.

During his first spring training after the new regimen, Finley was surprised to discover his new power. "I went to spring training that year [1999] and I had no idea what to expect, none whatsoever. I was nervous about how I'm going to feel. I went to spring training and my batting practice, in the first couple of days, I was launching balls to left field and left center, over the net, everything. I was like, 'Oh my God.' I mean, center field? I was hitting them anywhere I wanted to hit them, and it was easy. It was the same little easy flick I'd always had. And I was running around the outfield like a little kid. I called her up and I said, 'Edythe, this is unbelievable. I've never felt this good in my entire life!'"

"Usually, as a baseball player, you play so many games. If you have eight or ten games in a year where you're feeling perfect, nothing aches, it's a good year. There's always something that's aching or sore. Playing every day for nine innings—and you get 162 of them in 181 days, you're sore most of the time. There's not a player I can tell you that goes out there and they're 100 percent every single day. And in '99, after doing that workout, I was having four out of seven days when I felt perfect. I thought, 'This is unbelievable. I feel great every day. No Advil, no nothing.'"

Over the course of a season, as Finley jerks and twists his body, he feels pain and tightness in his muscles and hamstrings that could flare into a major injury. So he flies in Heus for consultations.

"She gets to the root of that problem to find out what muscles are not doing what they're supposed to do. I had a hamstring problem just a few years ago. I thought I was going to pull it. I mean, for three weeks, it was tight—I felt like it was just going to snap. Doctors and trainers are rubbing it, massaging it, doing ultrasound, everything. Nothing's doing anything. Edythe came here, she did a few muscle tests on me and finds out my low abs [were weak], there was nothing there, no strength whatsoever. She just pushed me right down and isolated those. She gave me four lower ab exercises. I did those for about four, five days, and it [the hamstring problem] just went away. My lower abs weren't supporting my pelvis in the right way, putting stress in my pelvis, therefore pulling my hamstring tighter over here. Those are the kind of little things that people don't think about. Some guy without that knowledge is going to end up pulling his hamstring, just trying to figure out what the hell's going on."

Manager Bob Brenly raves at Finley's physical condition: "He is one of the guys that has figured out how to best use his body to play this game—not to look good in a golf shirt, not to be big and strong and hit the ball six hundred feet, but in order to do everything you need to do well in this game."

◆ ◆ ◆

FIELDING IS A MENTAL game as well as a physical game. A great fielder needs a sense of where he is. A good fielder begins to run as the pitcher is throwing the ball.

As he looks in on the duel between Schilling and Spencer, Finley anticipates exactly where the ball will be hit. First he takes note of where the batter is standing in the batter's box—up closer to the pitcher and close to the plate. Then he studies where the pitcher releases the ball. Then he considers how the batter uncoils his body and puts his bat on the ball, the angle of the bat, and the quickness of the bat's jerk. Finley knows the tics and habits of most hitters, whether they are patient or impulsive, whether they pull the ball or hit it where it's pitched.

Other clues matter too—like the heaviness and temperature of the air, the breeze flowing through the field, the intensity and clarity of the light beamed down from above.

The sound of the bat hitting the ball also offers the fielder clues about where to go to catch the ball. When a bat makes a sound of a crack, the ball is hit well; when the sound is more of a clunk, the bat has not been hit as well.

Hitting the ball on the fat part of the bat—where the greatest power is generated—creates the fewest vibrations. Athletes call that part of the bat the "sweet spot." Hitting the ball there creates a vibration of around 500 hertz and produces the famous *crack* sound. On impact, 100 cubic centimeters of air explode out of the bat in one two-thousandths of a second. Hitting the ball on other parts of the bat produces a smaller air explosion, and smaller vibrations—with a sound frequency of about 170 hertz. (One hertz equals one cycle per second.)

The bat's sound—*crack* or *clunk*—gets to center field in about three-tenths of second. Sound waves travel at 1,100 feet per second, and center field is about 300 feet away.

On a noisy night, like tonight, fielders cannot depend on hearing the crack or clunk sounds. So they will use other cues to determine where the ball is going before it gets there.

"When you're playing in a big crowd like that, you can't hear the ball come off the bat," says the Yankees' outfielder Shane Spencer, the man at the plate. "In batting practice, you've got to work on fungo drills, you work on just seeing the ball off the bat. Sometimes the guys will wear earplugs in batting practice so they can just get breaks off the bat.... You figure out who the hitter is. You've got to scout him before and you know how your guys are going to pitch him. You see the catcher set up inside, or whatever, and that's when you start to move a little bit. You make one or two steps either way. If they're going to jam a guy, going to pitch him inside, or it's going to be an off-speed pitch, you can go to the pull side a little more. So you just make adjustments on how the pitcher's going to pitch the batter."

"He's just got great instincts," first baseman Mark Grace says of Finley. "I mean, there's no real reason other than that. He knows the hitters. He knows the pitchers. He knows their tendencies. He's kind of the Curt Schilling of center field. He knows where the ball's going to be hit before it's hit. And that's why he's been around so long. And he works his butt off."

◆ ◆ ◆

FIELDING IS THE LEAST celebrated aspect of baseball, but it requires the greatest virtuosity. Pitchers rear back and thrust their bodies forward, from the ground up, and then whip their arms forward in a terrible and violent action. Batters use their legs to power the movement of a bat through the strike zone.

Fielders do not exert such great power. But they do more with their bodies. They run hard, stop fast, jump, dive, change direction in an instant, move in one direction to avoid a collision while thrusting the body forward to complete a catch or throw. The game's glamour players are power pitchers and hitters. But fielders put on breathtaking displays of power ballet. To illustrate the parallels, the *Los Angeles Times* once published photographs of fielders and ballet dancers as they jumped, reached, and stretched.

The best center fielders—like Finley—take command on balls hit in the middle two-thirds of the outfield and balls just beyond the reach of the infielders. The best outfielders—like Willie Mays—play in shallow and glide back when a ball is hit over the head. Mays made probably the most famous catch in baseball history in the Polo Grounds during the 1954 World Series against the Cleveland Indians when he went full-speed on a drive by Vic Wertz, his back to the infield, caught the ball over his shoulders, and, in one motion, hurled the ball back to the infield, toppling after the throw.

Today, most outfielders worry about balls zipping past them. They play back, conceding the softly hit ball just beyond the infield.

"You talk to pitchers and they tell you two things," says Shane Spencer. "Sure, they care about the ones that are well struck and they're going to be over guys' heads. You don't want any extra-base hits if you can help it. But it's the shrimp hits, the ones that bleed, the ones that bloop in, that really get them upset. They love it when you play shallow because they take away the cheap hits, and if they do their job there's going to be outs. The best ones play shallow. Mike Cameron plays a little shallow. Andruw Jones plays shallow. Those guys, they take away the singles and it keeps guys off base. And that keeps guys out of big innings. The best ones, like Finley, can also go back and take away the triple."

◆ ◆ ◆

Steve Finley peers into the plate to anticipate where the ball might be hit. Shane Spencer stands at the plate in the top of the second inning with two outs.

Tino Martinez opened the inning by striking out on a fastball boring in on his hands. The next batter, Jorge Posada, stood off the plate, hoping he could bring the barrel of his bat on Schilling's hard inside stuff. But on a 1–0 pitch, the catcher swung late on a fastball on the outside part of the plate. Left fielder Luis Gonzalez loped across the grass for an easy catch.

As Schilling moves into his motion to pitch to Spencer, Finley does a quick hop. No matter where the ball goes, he needs a bounce in his step.

Spencer tries but cannot hold up on the first pitch. He swings through a fastball belt-high over the plate. It's a bad swing—but the pitch and swing have given him important information about the speed and movement and location of Schilling's pitches.

◆ ◆ ◆

When he's playing the field, Finley experiences what psychologist Mihaly Csikszentmihalyi calls "flow." Flow is a state of utter integration of the all aspects of the conscious and subconscious—physical, mental, and spiritual. In Csikszentmihalyi's own words, flow involves "being completely involved in an activity for its own sake. The ego falls away. Time flies. Every action, movement, and thought follows inevitably from the previous one, like playing jazz. Your whole being is involved, and you're using your skills to the utmost."

In that state of mindfulness, Finley is intense and relaxed, serious and playful, focused and aware of surroundings, in control and happy to let go. "That baseball slows down and you transcend time and space," says Edythe Heus.

Finley's play reflects the work of Rudolf Laban, who identified twenty-seven directions a body can move. The body moves in a vertical dimension (up and down), horizontal (right and left), and sagittal (forward and back). Physical activity requires a combination of movements. Pole vaulters move primarily along the vertical dimension, for example, while sports involving running are more sagittal. In baseball, all three dimensions need to be integrated in different ways on different plays. Each action in baseball has its own distinctive movement, timing, explosiveness, impact, stress, physical demands, and need for attention. When Steve Finley lopes after an easy fly ball, he operates mostly the horizontal dimension. But if the fly ball is hit on a line or has backspin, he might have to make a sudden leap or twist.

During part of his workouts, Finley closes his eyes to get a better sense of his body's movement in space. When you see everything you're doing, it's easy to lose the acuteness of the other senses. But close your eyes—when doing the dishes or moving across a room—and see how much you notice without sight. Finley's sense of space is more certain, much more of a real *feel,* when his body learns how to compensate for not seeing.

◆ ◆ ◆

SCHILLING THROWS THE next pitch a little higher, with a little less movement, over the plate. Spencer gets his bat around on this one and hits it 400 feet into deep center field.

Even before the crack of the bat, Finley moves.

The scouting reports say that Spencer can dump the ball in the outfield but does not hit a lot of line drives to the outfield gaps. The outfielder's job is to be prepared to run hard for the fly balls of all descriptions—short dumps over the infield that the shortstop and second baseman cannot reach, and right and left and back to catch the longer fly balls. Finley's job is to outrun the ball.

The large outfield expanse of the Diamondbacks' Bank One Ballpark might cut down on home runs, but it also creates more ground to cover. The BOB extends 407 feet to dead center field and 413 feet to right- and left-center field; compare that to 401 and 380 and 390 in Atlanta's Ted Turner Field. Or Fenway Park's right field pole—302 feet from home plate. The BOB's impact is captured in the Park Effect Index, a statistical measure of a stadium's effect on batted balls. The index shows that the BOB yields only about 90 percent of the home runs hit in other parks; triples, though, occur 60 percent more often in the BOB than in other parks. The BOB has a lot more room for the ball to bounce around than other parks.

As the general of the outfield, Finley covers enough room that the corner outfielders can play closer to the lines, where they can cut off potential doubles and triples. Playing right field, Danny Bautista has great speed and a strong arm and keeps runners from advancing from first to third base on singles and sometimes scoring from second on singles. Luis Gonzalez, the left fielder, is fast but has a poor throwing arm. If a ball goes to left-center field with a runner on base, Finley will take it and make the throw whenever possible.

Balls hit to center field tend to spin directly toward the fielder, while balls to left and right field tend to have odd spins. Even though it has a simpler spin, the ball hit directly into center field can be hard to gauge. When it's coming directly toward the fielder, it's sometimes hard to pick up because he does not see the whole arc of the ball.

Finley takes a peek at the wall before every pitch. "I look over there and I've got a snapshot of where Luis Gonzalez is, snapshot of where Danny Bautista is, a snapshot of where the wall is," Finley says. "If a ball's hit that way, I can guarantee you, I don't even have to look at the wall, and I'll know where I am. I'll know within a few feet of where I'm going to hit the wall. I don't count steps. It's just knowing where it is. It's spatial relations. And the same with the outfielders. I know their speed. I know what Danny likes to get to. If there's somebody new out there, it's a little more difficult because you don't know all their range. But when it's my same guys out there all the time, I get to know them very well and they know me very well, and we work as a great unit."

◆ ◆ ◆

WHEN SPENCER HITS the ball, Finley turns his back to the infield. He knows where the ball is going. He runs eighteen steps before turning back toward the infield to catch a glimpse of the ball.

In football, when a punter kicks the ball, you talk about "hang time"—how long the ball stays in the air before a receiver can catch it and start running down the field. Baseball people do not track the hang time of fly balls, but they should. The hang times of fly balls range from 4.3 seconds (a ball that lands fifty feet behind the fielder after reaching a peak height of sixty-five feet) to 4.6 seconds (a ball that reaches a height of seventy-five feet before landing in the fielder's glove) to 5.0 seconds (a high pop-up that reaches a height of a hundred feet before plopping in front of the fielder).

The hang time of this fly ball is probably somewhere around 4.4 or 4.5 seconds. From the time Spencer hits the ball to the time Finley catches it, 4.5 seconds pass. Even though he needs to move fast, Finley still has plenty of time to catch the ball if he does everything right.

Shortstop Tony Womack and second baseman Craig Counsell move to the outfield for a relay play if Finley cannot catch up with the ball.

Ten feet from the outfield wall, Finley looks up and sees the ball veering slightly toward right field. He twists his body, reaches up with his glove in his right hand, and catches the ball. The momentum of the run takes him another four steps into the padding of the outfield wall. He pulls up just short of the fence, gently putting both hands forward to hold the fence to break his stride.

When Finley runs, he glides. Other athletes chug-chug on the field, but Finley's body is operating with all of his muscles and nerves contributing to the body's movement. "I see people walking and running and ask myself, 'Why does that not look fluid?'" says Edythe Heus. "They're running almost as if they're dragging an extra fifty pounds with them. It's such labor."

When the upper body uses all of its muscles—especially when the micromuscles along the spine keep the length of the body loose and aligned—the legs have less to do. They do not strain under the weight of the torso.

"The human body is designed to work against gravity," Heus says. "When Steve jumps up and reaches for the ball, it's like he stretches his whole being. He's like an accordion. He has an ability to anchor the lower part of his body, even when he's in the air, so that he can twist the upper part of the body." Since his spine is strong, he can leap with his lower body and turn with his upper body. Finley is also ambidextrous, which gives superior quickness and range of movement in all directions.

His whole-body, multi-sensory training gives Finley a strong sense of where he is on the field, even when twisting and turning.

"Having to reach, to stretch—in a situation like that, because you're running hard and looking back over your shoulders, a lot of people would get disoriented," Finley says. "You're looking this side and you spin around. But what I love about our workout is that it helps you, your body, know where it is in space at all times. You watch figure skaters on ice, and they're holding somebody above their head and going down the ice. And they'll make it look super easy. Well, if somebody went out there and tried it, it's not going to work. They're very aware of their body in space, and that's the same thing this workout gives me. It makes me aware of my body in space, and when I make those catches it might look easy. They're not that easy. A lot of people couldn't do it."

Just as important as Finley's speed, quickness, and flexibility is his ability to slow down. "You need really good eccentric powers, which is braking and slowing down," says Heus. "You're not going to drive a car eighty miles an hour if you have brakes that don't work. You need to explode, run, stop, and explode in the opposite direction."

Finley's catch sets the tone for the early part of the game. The catch gives Schilling a break, arouses the Phoenix crowd, and of course prevents a run-scoring threat.

"I hit that right on the sweet spot," Spencer says, shaking his head. "Line drive up the middle. I had good backspin on it, and it just kept carrying. If it gets over his head, it's a for-sure double and maybe even a triple. And I have a chance, because he doesn't play real deep. And, you know, I'm always coming hard out of the box. And I was feeling pretty good. So that was a double or triple, and that's probably a difference in the game, right there."

Finley's speed and dexterity—and the agelessness he has won by using the training regimen of Edythe Heus—have robbed the Yankees' hopes for now.

Chapter Four

INSIDE THE DIAMOND

"Whenever I'm teaching younger players, what I ask is, 'Can you dance?'"

Matt Williams, the Diamondbacks' veteran third baseman who came to the big leagues as a shortstop in 1987, is ruminating about the art of defensive play in the four infield positions. Williams has become a philosopher of the game as he struggles to cool down his intensity and combine his God-given athleticism with his growing knowledge of the game.

Dancing—an activity that brings together focus and relaxation, grace and quickness, initiative and cooperation—provides Williams with the concept he needs to play his position. Dancing helps him understand when and how to stay loose but also when to move quickly. Keep light on the feet like a dancer, then you can attack and parry, as the play requires.

"That's all it is—you're just dancing through the ball. When your feet stop, when your feet get lead[en], your hand gets hard, when you don't adjust to a bounce, that's when you make mistakes."

◆ ◆ ◆

Leading off for the Diamondbacks in the home half of the second inning, Steve Finley hits a 1–0 fastball up the middle. Shortstop Derek Jeter hesitates briefly before playing the ball to his side. Jeter fields the ball, a hard one-hopper, cleanly. Reaching down with his six-foot-three body, Jeter flips it hard to first in one motion.

"You play short there's going to be a lot of plays that you're off-balance," Jeter says. "You just work at it, practice it, get better with time. Some may be kind of difficult because of how tall I am as opposed to a shorter guy. But that just comes with experience."

◆ ◆ ◆

Derek Jeter's fielding poses a dilemma. Depending on whom you debate, Jeter is either one of the best fielding shortstops in the game—or he is absolutely, positively the worst. The question is whether to believe your eyes when watching him.

Part of the difficulty in judging Jeter is that he is the winningest shortstop in an era of great shortstops. Players like Alex Rodriguez, Nomar Garciaparra, Omar Vizquel, Orlando Cabrera, and Edgar Renteria do not have the luxury of playing for consistently great teams. They seem to do more at their positions than Jeter. But Jeter is a winner. He has been on four World Series champions in five years, and now he's playing for a fifth title. He must be doing something right.

When baseball people gather to watch Jeter, they smile. They watch him charge balls in the middle of the diamond, range to the outfield and right-field line to gather pop flies, communicate with pitchers and infielders. They love his hustle, his willingness to risk his body to make a play; whether it's diving three rows into the stands or facing down a base runner barreling into second base. They watch the way he captains not only the infield but the outfield, too. They like the messages he gives other players. Years before, as a youngster, he confronted the Rubenesque pitcher David Wells when Wells had a hissy fit on the mound after an error. Jeter barked back on behalf of his teammates and they appreciated it.

Broadcaster Tim McCarver acknowledges that Jeter sometimes has a hard time picking up sharp hops. "I'm sure there are five or six shortstops who read a ground ball, a hop, better," says McCarver, a Jeter fan. "It's not one of his strong suits. He comes over and up on the ball. Sometimes he charges when he should stay back and stays back when he should charge."

McCarver pauses, looking for context: "But it's almost crazy to talk about that, he does so many things well."

Billy Blitzer, a major league scout for almost three decades, says Jeter is one of the best with the glove and arm. Blitzer tracks the Yankees and Mets for the Chicago Cubs organization and has watched Jeter since his days in the minor leagues. "You look at the highlights and he makes that play in the hole and I still don't know how he makes that play," Blitzer says. "I've seen him make that play so many times over the years." Jeter moves especially well on choppy grounders to the middle of the infield, reaching way down, on the move, for balls with strange topspin and odd bounces on different infield surfaces, scooping the ball, and throwing sidearmed in one motion.

Baseball people will always buzz about a play Jeter made in the American League Divisional Series against the Oakland Athletics. It was a spectacular play that might have ended in disaster, and it crystallizes the debate about whether Jeter is a great or a terrible fielder.

In the third game of the series, the Yankees were facing elimination but leading 1–0. With Jeremy Giambi on first base, the A's Terrence Long hit a shot that Shane Spencer fielded in the right field corner. Spencer threw the ball past both the cutoff man (Alfonso Soriano) and the backup to the cutoff man (Tino Martinez). The ball veered to the first base side of home plate. Jeter surprised everyone in the stadium by fielding the ball. In one motion, Jeter caught the ball and shoveled it to catcher Jorge Posada, who tagged Giambi chugging around to score the tying run. The play protected the Yankees' slender lead and helped them survive a two-game deficit and win the best-of-five series.

The most grizzled veterans, the most cynical reporters, were astonished by the play—not just Jeter's quick movements or his good sense to shovel the ball to Posada in one motion after catching the ball, but the very fact that he was in position to make the play. Most shortstops would have put themselves closer to second base, ready to take a cutoff throw and hold Long to a double. But Jeter was just a few feet from home plate. After the game, Jeter was asked about the play, and his matter-of-fact reply—"It was my job to read the play"—seemed to suggest that the spectacular is standard business for Jeter.

As great as Jeter was at that moment, he might have also contributed to a big A's inning with his positioning. What if Jeter doesn't make the swift shovel to Posada? What if Giambi slides (as he should) and avoids the tag? Who's covering second base? No one. Long can round second base widely and go for third base. No Yankee infielder is positioned to hold him at second. A 1–0 lead could easily have become a 1–1 tie and then a 2–1 deficit.

The Diamondbacks' third baseman Matt Williams has watched the play on endless television replays and still shakes his head. "That play with Jeter, the way it's drawn up in spring training, you never have a triple relay—but it was a head's-up play by him," Williams says. "It might have worked out badly. There's a batter-runner and there's nobody at second base and he [the runner] could go all the way to third. But you also go with your instincts."

Jeter remains blasé about the play. "I'm supposed to be over there for the cutoff to redirect the play to third if the runner scored," says Jeter. He does not care that most observers—including members of his own team—were surprised to see him near the play. "That's good," he says, "because then we got 'em." Some still question his positioning, but Jeter is adamant, in his nonchalant kind of way.

"I don't *think* that's where I'm supposed to be," he says. "I *know* that's where I'm supposed to be."

◆ ◆ ◆

HERE'S WHAT THE detractors say about Jeter's fielding.

Jeter has limited range. He doesn't always position himself well, so he does not make up for that limited range by being in the right place before the pitch. He has poor instincts, so he takes a split-second too long to react to batted balls. Sometimes he shuffles in the wrong direction as the pitcher throws the ball. He gets a bad jump on the ball. His hands are sometimes unreliable. His throws can be weak and off the mark, which result in more force plays and fewer double plays. He moves slowly to second base when he initiates a 6–4–3 double play.

He looks great on the ground ball deep in the hole, and he ranges far and wide on pop flies as far away as the left field stands and back into center field.

Jeter does not commit many errors, but that's because teammates compensate for his many weaknesses. Other infielders move toward the shortstop position and cover some of Jeter's ground, leaving gaps at their own positions.

◆ ◆ ◆

THE INDICTMENT AGAINST Derek Jeter's fielding finds its most forceful expression in statistics.

Most fans—and even many players, managers, and coaches—simply do not see enough with their own eyes to make independent judgments of fielding ability. In a given game, fielders make only four or five plays. Fielders need a wide range of skills—understanding hitters and the flow of the game, running, moving acrobatically to reach balls, throwing from different positions—but fans rarely see their full range of skills in a game or even a series of games.

The most common measure of defensive play is fielding percentage, a simple ratio of errors to chances. Players are usually considered good when they successfully field a ball and bad when they do not. But a better fielder might commit more errors than a lesser fielder.

The greatest difference between good and poor fielders is not what they do when they get the ball, but whether they get in position to make the play in the first place. The pitcher-hitter battle can be so riveting that few fans see how fielders position themselves. Even fewer fans have the knowledge of hitter strengths and weaknesses, pitcher strategies, and field conditions to know whether the positioning is smart or not.

Fans usually see only the end of the play, not the beginning—which is most critical, since it determines whether the fielder will get to the ball in the first place. Diving stops and over-the-shoulder catches often look like stellar plays but might be examples of poor positioning and poor reactions to batted balls. Fielders succeed when they get a quick jump on the ball, but few people pay attention to that split-second moment when the fielder moves into action.

A player's coordination with teammates has another major impact on the team's overall defensive excellence. The best fielders make their teammates better by covering more ground, communicating well before and during plays, and making reliable throws. But the coordination of different players on the field is hard to see and harder to measure.

Then there is the playing environment. The different sizes and configurations of ballparks make comparisons unreliable. Players in bigger parks—with bigger outfields and larger foul territory—have the opportunity to make more plays. Some fielders make more plays without necessarily having greater range—but sometimes they make more plays just because of their greater range.

On top of all this, the fielders have different demands and cannot be judged by the same measures. First basemen, for example, record more putouts than anyone else but mostly on easy throws from other infielders. Shortstops make more plays on pop-ups when other fielders yield to them. Catchers get credit for more putouts when the pitcher records a lot of strikeouts.

Analysts have developed a number of formulae to judge fielding.

Fielding Percentage: A simple calculation of successful plays made on attempts, fielding percentage tells whether a player is reliable when he gets to a ball. But this measure does not penalize fielders for not getting to balls that they should be able to field—and therefore penalizes players with great range and rewards players with little range.

Chances: The total number of attempted plays that a fielder makes, considered a good rough estimate of a player's range. Chances can be deceptive, however, since it might understate a player's skills if he plays alongside other players with good range.

Assists: Assists can be a deceiving number too. The best outfielders are often the ones with the fewest assists. Base runners do not attempt to take extra bases on outfielders with strong, accurate arms. They hold up on the base paths because of the specter of the cannon-armed outfielder throwing them out. But that does not show up in any stats.

Double Plays: Because they kill rallies and usually involve the cooperation of two or three players, double plays offer a good measure of fielding performance. DPs also provide useful comparative data. If Shortstop A makes more double plays than Shortstop B, even when playing with the same second baseman, you know something's wrong with Shortstop B.

Range Factor: The fielder's ultimate job is to get to balls, then field them. Range matters more than simply fielding easy plays. To show a player's range, RF figures the number of putouts plus assists per nine innings.

Zone Rating: Using data gathered by Stats Inc., a for-profit statistics firm, the ZR calculates the percentage of plays a fielder makes on balls hit into his zone. Stats Inc. assigns different fielders specific zones of the field and holds them responsible for making plays in those areas. In between the zones are "Bermuda Triangles," areas where a fielder cannot be expected to catch a ball. Scorekeepers paid by Stats Inc. chart fielders' performance on every batted ball. This measure represents a major advance for understanding fielding, but does not always account for the ways the different fielders work together or how getting into good position affects the plays.

Fielding Runs Above Replacement: Sometimes the best way to understand a player's value is to understand how well he performs compared to others at his position. By developing a measure that compares a player with an average "replacement" at the position, fielding runs achieves this goal. The formula for FR uses weighted measures for basic statistics (e.g., putouts, assists, errors, and double plays), equalizes those measures for innings played, and develops a comparison of particular players with the average statistics for that position.

Win Shares: The most elaborate—and probably the most reliable—measure of fielding comes from Bill James. The formula starts with a team's overall performance in preventing runs, and then gives credit to different players for that performance. The WS formula for shortstop tallies assists and expected assists, double plays and expected double plays, error rates, and the player's share of the team's putouts. The formula takes into account factors that would distort overall fielding numbers, such as the number of strikeouts, the ratio of pop flies to ground balls, whether the pitcher is right- or left-handed, and the size and makeup of the park. The end result is a number that expresses a player's contribution to a team's wins over a thousand innings, which is then converted into a letter grade. (Whew.)

In 2001, Jeter finished near the bottom of all statistical measures for fielding among the twenty-one major league shortstops who played in two-thirds of their teams' games. The numbers tell the same story: Jeter does not reach or field balls as well as other shortstops.

STATISTICAL MEASURE	Jeter's stats	Leader's stats	Jeter's rank
Fielding Percentage Successful share of attempted plays	.974	.989	10
Total Chances Number of balls in which the fielder attempted a play	570	772	15
Assists Number of times one fielder helped another player make a play	344	515	17
Double Plays Number of double plays executed	68	120	18
Range Factor Putouts plus assists per nine innings	3.81	4.97	21
Zone Rating Percentage of plays in fielder's zone	.789	.884	21
Runs Above Replacement Average Complex formula estimates the number of runs a player personally saves (positive number) or causes (negative) with his fielding	-17	31	20 (tie)
Fielding Runs Weighted measure that compares the player to the "average" player at the position	5	55	20
Win Shares Weighted number that shows what a fielder contributed to the prevention of runs in a season	5.9	13.5	11

The leaders in most of the categories included Orlando Cabrera of the St. Louis Cardinals, Alex Gonzalez of the Toronto Blue Jays, and Omar Vizquel of the Cleveland Indians.

Jeter also fares badly in statistical comparisons over recent history—and over all of baseball history. From 1998 to 2003, Jeter finished last among eighteen shortstops who had played at least 500 games, with a Win Shares score of 5.2 over the course of his career (the best of the class, Rey Sanchez, finished with a rate of 9.8). Of 290 shortstops that played at least 3,000 innings through the 2001 season—the equivalent of two full seasons of everyday play—Jeter had a better Win Shares rating than only fifty other players—putting him in the bottom fifth of all shortstops. Jeter had 4.11 Win Shares per 1,000 innings; the all-time leader was Bob Allen of the nineteenth-century Philadelphia Phillies, with 7.73. Jeter, in fact, does better than only two of the 102 shortstops who have played as many career innings.

◆ ◆ ◆

However well or poorly Derek Jeter plays shortstop, there is no debate that the position's impact extends all over the field. The shortstop creates the context for the rest of the defense. If Jeter gets to a ball in the hole on the left side of the diamond, the third baseman can play closer to the line; if he can range behind second base, the second baseman can move closer to first base and the first baseman can move closer to the right field line.

Fielding in the infield requires an ability to get into the rhythm of a play and then react quickly. The position requiring the greatest variety of moves is third base. A third baseman needs to be able to snare a sizzling drive down the line, charge on a bunt or spinning ground ball, dive to his right and left, range back and toward the stands on pop flies, grab ground balls at all angles and speeds, and throw from every conceivable position and angle.

Diamondbacks' third baseman Matt Williams explains how to approach the ball: "There are two philosophies I take—to have that rhythm and to be the hunter instead of the hunted. You take the approach that you're the tiger and that ball's the prey and you need to be aggressive. When in doubt, be as aggressive as you can, and things just tend to work. Once you get defensive or stand back on your heels, things tend to go wrong."

How players position themselves to be the tiger varies according to personality. Just as with hitting, the stance matters a lot—but the particular stance only works when the player feels comfortable.

"Some guys—take Carney Lansford [the former All-Star for the Oakland Athletics]—his feet were still and he crouched down. When I played third, I tried to stay standing up, because that's the way I move best. I would have this little hop before each pitch. And so I have this rhythm. As the pitch is on the way I hop off the ground a little bit. The idea is for my feet to hit the ground as the pitch was in the strike zone because oftentimes you have one step and a dive at third base—you don't have a lot of time."

The second baseman's movement is different—requiring less range and quickness and arm strength, but a greater capacity for taking twists and turns. When taking a throw from shortstop to turn a double play, the second baseman makes the play blind, without seeing the runner pounding down the base paths, then turns 80 degrees and throws the ball to first base in a split-second—as the runner does everything he can to upend him.

The second baseman plays in a box: with little time to react, a need to twist quickly on plays—and usually, with a weaker arm than the shortstop—he can't stretch out his limbs and range as widely as the shortstop. A second baseman has to respond quickly to a smash hit off a left-handed hitter's bat or—more often—catch and throw the ball instantly when a ball grounds or takes an odd angle on a slicing drive. The second baseman needs hands so soft that he does not grasp the ball completely on plays requiring a quick throw. He wears a small glove that enables him to grab the ball quickly for a throw. Unlike the shortstop, the second baseman needs to backhand throws to his middle-infield partners on many double-play balls.

The Yankees' Alfonso Soriano—once a shortstop and outfielder—has been learning the challenges of second basemen in his rookie year. Soriano uses one of the smallest gloves in the game, a piece of leather not much bigger than the cardboard he used in his native Dominican

Republic. As he reaches for a ground ball, he sometimes uses his right hand to push the glove an inch or two out of his hands to give the glove extra reach.

In the eleventh inning of Game Five, with the bases loaded and the score tied 2–2, Soriano made a diving catch of a line drive down the middle by Reggie Sanders. The athleticism of the play—quick reaction, soft hands—comes naturally. Soriano's challenge is to get into the right position, cover the base, and make the right cutoff plays. Those are thinking plays, anticipation plays; requiring tight attention to the game situation.

The infield's least appreciated player is the first baseman. Traditionally, first base has been the place to put human statues, bulky men and aging sluggers who lack the quickness and range of other players. It's where you go when you can't go anywhere else. The logic is simple: all the first baseman needs to do is catch balls tossed by other infielders, field an occasional weak grounder or pop-up, take a cutoff throw, and back up plays. It helps to be tall, so you can keep a foot on the bag while stretching for errant throws. Quick hands help, too, when left-handed hitters pull the ball hard down the line. But, according to conventional wisdom, first base is home of the one-dimensional athlete. As Mark Grace once said of the lumbering giant Mo Vaughn, the conventional wisdom is that the first baseman requires only "the range of a highway cone."

But the defensive play of Grace refutes the conventional wisdom. Grace understands that the first baseman's job is to reduce the errors and increase the daring and confidence of the other fielders. A winner of four Gold Glove Awards with the Chicago Cubs, Grace came to the Diamondbacks in 2001 because they had a chance to win a championship. As a left-handed fielder, Grace can move far to his right, toward second base. That enables the second baseman to move a few steps toward the middle of the diamond. With his sure hands, Grace can excavate balls out of the dirt and stretch long and wide for wild throws.

Even though Grace's defensive skills have declined in recent years—he does not move as quickly to his left or right as he once did—he knows the game well enough to compensate. He anticipates where the batter will hit the ball. He makes the awkward throw to second for a double play. Like a good catcher, Grace's biggest gift to his teammates is the utter confidence he gives them on throws to first base. Infielders can rush a throw to first because they know Grace will not let it get away for a two-base error—consequently they attempt more plays and get more outs. They can also play back a step or two—dramatically increasing their range—because they know Grace can weed low throws out of the dirt.

That, of course, is the critical element of all fielding. It's not the errors on the attempted plays that matter as much as being in position to make plays in the first place.

As Woody Allen once remarked, 90 percent of life is showing up.

Chapter Five

CALLING THE GAME

THE MOST UNFAIR expression in all of sports might be calling the catcher's equipment—mask, chest protector, big padded glove—the "tools of ignorance."

In fact, the smartest and most informed player on any team—and the toughest—is likely to be the catcher.

Catching requires the ability to catch a baffling array of pitches, gauge the pitcher's effectiveness, understand opposing hitters, tell the pitcher what to throw, direct the rest of the team, and act as the last line of defense as plays unfold. The catcher also must understand the psychology of pitchers. In fact, one of the catcher's greatest struggles is with his own pitchers. It's a struggle over what pitches to call, over which player sets the pace of the game—and who gets the tie-breaking vote when they disagree about pitch selection and other strategy.

Catchers prepare for the game by studying the opposing hitters, poring over reams of statistics, watching videos of pitch sequences, and talking with starting pitchers and relievers who might enter the game that day. As the catcher's experience accumulates, the information melds into his memory, available for recall in every different game situation.

The catcher adapts that knowledge as the game progresses. When batters move forward in the batter's box to cut off the break in a curveball, the catcher might call for a fastball in a curveball situation. When a hitter is swinging wildly at every pitch, the catcher knows that three or four pitches outside the strike zone might produce a strikeout. When the catcher sees the hitters eagerly swinging at first pitches, he can get the pitcher to throw the ball on the edges of the hitter's hot spots and induce a series of grounders and pop-ups—cheap and easy outs that might allow the pitcher to throw for an extra inning or two.

The best catchers control the game, but are so in sync with the pitchers that they make the pitchers think they're in charge. At the most important moment in the game, the catcher has to have the guts to tell the manager the pitcher is losing his stuff—which could make the pitcher lose confidence in himself and his backstop. It's like telling an old barrister that he's lost his edge in court. And the catcher has to do it a hundred times a year or more.

With Danny Bautista batting for the Diamondbacks, Roger Clemens and Jorge Posada struggle with the complexities of the relationship.

Bautista, a right-handed hitter, is trying to make Clemens labor on the mound. He takes the first pitch high and inside. The Yankees' pitcher hits the outside corner for a strike and then gets Bautista to swing late at a splitter in the dirt. Bautista lays off two more tempting pitches—a low-and-away splitter and a fastball just low over the plate. On a full count, Clemens throws the next pitch high and hard. Bautista walks.

Clemens is an emotional pitcher and over the years has lost his composure in the early innings of crucial games. If he cannot regain control, he falls behind in the count and then he has to throw the ball over the plate—where hitters can hit it. But when he controls his emotions and energy, he can be unhittable—alternating up-and-in pitches with low-and-away pitches, in turn overpowering and baffling hitters.

Part of Posada's job as catcher is to manage Clemens's emotions. Since he took over from Joe Girardi behind the plate in 1997, Posada struggled to find a rhythm with his pitchers. Posada and his pitchers often disagreed about pitch selection, sometimes passionately. Posada crouched behind the plate, wiggling his fingers in a series of signals, and the pitcher shook his head again and again. Occasionally, the disagreement went on long enough that the pitcher, exasperated, called Posada out to the mound to talk it over.

Too often, Posada got confused on signals and pitch location. He gets ready for a curveball low and away and was handcuffed by a fastball inside and high. Even worse, pitchers complained that Posada allowed base runners to read his signs, who then passed along the intelligence to hitters at the plate. Posada and his pitchers also got out of sync on holding base runners to first base, pitchout plays, and bunts in front of the plate.

When Posada first took over for Girardi, pitchers became visibly upset when their young backstop missed a sign or dropped a ball. *Can we please get on the same page?* Posada sometimes responded with glares and barks of his own—a cardinal sin for working with the fragile psyches of pitchers. Posada's most celebrated battles involved Orlando Hernandez, the volatile Cuban exile who occasionally shouted at his catcher when they got back to the dugout. The two argued, in Spanish, for hours and sometimes days.

Posada's temper spilled over into his relations with umpires. After a borderline call, Posada would snarl at the umpire—not a smart idea when trying to widen the strike zone for the pitcher. After one game, Posada complained to the media about umpire Greg Kosc's physical condition—implying that the arbiter's heaviness was getting in the way of doing a good job. Joe Torre made him apologize to Kosc, a humbling experience for the struggling backstop.

"He was a second baseman when he signed, and he was brutal behind the plate—just *brutal,*" says Shane Spencer. "He had a great arm. He could run. He was a lot faster than he is now. But he couldn't catch. The ball was just popping out of his mitt all the time. And he was throwing the ball into center field. He had a tough time."

But in the past year or two, Posada has found confidence and rhythm behind the plate. He still has his mix-ups, but Yankee pitchers have started to appreciate his hard work, his eagerness to call a better game, his willingness to put his body at risk on plays to the plate. The transition has not been easy, but Girardi has patiently schooled the man who took his job. Torre, a former catcher himself, has tried to teach him to take things as they come.

Posada acknowledges his early unsteadiness.

"It comes with experience," he says. "Torre put his trust in me, but you don't develop those tools on the bench. You develop them as you play the game. Calling the games, the pitchers are so focused on getting this guy out that when I call the game it helps them concentrate. But it takes a long time to understand what pitches to throw when. Do I have to throw a curveball here?"

With daily experience—crouching behind the plate, catching thousands upon thousands of pitches—catchers develop the knowledge they need to call a good game. No other position depends so much on experience. Some catchers struggle to obtain the experience they need to be rewarded with the starting job; like entry-level workers in all businesses, they are told to come back when they have enough experience. The Diamondbacks' Damian Miller started to get his experience when he developed a good working relationship with Randy Johnson; in 1998 he became Johnson's "personal" catcher and the next year shared the catching job with Kelly Stinnett. Finally, in 2001, he won the full-time job.

Torre did not give Posada the everyday job until he demonstrated the maturity and consistency that only a former catcher like Torre can understand. Even then, he challenged his young catcher. "Georgie, I think, hated me when he first came up," Torre says. "He wanted to be in there every day and we had Joe [Girardi]. He was frustrated. But he had to learn how to catch, how to work with pitchers. It's not easy. It's the most demanding position on the team."

Whatever experience he gets, Posada is always seeking the advice of his coaches. "I see Mel Stottlemyre every day and talk about it," he says. "We have a scouting report every series, but sometimes they don't work because a pitcher is not on—he's getting the ball up or doesn't have a good splitter or something [else]. I say, in the game, 'Hey, Mel, I don't have a feel for this game, I don't know what to do.' Mel will tell me what's happening—the pitcher's trying to work too hard, he's not looking at the target, his body is flying open—and he'll tell me what to do to get him to stay back and get him to [pitch to] the other parts of the strike zone."

Posada has modeled himself after great defensive catchers of two eras. After the 1996 season, he started working out at the University of

Puerto Rico in San Juan with the Texas Rangers' Ivan Rodriguez. Rodriguez uses demanding running drills to strengthen the legs, which take endless wear as the catcher squats behind the plate and moves quickly to back up plays at first base. At the same time, Posada has embraced the rugged ethos of the late Thurman Munson. Posada has taped a quotation from Munson on his locker: "Look, I like hitting fourth and I like a good batting average. But what I do every day behind the plate is a lot more important because it touches so many more people and so many more aspects of the game."

◆ ◆ ◆

THE CATCHER IS the only player who plays his position in foul territory. Squatting behind home plate, he has a view of the whole field and the best sense of the pitcher's power, control, and psyche. He takes the role of the field general, not only calling pitches but also positioning fielders and directing traffic on bunts, pop-ups, and relays.

Watching the catcher provides subtle clues about how the game is progressing.

The catcher starts by crouching behind the plate, signaling with his fingers, and shifting to the part of the strike zone where he wants the pitcher to throw. With no base runners and fewer than two strikes, the catcher can rest his weight on his right instep, with the left foot a few inches forward. That stable foundation can help him to shift slightly to catch the ball and frame it for the umpire. With base runners or two strikes, the catcher leans slightly forward on the balls of his feet, ready to make a quick throw or chase an errant pitch.

The catcher needs to give the pitcher a target and then frame the pitch, especially when the ball comes in on the edge of the plate. Ideally, the pitcher screens out all distractions and throws to the catcher's glove. If the catcher sets his target too soon, the batter might sneak a peek to see where the pitch is coming. Just as the pitcher rocks into his motion, the catcher puts his glove where he wants the ball.

Framing the pitch is an art of its own. When a pitch comes in near the edges of the strike zone—inside or outside, high or low—the catcher needs to grab the ball and hold it as if he's hitting the pause button on a VCR so the umpire can get a good look. The best way to show the umpire where the ball lands is to catch the ball on its outer side—for example, the right side of the plate for a right-handed batter—and then turn the glove so the umpire can see the part of the ball that hit the plate. Catchers cannot jerk balls into the zone or they'll lose credibility with the umpire. The catcher's framing should help the umpire, not try to force him to make a favorable call.

Over the course of a game, the catcher gets battered by foul balls and pitches in the dirt. The catcher's objective is simple: keep the ball in front and avoid endangering his hands. Until the 1970s, catchers put their throwing hands behind the glove so they could make a quick transfer for a throw. But Johnny Bench pioneered keeping the whole throwing arm behind his back until he caught the ball.

To stop an errant pitch, a catcher has to decide in a split-second whether to block the ball with his body—falling on his knees in front of the ball—or whether to grab the ball like a hockey goalie. Falling in front of the ball creates a bigger barrier, while the goalie grab offers greater range and flexibility.

Catchers need to have the strongest arms on the team. They need to throw the ball more than 120 feet to second base on attempted steals, often from a crouched position. They need to snap throws to first and third base for quick pickoff plays. They often make these throws as batters put their bats or bodies in the way.

The catcher takes charge of the field as plays unfold. When the hitter drops a bunt or lifts a fly ball over the infield, the catcher has the best sense of the ball's spin and movement and which player is in the best position to make what play. The catcher calls most plays on bunts, telling the pitcher or corner infielder where to throw the ball.

To perform all these feats, the catcher needs a strong knowledge of the hitter's abilities with the bat, the hitter's speed, the base runner's speeds and styles, and his own teammates' styles on the field.

But the most important job is guiding the pitcher throughout the game.

◆ ◆ ◆

Catchers have to develop strong working relationships with their pitchers—and every pitcher takes a different approach to working a game. Some want the catcher to call the game so they can concentrate on just throwing the ball. Others want the catcher to suggest pitches, but hold a veto option on those calls. A few want to direct the game themselves, pitch by pitch.

Curt Schilling sets the game plan and challenges catchers to come up with a better idea. He explains the silent dialogue he develops with catchers over the course of the game: "I've told all my catchers [that] if I shake you off and you call a pitch you want, put it back down [repeat the signal] to make me understand that you have an idea. A lot of guys don't want to take that responsibility. They want to call the game and put down the fingers you want them to put down. I ask a lot of my catchers and the guys playing behind me. Sometimes they give it and sometimes they don't."

Randy Johnson does not take Schilling's activist approach to studying opposing hitters, but he insists on calling his own game: "I'm the one that has to answer to the media. If I feel more comfortable with a particular pitch in a situation, with a particular hitter, then I'll shake the catcher off and throw the pitch. Sometimes I give a hitter a home run on a pitch, and maybe I shouldn't have thrown that pitch—but you know what, it was a pitch that I felt confident with. Before you throw that pitch you've got to be confident with that pitch, have 110 percent confidence that you can execute that pitch. If there's any doubt, step off the mound or shake that pitch off that he's putting down because that's not the pitch you want to throw." Usually, Johnson and Miller are on the same page. "When things are in the flow of the game, I'm not shaking them off."

Most pitchers need their catchers to think for them so that they can concentrate on throwing the ball. Recalling his seventeen years with the Cincinnati Reds, catching great Johnny Bench says: "Look, they had no clue. I mean, most of them had no clue, and if they did you admired them and respected them. If [Tom] Seaver was pitching, you let him shake you off. If another guy was out there, you walked out to the mound and said, 'Don't you ever shake me off again.'"

Fellow Hall of Famer Carlton Fisk agrees: "I let him know I was in charge and he was not in charge. If he thought that pitch was going to get somebody out, he was sorely mistaken. What I try to do behind the plate is think, which was something the pitchers never did." The pitcher's job is so physically and mentally taxing that he needs another brain to help him think through pitch selection and long-term strategy. The catcher is the one who sees close-up how pitches cross the plate, whether they have good movement and location, and how the batters react to the pitches.

Most pitchers and catchers talk between innings. The pitching coach sometimes joins the conversation. They keep tabs on how well the pitchers are throwing—and how the hitters are setting themselves up against the pitchers. When they talk on the mound during crises, the conversation is limited. If they need to discuss a strategic move—*Should we intentionally walk the next batter? Should we play the infield in?*—mound meetings can have some substance. But the discourse is usually limited to recitations of the game's simple verities. "Get strikes, but don't give him anything good to hit," the catcher or pitching coach will say. "Mfmph," the pitcher will respond. *Easy for you to say,* the pitcher will think to himself.

The catcher nurses the pitcher's psyche during the game. When Randy Johnson doesn't get calls from the umpire, he gets upset. Damian Miller works to keep Johnson focused—to use his pitcher's anger to focus his attention. "Randy puts a lot of faith in me. He wants me to do whatever I can to get him through seven or eight innings. If I have to yell at him, I yell at him. One thing about Randy: he's got the three Cy Youngs, but if I've got something to say he looks me right in the eye and listens to it. He doesn't feel like he's above his catcher. He wants his catcher to get in his face."

Miller does not have Posada's high profile, but he has earned the respect of his pitchers. Earlier in the year, the Diamondbacks made a video of Miller's work behind the plate and sent it to other teams to campaign for Miller to win the Gold Glove Award.

"He's kind of a clown type of guy, funny guy, but what really matters is that he's a great defensive catcher," says Mark Grace. "He will throw a guy out, he blocks everything, he has a big old ass and keeps everything in front of him. You know, he's not going to knock your socks off with the bat, but we had plenty of hitters. So his job is just to keep

Johnson and Schilling and the rest of the guys focused and on them. Randy doesn't like to shake off signals. Randy just likes to go with what you call. And Damian knows Randy like the back of his hand. And you know, with Curt and with Randy, you're going to have a lot of balls in the dirt—splits, sliders. So you're going to bounce around a lot back there. He did. He did a great job."

◆ ◆ ◆

STEVE RIPPLEY STANDS behind home plate with the power to set the pace of the game, determine whether Curt Schilling and Roger Clemens get ahead or behind in the count, and make the calls on close plays at the plate.

Rarely do umpires affect a game by making a spectacular mistake. Ken Burkhart gave the Baltimore Orioles the opening game of the 1970 World Series. Baltimore catcher Elrod Hendricks tagged Cincinnati Reds' Bernie Carbo with an empty glove—and Burkhart called Carbo out, securing a 4–3 win for the Orioles. In the sixth game of the 1985 Series, with the St. Louis Cardinals leading 1–0, Don Denkinger called the Kansas City Royals' Jorge Orta safe at first base in the ninth inning. Replays showed Cardinals' pitcher Todd Worrell beat Orta to the bag. The Royals rallied to win that game and the Series.

But the umpire's greatest influence, day after day, is behind the plate. Umpires call different strike zones and control the tempo of the game differently. When a pitcher struggles to find his groove in the game's early innings, the umpire's personal strike zone could determine whether pitchers get ahead or behind in the count—and that could shape the course of the whole game.

The umpires call the strike zone that the teams and players allow them to call. Mark Hirschbeck, one of the game's best, explains: "You come up from the minor leagues as a young umpire and all the sudden you're trying to work the plate. On a pitch up at the high waist, you call that a strike and the dugout goes crazy, and you say, 'Well, that's a little too high, let me bring it down a little.' And you go down a couple inches and you call that one a strike and they go crazy again. And you go down a couple inches and you're at the belt now and all of a sudden you don't hear them say anything, so you say, 'Okay, that's where the strike zone ends.' It's trial and error."

To compensate for the low strike zone, some umpires allow any pitch that nicks just a small part of the plate to be called a strike. "If the ball's half and half [over the plate], you're not sure if it's a strike. We're not that good where we can see something within a quarter of an inch, where the ball's coming in at 96 miles an hour and it's a blur, with movement. It's easier to call a strike if you have to make sure the whole ball's on the plate."

At times, even balls off the outside part of the plate are called strikes.

Before the 2001 season, Major League Baseball ordered umpires to strictly follow the strike zone prescribed in the rule book—above the bottom of the knee to the middle of the torso, and over the seventeen-inch plate.

Players and coaches grumbled that the old system of umpires having their own zones was often more predictable. One manager complained: "You hear that they aren't going to be calling them off the plate and sometimes they do and sometimes they don't. You hear they are going to be calling them high, and sometimes they do and sometimes they don't. That kind of messes you up. You don't know what to take and what to swing at." Steve Rippley sighed in early May: "It's definitely a change. It's a work in progress. We're trying to be as consistent as possible with it. The players are used to looking at a different zone, and they're adjusting also."

Baseball's effort to standardize and expand the strike zone has made life easier for many pitchers. In 2001, the average number of runs per game declined 8 percent and 6 percent in the American and National leagues, respectively. The number of walks declined 15 percent and 12 percent, and the number of strikeouts increased 4 percent and 3 percent.

Rippley has a reputation for giving the pitcher close calls. He calls a large strike zone, forcing hitters to swing at borderline pitches. The big strike zone keeps everyone alert—pitcher, hitter, fielders—and makes for a quicker and livelier game. In games recorded by Retrosheet, an Internet site dedicated to archiving statistics from every baseball game, Rippley's reputation is confirmed. When he works the plate, pitchers for both teams averaged about one more strikeout per game than they do for other umpires and almost a half a walk less. His reputation for calling a pitcher's game—and keeping the game moving—is usually enough to get pitchers to throw more strikes and batters more prepared to swing.

Tonight, Rippley is calling strikes on anything close to the plate. Rippley has made a number of strike calls that could have gone the other way: in the first inning, on Derek Jeter (strike three on an outside pitch) and Tony Womack (strike two on a ball inside); in the second inning, Danny Bautista (strike one on an outside pitch) and Curt Schilling (strike one on an outside pitch, strike three on a ball high); in the fourth inning, Jeter (strike two on a pitch outside) and Paul O'Neill (strike one on an outside pitch); and in the fifth inning, Tino Martinez (strike one on a pitch outside) and Jorge Posada (strike two on a ball outside). The only complaint against Rippley came on the first close call, when he established his wide zone, and on the first pitch to Posada in the fifth, when he called a borderline outside pitch a ball.

The true sign that an umpire performs his job well is that no one notices. "The staggering anonymity of the umpires [in the seventh game of the 2001 World Series] at least implies that Rippley was calling a remarkable game," says broadcaster Tim McCarver.

◆ ◆ ◆

UMPIRES UNDERSTAND THE pitcher-catcher battery as well as anyone on the field. Umpires develop an unusually intimate relationship with catchers as the two spoon behind the plate for every pitch. They move in sync. They share the joys of a disciplined and fast-working pitcher and the miseries of a wild or inconsistent pitcher. Hirschbeck, the veteran umpire who worked the 2001 World Series, gives Posada high marks for his work with Clemens and other Yankees pitchers.

"Good receivers are ones that catch the ball nice and soft and make everything look good," Hirschbeck says. "Jorge gives you a good look at the ball. He'll put the glove out and just hold it there. He won't swat and lunge at pitches, he'll just catch the ball. In my whole career there were just one or two guys that you thought, 'Oh no, I'm going to get killed back there,' and you did because they stunk."

In an era when pitchers change teams frequently and expansion has thinned their ranks, catchers have become the most important players for many pitching staffs. "You used to look up the pitching matchups and say, 'Oh good, today I got Maddux and Schilling,'" Hirschbeck says. "But catching has become so important that umpires nowadays say, 'Hey, who do I have catching today?' A good catcher can work wonders for even a fifth or sixth pitcher on the staff. He can actually make the pitchers look good. If a guy is a butcher, you don't want to go back there as an umpire."

With an unsteady catcher, umpires have a hard time seeing pitches. Hirschbeck talks about one catcher who used to undermine his pitchers in every game. "If you had a great pitcher on the mound he's going to make everything look like shit," Hirschbeck says. "I couldn't stand working behind him. I had a very difficult time behind him—a horrible time. It seemed like he always set up late, when a pitcher was getting ready to throw. He's a good guy and everything, but I couldn't handle working behind him—[there was] movement, up and down, herky-jerky. It seemed like every time he caught the ball he was sweeping down and beating the ball into the ground, always moving. So if he caught a pitch knee-high and that little bit of movement made it look like the pitch was low. And the pitcher gets pissed." Hirshbeck pauses as if to answer: "Well, don't blame me. Blame your catcher."

◆ ◆ ◆

WITH ONE OUT and a runner on base in the bottom of the second inning, Mark Grace, a left-handed hitter, bats. Grace lines a 1–0 pitch on the outside part of the plate to left field for a hit. The Diamondbacks now have runners on first and second base. Behind in the count after throwing four straight balls, Clemens comes in with the pitch and Grace is ready. A master of bat control, Grace leans out over the plate, offering his bat with both hands and going with the ball where it's pitched, avoiding the temptation to pull the ball. Good hitters often take weak swings because they are overeager, so determined to smash the ball that they are fooled by the pitch's speed or location. Grace tracks the ball all the way to the bat. Grace leans his body toward first base as he hits the ball.

The hit comes on a hit-and-run play. Manager Bob Brenly wanted to get Danny Bautista to third so he could score on an out. But Bautista hesitated on the base path, uncertain whether Grace's hit could be caught. As he runs to second base, Jeter blocks the bag. Bautista probably had no chance to get to third base, but Diamondbacks manager Bob Brenly complains that umpire Dale Scott should call interference on Jeter and award Bautista third base. Even if Jeter did not come into contact with Bautista, he forced the runner to break his stride.

◆ ◆ ◆

THE DIAMONDBACKS HAVE an opportunity to score with runners on first and second base and one out. Catcher Damian Miller, a right-handed hitter, steps up to the plate. After a couple of balls, Clemens throws a fastball on the outside part of the plate for a strike. Posada got crossed up on the pitch—he was expecting a changeup and got a hard fastball. Clemens and Posada have had a hard time agreeing on what Clemens would throw and where.

The mix-up causes no damage. Miller fouls back the next pitch and then strikes out on a splitter on the outside part of the plate. The ball looks destined for the outside part of the plate and then bends over the plate. Clemens has settled down with three straight strikes. Now he can finish the inning with an easy out. Curt Schilling, a poor hitting pitcher, steps to the plate.

◆ ◆ ◆

HISTORICALLY, THE MOST athletic pitchers have helped their own cause by swinging the bat well. But Schilling is not comfortable hitting. Clemens gets ahead in the count right away. Schilling looks at the first pitch catch the outside corner like a pedestrian uncertain whether to confront a street nuisance. He waves through the next pitch over the plate.

After getting ahead in the count 0–2, Clemens struggles to put Schilling away. The next pitch sails up and away for a ball. Posada has to stand to catch it. The next pitch also sails up and away. Posada's troubles with Clemens continue.

Finally, Schilling strikes out when he checks his swing on a 95-mile-an-hour fastball that bites the inside part of the plate.

Chapter Six

DRAMATIS PERSONAE

As the finale of the 2001 World Series assumes its own rhythm, the ballpark moves from a frenzied noise to a steady murmur of a midsummer game.

Bank One Ballpark (known as "The BOB") is a hybrid of airport hangar and warehouse. Red brick and green structural steel create a rectangular box large enough to hold eight professional basketball arenas. The façade of the old Arizona Citrus Growers Packing House forms the south side of the stadium. Inside, advertising signs and luxury seating wrap around the building's upper deck. A food court rings the stadium, a restaurant hangs over left field, and a swimming pool lies beyond the right field fence. The engineering feat of the stadium is a retractable roof, which opens or closes in five minutes. In the steamy summer months, the open roof allows the sun to nourish the grass during the day, then closes just before the game begins. The air-conditioning system—a must for every home in Phoenix, where the temperature exceeds 100 degrees ninety days a year—uses one to three million pounds of ice produced on the premises. Tonight, the roof is open.

The real grass, the open sky, the steel beams stapling together the corners, the liberal use of bricks and the green paint, the rumble of the trains next door—all bring an early baseball feel to the modern facility. In some strange way, a dirt path between the mound and home plate evokes an era of "base ball" a century before, when players wore collar shirts and handlebar mustaches. Evocation of yesteryear was not the inspiration for the path. The team's original manager, Buck Showalter, dreamed it up to create odd rolls on soft grounders, which would create a home-team advantage.

Downtown Phoenix, home of the BOB, is a small cluster of glass and concrete buildings. As recently as the 1980s, the city boasted just four skyscrapers. The skyline is not much bigger today. An exception is the downtown's tallest building, the forty-floor brick-and-glass Bank One Center. Key attractions downtown include the Civic Plaza Convention Center, a Hyatt Hotel, and the Herberger Theater. The most famous buildings downtown are sports arenas named after corporations. The America West Arena is home to the basketball Suns and the hockey Coyotes. The city's only nod to the past is a historic district consisting of a small block of old wood houses. Parking garages fill in gaps—and *create* gaps—all over the central business district. Downtown stands empty after business hours, except when a sports event takes place—and then the hubbub is all about getting in and out, not actually congregating in public spaces.

Phoenix is just part of the sprawling Valley of the Sun. Frank Lloyd Wright once celebrated the area's stark beauty: "The desert, with its rim of arid mountains, spotted like the leopard's skin or tattooed with amazing patterns of creation, is a grand garden the likes of which in sheer beauty of reach, space, and pattern does not exist, I think, anywhere else in the world."

Dams made it possible to grow cotton, citrus, melons, and dates—and tract housing, the most plentiful fruit of recent years. A broad lattice of highways and arteries sculpts the landscape. Sand-colored strip malls and housing tracts line the edges of the highways. Those highways are Arizona's common denominator. Highways bring Arizonans from home to work and back, to nationally renowned hiking and camping spots, to ski slopes in snow-capped mountains and lakes for water skiing, and to golf courses everywhere.

The highways also bring Arizonans to baseball diamonds around the Phoenix area. Baseball has become the premier game in Arizona, thanks to year-round warm weather, a population and economic boom, an increase in major leaguers past and present living in the area, twelve teams in the spring-training Cactus League, and a proliferation of amateur leagues. The state's youth leagues are as good as the leagues in California and Texas, long the nation's best.

"Ten or fifteen years ago, every kid here wanted to be like Charles Barkley," says Lou Klimchock, a former major leaguer who has been a major force for amateur ball in the state. "Now all you hear out of the kids is baseball, baseball, baseball. The Diamondbacks are the only game in town, and that fact is shaping how a generation of kids from this city view sports."

Baseball in Arizona is like baseball in Latin America—with the added advantage of affluence. That's a long way from 1947, when Bill Veeck moved the Cleveland Indians training camp to Arizona to avoid the segregationist policies of Florida.

◆ ◆ ◆

THE ARIZONA DIAMONDBACKS were built to win right away. Created in 1998, the team won just sixty-five games in its first season. Nothing remarkable about that. Every expansion team suffers years of ineptitude before competing for a championship. But the Diamondbacks panicked when season-ticket sales fell 25 percent after the first year. Rather than build a team slowly through the farm system, Diamondbacks owner Jerry Colangelo decided to spend money on established players. He brought in Mark Grace from the Cubs, Matt Williams from the Indians, Todd Stottlemyre from the Rangers, Jay Bell from the Royals—and of course, Randy Johnson from the Astros and Curt Schilling from the Phillies. All were All-Stars, but none of them had ever played for a World Series winner.

Colangelo was so profligate that one of the objects of his desire expressed concern about the team's financial capacity. "If I were to sign with you, you're not going to have anything else to get any other players," Randy Johnson said.

"You don't worry about that. I'll figure that out," Colangelo answered.

He did. Taking a page from the Broadway play *Damn Yankees*—in which a faithful Washington Senators' fan sold his soul to the devil to lead the Senators to victory over the dynastic Yankees—Colangelo brought the best players to Arizona on a buy-now-pay-later arrangement. By 2001, the Diamondbacks had a payroll of $94 million plus $53 million in deferred salaries. The organization would have to play players for years to come, long after their playing days were over. Spending brought quick success. In their second season, in 1999, the Diamondbacks won 100 games.

In their fourth season—they had existed as a team one year less than Arizona's Senator John McCain spent as a prisoner of war in Vietnam—the Diamondbacks were playing for a championship.

The Diamondbacks began the 2001 season with the second-oldest lineup in baseball history—an average age of thirty-four years and seventy-two days. The injury reports confirmed the team's seniority. Schilling was still working to recover fully from his 1999 shoulder injury. Matt Williams and Jay Bell were also nursing themselves back to health after injury-hobbled seasons in 2000. Todd Stottlemyre was lost for the season after his second surgery. Closer Matt Mantei was out for the year—after playing for just one month—following elbow surgery. By the end of the season, eight other players went on the disabled list.

But the Diamondbacks won the division by two games over San Francisco, winning thirteen of their last nineteen games. And then they roared through the playoffs, beating the St. Louis Cardinals and the Atlanta Braves to win the National League pennant.

◆ ◆ ◆

CALLING THE YANKEES the premier team in professional sports is like calling Stephen Hawking smart. Starting in 1923, a period of seventy-six years, the Yankees won twenty-six championships—better than one every three years. The Yankees invented the dynasty in American sports. Every era of Yankees dominance can be identified with its legendary players—Babe Ruth and Lou Gehrig, Joe DiMaggio and Mickey Mantle, Reggie Jackson and Thurman Munson, Derek Jeter and Roger Clemens—and an ever-changing parade of lesser stars.

After a decade of failure, the Yankees rediscovered the formula for success in the mid- and late-1990s. The Yankees won three straight championships—winning sixteen of their last seventeen World Series games—by getting players who not only possessed great athletic ability but also a willingness to play in Manager Joe Torre's system. Torre played aggressive baseball, insisting that players submit to his authority and do the little things that win games—work the pitchers hard in every at bat, sacrifice themselves at the plate, run the bases aggressively, hit the cutoff man. Torre praises his players liberally but is uncompromising when players cross him.

Torre's way has given the Yankees an unusual edge in close games—during the season and even more in the playoffs and World Series. From the beginning of their three-year run of championships through Game Six of the 2001 World Series, the Yankees played in twelve games decided by one run. The Yankees won every one of those games.

Torre enlisted veterans like Paul O'Neill, Tino Martinez, Jorge Posada, and Derek Jeter to serve as unofficial disciplinarians for the rest of the team. Torre worked hard to instill in the Yankees an "inner conceit"—not cockiness *per se*, but a deep drive and confidence that tells them they'll prevail somehow in the end, no matter what the matchup. "We grind," Torre says. "We play nine innings. That's the highest compliment I can give."

Torre's demanding and deft touch would mean little without owner George Steinbrenner's money. Because baseball gives franchises exclusive rights to their regions—and the Yankees' formal territory encompasses a population of better than fifteen million people, stretching over three states—the Yankees are given far more in TV and radio money than other teams. The Yankees estimated the value of their broadcasting rights to be $2.4 billion over ten years, ten times as much as most other teams and more than twenty times the broadcasting revenue of small-market teams in St. Louis, Milwaukee, and Minneapolis. In recent years, the Yankees pioneered multi-sport marketing and broadcasting deals, creating partnerships with the New Jersey Nets of the National Basketball Association and the New York Giants of the National Football League—and, later, Manchester United, the world-famous British soccer team.

The Yankees' opening-day payroll in 2001 was $107 million. Before the season, the Yankees invested $277.5 million on multi-year contracts for just two players, shortstop Derek Jeter and pitcher Mike Mussina. Historically, the Yankees have always found a way to monopolize talent. From the 1920s to the 1950s—before baseball instituted a draft of amateur players to give other teams access to the best players—the Yankees assigned a fleet of scouts to scour the landscape for high school players. The Yankees also bought top players from bankrupt franchises like the Kansas City Athletics.

The Yankees have reinvented that old formula, not only trading for poor teams' best players but also scrambling to sign the best free-agent players and cornering the market for international players.

◆ ◆ ◆

LAS VEGAS WAS ambivalent about the seventh game of the World Series.

Until the playoffs and World Series, gamblers do not pay much attention to baseball. About 70 percent of all gambling dollars go to college and pro football, and another 25 percent goes to college basketball. Only about 4 percent of all bets go to baseball, and almost all of them are for playoff and World Series games.

"I'm a typical sports bettor in that during the season I don't watch a single inning of baseball, but once the World Series comes around I watch every single inning," says Wayne Allyn Root, one of the leading handicappers in Las Vegas and the author of *The Zen of Gambling*.

Root's job is to beat the lines set by oddsmakers. He makes most of his money on football. Every week, he identifies three or four games of the fifty big-time games where the oddsmakers have misjudged the competition. He exploits the occasional ignorance of oddsmakers and the common ignorance of bettors. "In the old days, people made bad decisions because of what the TV and newspaper reporters were saying about the games," Root says. "Now the Internet allows people to share statistics, but they're usually sharing the wrong statistics. People think they know everything but they always make the wrong bet."

Ken White, the chief operating officer for Las Vegas Sports Consultants, the world's largest oddsmaking company, figured that the Diamondbacks would win the game. A former minor-league player in the San Francisco Giants organization, White uses his own analyses to set the odds for the World Series. Noting Schilling's strong performances in Games One and Four—as well as the Diamondbacks' blowout win in Game Six and a slight home-field advantage—he figured the time was ripe to end the Yankees' string of championships.

"Pitching is 75 or 80 percent of the game, and both teams had great pitching and defense," he says. "The Yankees had better hitting but they were playing without the designated hitter, so the teams were now even. You can't really take momentum from one game to the next. It still comes down to one pitch at a time. It was close, but the Diamondbacks' win in Game Six increased their value by 25 cents."

By the game's first pitch, the line was $1.35 for the Diamondbacks—meaning that a bettor would have to bet $1.35 on Arizona to make $1. While White personally crunches three years' worth of data to set the odds, Root relies on his gut. Betting on a World Series game, he says, is a crap shoot. "The truth is that there is no edge in championship games because the teams are so evenly matched and there is no misinformation for games that everyone is watching and talking about," he says. "I look for a team that wants to get revenge after they've been embarrassed," he says. "Anytime someone loses 15–2, like the Yankees did in Game Six, it's embarrassing and they're going to come back the next day and fight hard. And the team that wins big isn't going to be able to score runs the next day."

Root put his money—how much, he won't say—on the Yankees.

◆ ◆ ◆

THE DIAMONDBACKS PROFESS respect for, but not fear of, the Yankees. After hearing for days about the mystique and aura of the Yankees, Curt Schilling cracked: "Mystique and Aura, those are dancers at a nightclub, not things we concern ourselves with on the ball field." Manager Bob Brenly protested, "The uniform doesn't beat you, the ballpark doesn't beat you, the fans don't beat you, the history of that organization doesn't beat you."

But the mystique remained. When the World Series moved to New York after two games in Phoenix, the Diamondbacks' veteran Mark Grace wandered around Yankee Stadium, awestruck. "I defy anyone to try to wipe this smile off my face. I've had a lot of trouble controlling my anxiety. I'm going to have to try to control my emotions, not go off the deep end, having to be thrown into a straitjacket."

Photos courtesy of Arizona Diamondbacks

Craig Counsell (left) and Matt Williams (right) both displayed their batting strength on Saturday's victory over the New York Yankees.

...laying with my life, but it's ... doesn't have the ... ll of a su...

* * *

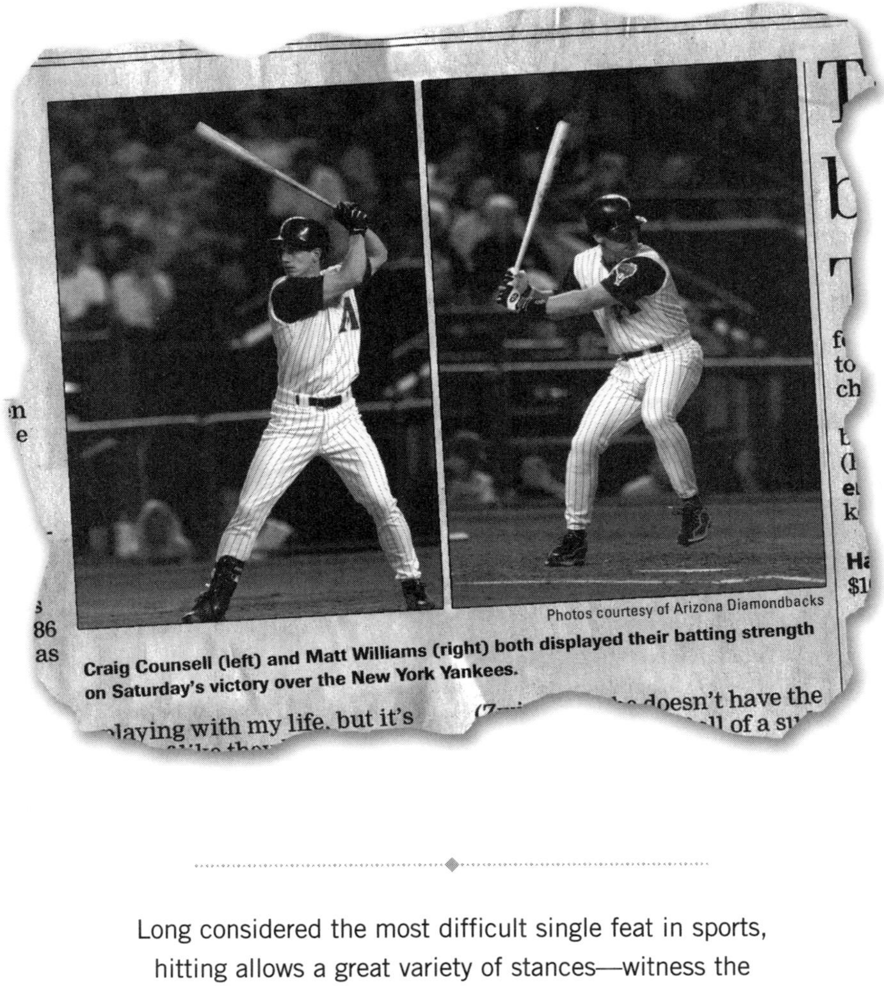

Long considered the most difficult single feat in sports, hitting allows a great variety of stances—witness the sky-scraping posture of Craig Counsell. Matt Williams shows a more classic approach to hitting, with a rapid-fire sequence of movements from feet to legs to hip to arms to hands.

THIRD INNING

In which hitting—the "the hardest single act in sports," according to Ted Williams—is explained by the gritty Matt Williams, the surprising Luis Gonzalez, and a group of scientific researchers that almost no one knows

Chapter Seven

STANDING AT THE PLATE

BASEBALL PEOPLE AGREE that there is no one right way to stand at the plate. The only thing that matters is getting ready to swing the bat—the legs anchored but ready to generate power with a forward thrust, the eyes trained on the pitcher's release, the arms stretched back like a rubber band, ready to snap the bat across the hitting zone.

Over the years, players have used every conceivable stance. Willie Mays planted his feet wide apart with his knees bent slightly, which gave him a short swing—and great control over his body and bat. Stan Musial bent and turned away from the pitcher in a closed stance, coiled and ready to attack the ball. Pete Rose crouched and nervously wagged his bat, while his teammate Joe Morgan flapped his back arm against his side. Jeff Bagwell squats, Ken Griffey Jr. stands erect, and Ichiro Suzuki leans by the plate ready to slap the ball and dart to first base in the same motion.

Ultimately, the stance is just a setup to the real work of hitting, putting the legs and hips and bat in motion. Whether holding the bat high or low, behind the plate or almost over the plate, the point is to be comfortable before going into a swing.

◆ ◆ ◆

DIAMONDBACKS ACE CURT SCHILLING sets the Yankees down in order in the top of the third inning.

As he steps to the plate in the bottom of the third, second baseman Alfonso Soriano looks like fettuccini being dropped onto a plate. Soriano's loose batting stance helps him coil his flexible body back to swing at whatever pitches come his way.

True to the pattern he established over the course of his rookie year, Soriano watches the first pitch, a called strike, and swings through the second pitch. Then he golfs an outside pitch to right fielder Danny Bautista for the inning's first out.

Third baseman Scott Brosius does Curt Schilling a favor by lifting the first pitch to first baseman Mark Grace. Easy out.

And then pitcher Roger Clemens watches a ball low and away before swinging though three pitches for a strikeout.

◆ ◆ ◆

TWO OF BASEBALL'S oddest stances belong to second baseman Craig Counsell and left fielder Luis Gonzalez of the Diamondbacks.

After second baseman Tony Womack strikes out on a foul-tip to catcher Jorge Posada, leading off the bottom of the third inning, Counsell steps to the plate.

Counsell holds the bat up high and behind his head, with his left elbow well behind his back. Manager Bob Brenly smiles at the sight. "He looks like he was trying to knock a spider off the ceiling with a broom," he says. "It's just such an odd-looking thing. And the grip that he has on the bat, it's way up in his fingertips, and his hands are down off of the knob. And you know, the bat is way above his head."

"Hitting a baseball seems like the absolute last thing he can do from this position," says Leigh Montville, a writer for *Sports Illustrated.* "He's beautiful."

But it's not the original stance that matters, it's where the hitter holds the bat as he gets ready to launch a swing. "If you look at a videotape, when that pitcher is at the point of release, his bat is in a good hitting position and he is balanced," Brenly says.

Counsell has answered endless questions about his stance. "A lot of people get fixated on where the stance starts. But go forward five frames and I look like everyone else."

The sky-scraping stance has a reason. The Los Angeles Dodgers released Counsell before the 2000 season. When he signed with the Diamondbacks he was afraid he would be cut loose again. He knew he would never be a power hitter—in fact, as he rose through the minor leagues he modeled himself after the light-hitting shortstop Walt Weiss—but he had to hit better than other defense-oriented infielders.

"I got released by L.A. because I wasn't hitting," he says. "I was looking for something to turn it around. I was working on the back fields in spring training and it felt comfortable. I always had problems with my hands dipping too low. It created a bad swing path. I figured an exaggerated height would prevent me from dropping my hands too low."

Counsell's swing gives his slender arms elasticity as he whips the bat into the hitting zone. He holds the bat loosely and away with the expectation of moving it forward in a snap on a good pitch. As Clemens rocks into his motion, Counsell slowly pulls the bat down and back. As the pitch approaches the plate, he gets ready to attack. "That's the stage where you're loaded and coiled, where you create the energy to drive the ball," he says. "That's why you stride, flex your knees, turn the shoulders."

Batting with one out and no one on base, Counsell steps forward on Clemens's first pitch but lets the ball go outside for a ball. On the next pitch, a belt-high fastball on the outside part of the plate, Counsell whips the bat through the zone, under the ball, his body twirling on the follow-through but not losing his balance. He seems to be running off the pitch, not quite stepping into the bucket but facing the pitcher as he swings—a swing that's not going to generate much power except through the elastic snap of his arms and their endpoint, the wrists.

The next pitch is perfect for Counsell—out over the plate where he can swing through the ball and send it up the middle and into center field. The Yankees' catcher, Jorge Posada, wanted Clemens to throw the ball farther outside and higher, but the pitch comes out over the plate. Counsell gets the fat part of the bat on the ball.

As he turns on the ball, both legs bend, allowing him to fling the bat wherever the ball comes. As he follows through on his swing, Counsell looks like he's doing a dance, with his arms and legs all falling apart from his body. The point of hitting for Counsell is not to concentrate power and force, but to direct his hands and bat wherever the ball is pitched.

◆ ◆ ◆

WITH A RUNNER ON base and one out in the home half of the third inning, baseball's most improbable power hitter steps to the plate.

Before Luis Gonzalez opened his stance, he was a singles and doubles hitter. When he played for the Detroit Tigers, teammate Bobby Higginson encouraged him to exploit Tiger Stadium's short right field fence. Experimenting with different stances, Gonzalez found that he could take a completely open stance. Hitters are traditionally taught to stand perpendicular to the pitcher, turning their heads to see pitches come to the plate. That sideways stance enables them to twist their body into the ball, generating power. Gonzalez faces the pitcher directly with his open stance so he can track the ball with both eyes. Most hitters disdain the open stance because they fear losing the power of the twisting body. But by stepping into the pitch, Gonzalez can twist his body into the ball, too.

But Brenly wonders why more hitters do not take an open stance to see the ball and then step into the pitch to generate power. Brenly's own discovery of the open stance occurred, he said, when he realized his outsized nose impeded his vision. "I wasn't seeing the pitch with my right eye as well as I should be," Brenly says. "I was wondering, 'Why in the hell am I not hitting better?' And then I looked at some videotape, and I realized that, from the center field camera, I can't see my right eye. So that right eye is obviously not seeing what it's supposed to be seeing. So I ended up opening up my stance. And a lot of guys do, just to make sure they see the ball a little bit better."

Research in ophthalmology shows, not surprisingly, that batters get greater depth perception when both eyes work together. Binocular vision takes the images produced by both eyes separately and puts them together into one image with a more three-dimensional view of an object's location and movement in space. In one experiment, researchers placed a filter over a batter's left eye and then over his right eye during a hitting exercise. The batter did much better when he used both eyes. Just how much the binocular vision helped depended on the timing of the impulses from the eyes to the brain—and that depended on the angle of the batter to the mound.

Gonzalez checks his swing but Clemens hits the outside corner of the plate for a strike. After a ball, Gonzalez waves at a pitch on the outside corner—a hanging splitter—and pulls it down the right field line, foul, for strike two.

Would Gonzalez hit the ball more squarely with a standard stance? Maybe. But then again, he might not have seen the ball well enough to make contact.

Clemens wonders what he has to do to get Gonzalez out. Clemens tries the outside part of the plate again, suspecting that Gonzalez's open stance doesn't allow him to whip his bat all the way around to pull with authority. But the pitch gets too far up and outside. Posada has to stand to catch the pitch. Then Clemens comes inside with a fastball—and Gonzalez cannot get around on it. He whiffs, the bat barrel circling his body long after the ball is past him for strike three.

◆ ◆ ◆

ON THE GONZALEZ strikeout, Posada snaps a throw to first base to get Counsell lollygagging off the bag. Tino Martinez rushes in to catch the ball, moving in front of the bag and then sweeping around in a counterclockwise movement to slap his glove on the bag—but Counsell's foot gets to the base a split-second before Martinez's slap. The throw takes everyone by surprise. Even though Counsell gets back safely, Clemens and Posada have taken the spring out of his step. Counsell probably won't get a long lead or get a good jump the rest of the inning. He will be leaning toward first base.

Now the Diamondbacks have two outs. Counsell remains stuck at first base in the bottom of the third inning. The Yankees' infielders now can lean back on the grass. They have more time and room to field the ball. For now, they can relax.

Chapter Eight

SWINGING STYLES

MATT WILLIAMS, FOLLOWING the teachings of his onetime coach Dusty Baker, says the best approach to hitting comes from the "One-Hand Fred."

No one has ever seen this mythical Fred character, but he represents an approach that combines the two classic approaches to hitting. In baseball's dead-ball era, hitters were happy to make contact with the ball and put it into play. They followed the linear approach, bringing the bat across the plate in a line. After the Babe Ruth revolution, hitters whipped the bat around the plate in a wicked circle. That's the rotational approach.

The One-Hand Fred combines the linear and rotational approaches. Williams is the embodiment of this hybrid approach to hitting.

The Diamondbacks' third baseman, the most accomplished power hitter playing in the 2001 World Series, has hit 362 home runs over a fifteen-year career with the San Francisco Giants, Cleveland Indians, and now the Diamondbacks. Williams has hit over .300 three times, including .336 in 1995. Playing for the Giants in 1994, Williams hit home runs at a pace that would have enabled him to break Roger

Maris's single-season record of sixty-one. When labor strife ended the season in July, the sports analysis company Stats Inc. conducted a computer simulation and projected that Williams would have hit sixty-two home runs had the season continued.

Williams stands six feet, two inches, and he weighs 210 pounds. He has muscles all over, coated in a light layer of baby fat. But his most distinguishing characteristic is his bald head. He looks like Uncle Fester in the old Charles Addams cartoons. When he's intent—which is often—forehead wrinkles and veins stretch across his forehead. His face is soft, but worn by years in the sun. Sometimes he looks like a hardened truck driver, but you can catch him looking like an innocent child too. His smile is a shy one.

His voice is quiet, sometimes halting, searching, earnest. He says he is on a "journey" to figure out how life works, through the medium of hitting.

These days, Williams estimates that he swings only 80 percent as quickly as he once did, but he's also a lot smarter now. Williams sometimes lacerates himself when he strikes out, but he has learned to ease up on the self-abuse and refocus his mind after a tough at bat. Like other dedicated students of hitting—from Ted Williams to George Brett—Matt Williams comes to the ballpark early every day. He practices everything, including bunting, something that he has never actually done in a game. Against his better judgment, he takes extra batting practice when he's doing well (to stay in the groove) and when he's doing badly (to get in the groove). Sometimes he practices so much that he's tired by the start of the game and his hands are raw from swinging the bat so hard and so long.

When Williams walks to the plate in the bottom of the third inning, his bat folded under his right arm, neither team has shown much ability with the bat.

◆ ◆ ◆

FOR YEARS, MATT WILLIAMS participated in a baseball equivalent of the Algonquin Round Table. Like the literary set that met at New York's Algonquin Hotel in the 1920s—Dorothy Parker, Robert Sherwood,

Harold Ross, Harpo Marx—a group of players, gathered by Dusty Baker, met around the batting cage to talk about hitting.

Dusty Baker was the hitting coach for the Giants during Williams's years in San Francisco. Rather than having his hitters just take their cuts in the batting cage, Baker invited Williams and other players to be part of an ongoing conversation about hitting. The conversations continued in clubhouses, restaurants, and hotel bars.

Baker tried to improve his players' hitting by *forgetting about* hitting. Baker brought a boom box to the cage and played the role of a disc jockey. When the Giants were facing a power pitcher like Curt Schilling, Baker would play hard, driving music like AC/DC. When the Giants faced a finesse pitcher like Greg Maddux, he would play soft stuff, like 1970s oldies. Baker would play the songs he wanted the players to blend into their subconscious and then send them in to hit. Baker's strategy in the cage was to coax the players into grooving and swaying with the music.

The science of the brain supports Bakers approach. Researchers have found that a set of circuits in the front of the brain keep rhythm and melody in the head long after the music is heard. That's why you cannot get a song out of your head, whether it's a bad radio jingle or Beethoven's *Ode to Joy*. That part of the brain—called the rostromedial prefrontal cortex—not only processes music but also controls the body's movement. The brain's circuitry for music is also the circuitry for dance—and for moving around a baseball diamond. "The experience of the groove in music is a state where our perceptions and actions are meshed together," says Petr Janata of the Center for the Mind and Brain at the University of California's Davis campus.

◆ ◆ ◆

HITTING REQUIRES MORE than getting in the groove. It also requires understanding the lightning-fast mechanics of the swing. That's why the One-Hand Fred entered the conversations.

For a century, baseball people have debated two basic approaches to hitting.

The linear school of hitting dominated baseball from the late nineteenth century until Babe Ruth changed the game in the 1920s. The linear school taught batters to bring their bat over the plate in a straight, even line. Using fat bats with fat handles, hitters just wanted to make contact with the ball. The goal of hitters like Ty Cobb and Wee Willie Keeler was to put the ball in play— "hit 'em where they ain't," to use Keeler's famous expression—and play for one or two runs at a time. If the goal was to get the bat on the ball, hitters could not generate much power. In an era of low-scoring games, power was not needed.

In modern times, the legendary hitting coach Charley Lau revised and revived linear hitting. Over the course of three decades, Lau tutored dozens of players like George Brett, Harold Baines, Carlton Fisk, Wade Boggs, Tony Gwynn, and Bill Buckner. In 2001, a Japanese sensation named Ichiro Suzuki brought a new set of linear moves to the batter's box.

Lau's basic insight was simple. The smoothest swings occur when the batter keeps the body's many moving parts moving freely, each in sync with the others—and against the ball hurtling toward the plate. Batters succeed when they coordinate their body parts; they fail when they allow those body parts to get tied up and contorted.

Lau's hitters look as though they are flinging their bats at the ball rather than using the full force of their bodies to power the ball. That way, they achieve a freer swing, absent the resistance of their own bodies. Rather than squeezing the bat with both hands through a circular swing, Lauist hitters let go of their top hand as they hit the ball; their lower hand swings all the way through, "finishing high"—lifting the bat high in the air after their swing, as if they are pointing to a distant star.

The second approach to hitting is known as rotational. As the name suggests, the hitter's goal is not just to meet the ball, but rather to bring his bat around in a circle with great power. The champion of the rotational approach was Ted Williams. Williams taught that the hitter generates power by shifting his hips forward. The hitter swings hard, bringing the bat around his body in a wicked arc. He holds the bat with both hands all the way around. All of the body's forces are brought to bear on that five-ounce ball hurtling toward home plate at 85 to 95 miles per hour.

Once Babe Ruth popularized the power game in the 1920s and 1930s, the linear approach to slapping hits faded away. Why settle for a series of singles when doubles and homers can clear the bases and bring home more runs? The goal of the game, after all, is to score as many runs as possible. The modern era has been dominated by rotational hitters—Ted Williams and Joe DiMaggio, Mickey Mantle and Harmon Killebrew, Willie Mays and Hank Aaron, Reggie Jackson and Mike Schmidt, Barry Bonds and Sammy Sosa.

Power gets generated from the ground up—with the legs driving the hips, which drive the torso, which in turn drive the arms—and direct that power toward the end of the bat. The end of the bat responds like the end of a whip when it's snapped. To create this end-of-bat torque, a long circular swing pushes the bat away from the body (centrifugal force) while at the same time bringing it back in (centripetal force).

Scientists studying hitting have found that the ideal swing includes both linear and rotational components. The rotational elements are essential for power, and the linear elements are essential for balance and control.

Even when whipping the bat around in a wicked arc, the hitter sometimes needs to shorten his swing to cover as much of the strike zone as possible. A hitter shortens his swing when he gets fooled on a pitch and needs to hold the bat back for milliseconds, gaining enough control of the bat to make simple contact with the ball. Or when he's facing a pitcher like Mariano Rivera, who burns the ball inside and doesn't allow the hitter much chance to extend his arms.

What's happening in this split-second adjustment is a shift from Ted Williams's rotational motion to Charley Lau's linear motion. Rather than whipping the bat around ferociously, just put the bat out in front, covering more of the hitting zone with the fat part of the bat. Step toward the plate with the bat, lay the bat over the plate, and *let the ball hit the bat.* By stepping toward the pitch, the batter does not have to exert the same kind of precision to his swing. Just put the bat on the ball.

That's what Dusty Baker and his merry band of sluggers called the One-Hand Fred.

No one knows where the name Fred originated. Baker could have called his mythical friend One-Hand Willie or One-Hand Harry. All

Baker cared about, as a teacher, was getting his hitters to embrace this character when they needed to shorten their swing.

"A ball that you're fooled by—when you would release your top hand to stay through that ball—we used to call it the One-Hand Fred," Matt Williams remembers. "When you're fooled by it, there's only so far you can go. So you're going to swing by taking that hand off the bat so you can extend the bat out through the ball and keep yourself out on a plane. You'd get fooled but get your bat on the ball, then you'd come back to the dugout, and Dusty would say, *'Ohhhh, One-Hand Fred!'* It became a term we would use. If you're on time and on a plane, use two hands all the way. If you're fooled or you need a chance to extend the bat and stay on that ball, you One-Hand Fred it."

Reaction time is critical to the One-Hand Fred. Reaction time requires one part physical conditioning and one part mental training. The body's 640 muscles—and the hitter's brain—have to be ready to respond to events in small fractions of seconds.

◆ ◆ ◆

WITH A RUNNER ON BASE with two outs, Matt Williams stands at the plate in the bottom of the third inning. A right-handed hitter, Williams stands upright. In his practice swings before the pitch, Williams wags the bat below the strike zone, almost scraping the ground. He's in the rhythm. He's going to let his athleticism, his fast-twitch muscles, do all the work, from the memory of millions of swings stored in his body. No point in thinking too much.

Matt Williams lifts his leg as the pitch approaches the plate, then lets the pitch fall just outside the zone for ball one.

Why the leg kick? Williams can't figure it out himself. He's tried to change it. Early in his career, his coaches worked with Williams to eliminate the leg kick. A kickless stride worked in batting practice, but not in games. "I tried to change a million times. I tried to take my leg kick out, I tried to take my hitch out, hold my hands here [in the middle of his frame, just slightly behind the body], and just swing—and I couldn't do it. I'd think I was doing it and I would go back and look at tape and see I was doing the same thing. I would spend all winter doing it, and in batting practice I'd do it, and I'd be fine, and I'd think, 'Hey, this is perfect, I'm taking this into the game,' and as soon I got into the game and the first pitch was thrown I would revert back to the leg kick and the hitch and everything else. When you get in a pressure cooker you revert back to who you are."

Something in Williams's subconscious wanted to keep the leg kick. "I only knew one way and I guess there were enough good things about that one way to keep me around," he said. Eliminating a quirk in hitting style doesn't make sense if it causes anxiety. As Dusty Baker would say, get in the groove and let the body take over.

The Diamondbacks' aging star might not like to think too much about his swing, but the leg kick plays a functional role. The leg kick breaks the swing into two key component. Rather than lurching and moving the body forward before he's ready to swing, getting the hands out in front too soon, the leg kick creates a pause in the action that allows the hitter to move his body forward in the proper sequence: kick the legs, step forward, move the hips, turn the torso, and snap the hands. Hall of Fame third baseman Mike Schmidt, in fact, now markets a mechanical device that forces hitters to do what Williams does naturally—namely, stride, wait, and then swing. "The machine was developed to teach a hitter not to react to what they see from the pitcher," Schmidt says matter-of-factly, "but to get in position to wait on the ball." Which is what the leg kick does.

But the kick does something else. Lifting the front foot and then putting it down again shoots energy down the leg, and that energy then shoots up the leg and to the hips and torso where it can power the swing. Coop DeRenne, a researcher at the University of Hawaii, has broken down the swing after viewing slow-motion videotapes of elite hitters. The key moment in the swing, DeRenne says, occurs when energy shoots up the front foot. As the hitter strides forward and puts his front foot down, the ground pushes back against the body; in DeRenne's words, "The ground's reaction force is applied to the body." It's as if the ground were pushing up against the body. The batter generates power for his swing with the ground force upward on the legs, hip, and torso.

Matt Williams fouls back the next pitch, a ball low and over the plate. On a 1-and-1 count, Clemens gets Williams reaching on an outside pitch—a splitter even further outside than catcher Jorge Posada wanted. Williams bounces a high pitch down the third base line. Scott Brosius bare-hands it and throws late and wild to first base. Tino Martinez can't handle it. It's a hit, but not one that makes Williams proud.

It's the One-Hand Fred. Williams was fooled. He saw a fastball coming out of Clemens's arm slot and what he got was a hard, diving splitter. He uppercut the low pitch and hit it weakly down the line.

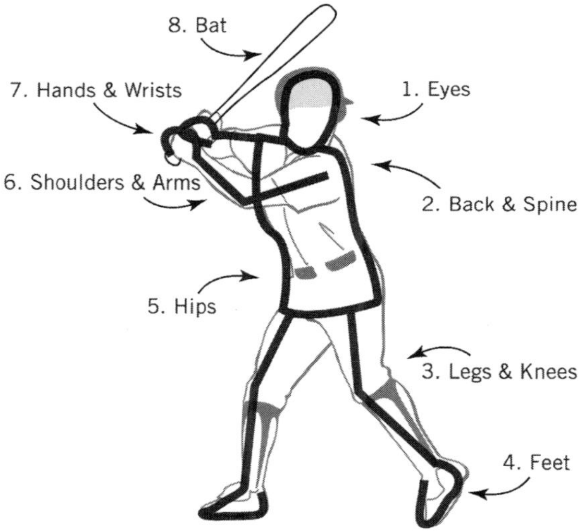

Scientists have identified a clear sequence of movements that occur in batting. A stick figure drawn from a photograph of Matt Williams shows the body parts used in the sequence. As the batter holds his head and eyes steady (1), he also maintains a straight back and spine (2). The batter flexes his knees (3), and often lifts his front foot (4), before quickly twisting his hips and torso (5). The batter brings back his shoulders and arms to create elastic tension (6), before the hands and wrists move forward (7). Finally, the hitter whips the bat forward across the hitting zone (8).

(Graphic by Matthew Chenoweth)

IN THE LAST GENERATION—with the benefits of high-speed video analysis and a greater emphasis on power hitting—baseball has discovered that the linear and rotational approaches can be combined into one hitting system. To understand the scientific approach to hitting, you need to understand the body's different parts and how they move in a rapid-fire sequence.

Researchers at Human Performance Technologies in Jupiter, Florida, filmed thirty-nine professional hitters. Under the direction of Christian Welch, the president of HPT, the researchers used video cameras and computer-imaging equipment to measure the movements of different body parts at a rate of two hundred frames per second. By placing electronic plates in the batter's box, which record data the shifts of the batter's body weight, researchers measured the force of the body on the ground at intervals of 1,000 samples per second. The results, published in the *Journal of Orthopedic and Sports Physical Therapy* in 1995, reveal every twitch and movement in the batter's box.

That research—and dozens of other articles published since then—break down the swing into eight key elements.

1. Head and Eyes: The eyes must see the ball and send information to the brain. To get the best information about the pitch—coming at variable speeds of 80 to 100 miles per hour, to different areas inside and outside the strike zone—the eyes need to pick up the ball at different points of its journey. The head has to be steady so the eyes can get the most reliable information. The more the head moves, the more false information the brain gets about the ball's movement.

The pitcher's release point determines where the hitter looks for the ball. The hitter looks first at an imaginary box or oval just beyond the pitcher's release point to where his eyes can pick up the ball. It's a process that eye specialists call "soft centering": looking in a general area, rather than locking the eyes on a single spot.

What the hitter cannot do is watch the ball all the way. Forget what the Little League coach says about keeping your eye on the ball—*it cannot be done.* Instead, says Donald Tieg of the Institute for Sports Vision in Connecticut, the batter should look for the ball at select points along the pitch's path—out of the pitcher's hand, into an imaginary box eight or ten feet beyond the ball's release—to make a judgment about where the ball will end up near the plate.

Using a mental library of thousands of images stored in his brain, the hitter makes an educated guess about the pitch's speed and movement and location. A ball will go one way if it is hurled by a tall pitcher with a certain push of the legs off the mound, with a certain angle of the arm, and with a certain whip of the wrists. The ball will go another way if the pitcher's leg push, arm angle, and wrist snap are different. Pitchers send off as many intricate signals as there are variations in the movements of body parts—legs, knees, feet, shoulder; elbow, wrist, hand, fingers; eyes, head, neck, chin, mouth. Batters must use their mental library of images to guess where the ball will go, how fast, and with what movement.

The mental library of pitches gets hardwired into the very muscles and fibers of the body. This "body memory" enables the batter to pay attention to the particulars of the situation and allow his body to do the rest without much effort and even less real thinking.

The hitter's ability to make a smart decision based on fragments of information—putting the data together in some kind of superhuman hyperspeed—has come to be called "thin slicing." The brain stores so much information, and makes it available in such miraculous ways, that people can make smart decisions based on very narrow "slices" of the total information stored in the brain.

Author Malcolm Gladwell argues that virtually every aspect of life requires such rapid cognition. Whether assessing a job candidate, calculating the danger of a scary-looking city street, understanding the wiliness of a salesman—or hitting a baseball—people have a great capacity to call up, sort, and analyze massive amounts of information. By understanding patterns, people can make snap judgments that are often better than deliberate judgments. In some cases, like hitting, there is no other option given the lightning speed of the challenge. The critical fact for hitting is that this process of instant decision making can be trained and improved.

2. Back and Spine: To keep the head steady—and to create a stable foundation for the swing—the back and spine need to make a straight vertical line through the body.

The back and spine not only give the body stability, but also make it possible for the hitter to twist his body back to generate power. The spine acts like the center of a spinning top; when stable, it provides a strong foundation for the rest of the body's actions. The stronger and steadier the spine, the greater the force the legs and torso and arms can exert on the ball. If the center of the body is wobbly, the hitter cannot generate power with his hips, torso, shoulders, and arms; instead, power dissipates during the swing.

3. Legs and Knees: The knees need to be flexed—to help the hitter move his legs easily and to give them some springiness. The batter's critical movement occurs when he steps forward from the back foot to the front foot. That step varies with different hitters. Followers of Ted Williams tend to plant the back foot as they step forward with the front foot; followers of Charley Lau tend to lift the back foot as they step forward. The back leg supports the front leg as the batter drives forward toward the pitch.

4. Feet: Even though batters succeed with a wide range of batting stances, the feet need to be planted firmly enough so that the batter not only has that steady base and vertical spine, but also so that the legs can generate as much energy as possible and distribute it up the body to the hips, torso, and arms. If a coach can push a batter over in his stance, the legs are not an appropriate distance apart. The feet need to support the batter's stride forward. Even if the batter simply lifts his front leg and puts it in the same place again, he still needs to move his body up and forward.

The stride powers the swing. When the hitter picks up his front foot and puts it down on the ground—ideally, just under three feet in front of the back foot—the amount of force put on that front foot is equal to about 123 percent of the batter's body weight—or about 1,007 newtons. (For a point of comparison, consider that a hard collision in the National Football League, in which opposing players hit each other at a rate of ten meters per second, produces about 9,000 newtons of force.) That force shoots energy up the leg, where it powers the hips, torso, shoulders, and arms.

5. Hips: The first recipient of the ground-up power is the hips. The hips take that power, twist back and then forward, generating their own forward (rotational) movement. The hip movement is scarily fast—about 714 degrees per second, according to one scientific analysis. To understand the speed of that movement, consider that the hips would turn around completely almost twice in one second. That rotation creates the energy needed to power the torso and arms.

6. Shoulders and Arms: In a process known as "elastic loading," the batter brings his bat behind his shoulders and back. Like a rubber band stretched before snapping, the bat gets extra force from the muscles' elasticity. As the bat moves forward, a snapping action occurs—creating as much power as possible on the bat.

The shoulder moves forward at a rate of 937 degrees per second and the arms move forward at a rate of 1,160 degrees per second. The shoulder has a shorter distance to turn, but both the shoulder and arm move forward fast enough to do about three full circles in a second. Before one movement moves anywhere near a rotation, another rapid-fire movement takes over.

When a hitter moves into launching position, he stretches his muscles by as much as 20 percent, which produces 15 percent greater tension and 30 percent more work. Muscles can also contract to as little as half their natural length. Both expansion and contraction matter for an athlete's actions, since the force of the muscles is the speed of contraction. Muscles are very inefficient—transforming only 15 to 25 percent of calories into energy—so athletes need to do everything they can to create smooth movements.

Muscles make up about half of the athlete's total body mass. Go back to high school biology. Remember that muscles are bundles of cylindrical cells, like strands of spaghetti. Electrical pulses from nerve cells cause muscles to twitch—contract and then relax—in periods ranging between ten and a few hundred milliseconds. Muscle actions quicken when twitches overlap each other; like singers around a campfire doing rounds of "Row, Row, Row, Your Boat," muscle twitches overlap each other rhythmically. New rounds start before the old ones are completed. Some muscles simply twitch faster than others—capacities that are set at birth by the thickness and cross-sectional density of the fibers.

Fast-twitch muscles provide short bursts of energy good for tasks like hitting a baseball or throwing a discus; slow-twitch muscles provide less explosive but more enduring aerobic power for activities like long-distance swimming or running. The difference in the two types is not how much force is exerted in each contraction, but how rapidly muscle fibers fire. Most people have roughly equal shares of these two muscle types, but the ratio of fast- to slow-twitch muscles varies greatly for specialized athletes and physical laborers. A defensive lineman typically has a 4-to-1 ratio of fast- to slow-twitch muscles, while a marathoner usually has the opposite ratio. Much of the athlete's muscular makeup is genetic, but training can alter the ratio at the margins.

7. Hands and Wrists: Batters hit best when holding their bats lightly. When batters get tense and squeeze the bat, energy gets locked up; it's harder to get the swing to transfer energy from the torso to the arms and hands to the bat.

At a critical moment of the swing, the hands stop. By arresting their forward movement, energy moves from the hands to the bat. The more the batter can hold his hands close to the body during the swing, the greater the amount of force that is generated at the end of the bat. For the past fifty years, bat handles have gotten thinner and thinner; the average circumference of the handle has declined from 1.2 inches to 0.7 inches over the last half-century. With a smaller handle, the bat's weight can be moved toward the barrel—and the bat can be whipped around viciously, like a rock at the end of a string.

To maximize the bat speed, the hitter needs to keep his hands close to his body. John White, a retired physicist for the Lawrence Livermore National Laboratory, likens the rotational approach to a spinning ice skater or a top. By maintaining a strong center of gravity—with a balanced stance, hands close to the body—the batter develops the maximum amount of energy. That energy gets transferred out to the hands, arms, and bat during the swing. The lower arm pushes the bat away from the body and the top hand directs the bat through the zone.

The two hands, in a subtle way, work against each other to maintain the handle's steadiness while driving the end of the bat through the hitting zone. The upper hand pulls back toward the catcher, and the bottom hand drives forward toward the pitch. The hands move on a circular path. The wrist action is really a snap that comes from opposite forces being exerted on the hands. The heel of the bat moves forward, while the bat head stays back for an instant. The bat's whipping effect comes from the push-pull action of the arms as the hands move in a circle.

Rotational and linear hitting theorists disagree vociferously about the importance of the wrists. Rotational advocates insist that the top hand stay on the bat through the swing to impart extra power to the swing. Linear advocates say the wrists don't matter much, so taking the top hand off the bat during the swing is okay. Research shows that the wrist roll does not occur until after the bat hits the ball. By the time of contact, the ground-up batting motion has already generated the bat's energy. However impressive strong wrists look as they roll over in a swing, they do not have much impact on the swing's power.

8. Bat: When the bat hits the ball, a collision of two opposite forces occurs. The force of the bat, whipping forward at 70 to 85 or more miles per hour, counteracts the force of a ball, traveling from 80 to 100 miles per hour. When the two collide, energy transfers from bat to ball. The bat first stops the momentum of the ball and then reverses it. For a split-second, maybe 1/1,000th of a second, the ball stops. At the moment of collision, most of the energy dissipates in the heat and the distribution of energy along the bat. The faster the bat comes around, the greater the distance the ball travels. Mark McGwire and Sammy Sosa swing their bats at 80 miles per hour; Barry Bonds swings his even quicker, as fast as 85 miles per hour. Every extra mile an hour of bat speed adds seven or eight extra feet of distance.

A difference in timing the swing of 1/100th of a second can mean the difference between hitting a long home run and a weak foul ball. A difference of 1/200th of a second determines whether the ball flies to left, center, or right field. The bat itself only moves about an inch during contact with the ball.

At the 1/1,000th of a second's moment of impact, the batter exerts about 8,000 pounds of force, equivalent to an elephant putting all its weight on the ball at that moment. In the last twentieth of a second before contact, the batter generates about ten horsepower of energy—about seventy times what a construction worker exerts in an entire shift.

Batted balls rotate as fast as 2,000 rotations per minute, or about 33 rotations per second. A ball with backspin (as opposed to topspin) can carry an additional thirty feet.

The uppercut helps to produce backspin on the ball. By getting under the pitch a centimeter or two, the hitter rotates the ball backwards toward the plate, which gives the ball some extra lift.

Old-timers often disdain the uppercut. In its early days, baseball was a game of singles and doubles. Hall of Fame players like Ty Cobb, Honus Wagner, and Nelson Fox mastered the art of getting their bat on the ball, punching the ball through infield holes and outfield gaps. In an era dominated by pitching and fielding—as well as a Puritan ethic of small, unpretentious contributions to a team's offense—batters learned to swing *down* on the ball.

Uppercutting often breeds bad habits—long, loping swings that take more time, and therefore require the hitter to begin his swing before really knowing where the pitch is going to be. That means more strikeouts—a virtual gift to the pitcher, and bad habit for hitters. By not putting the ball into play, big swingers do not force the defense to make the plays—and deprive their own team of the chance for something big to happen.

But it doesn't matter. Modern baseball is a power game all around. Pitchers throw harder, and batters swing harder. The big hits and misses are both more dramatic.

◆ ◆ ◆

WITH TWO BASE runners, Steve Finley has a chance to put the Diamondbacks on the scoreboard in the bottom of the fourth inning.

Finley plays Clemens's inside-out game. He watches Clemens's first pitch come inside for a ball, then the second pitch catch the outside of the plate for a strike. Then Clemens comes inside again—his specialty: a high, hard fastball. Finley swings though the ball for strike two.

After laying off a high and inside fastball for ball two, Finley waves at a pitch on the outside part of the plate for the third strike. Another frustrating inning ends for the Diamondbacks. Despite two base runners, the Diamondbacks cannot manage a run against Clemens.

It looks like it's going to be a long night for the hitters. Whatever wildness Clemens has now is working to his advantage. He not only has the sizzle of a younger pitcher but an exquisite balance of predictability and unpredictability that marks baseball's great power pitchers.

Dominant pitchers—like Curt Schilling and Roger Clemens—derive their power from their lower bodies.

Photos courtesy of New York Yankees and Arizona Diamondbacks

FOURTH INNING

In which two of baseball's premier power pitchers explain how pitching works—from the development of a game plan to the execution of pitches in every conceivable situation over the course of the game

Chapter Nine

THE PHILOSOPHY OF PITCHING

Elite athletes wrap everything they do around a single psychological trait. Ted Williams's single-mindedness, Willie Mays's exuberance, Sandy Koufax's pinpoint intensity, Pete Rose's hustle, and Greg Maddux's in-the-moment deliberateness—to name just a few examples—gave focus to every pitch of every game.

Curt Schilling's defining trait is his preparation for games.

The Diamondbacks' pitcher studies every batter, every game situation, more thoroughly than any player on any team. Working with a video company in Los Angeles, Schilling maintains a vast electronic library of images of hitters he might face. Over six years, Schilling has accumulated clips from twenty thousand at bats. He studies the clips to develop strategies for the batters he expects to face in the next game, looking for patterns and tendencies in different situations that he can exploit in game situations.

Every aspect of Schilling's personality—his training regimen and between-start workouts, his gregariousness between starts and intense silence on days he pitches, his love of media attention, his dramatic assumption of responsibility to carry the team, his desire to dominate the opposition utterly, a camaraderie with teammates that sometimes dissolves into mutual antagonism, his charity work on behalf of Lou Gehrig's disease, and his life as a born-again Christian—now revolves around his messianic zeal for preparation.

Schilling is like a dramatic actor who has figured out his "through-line," the statement that captures his character's motivation for every thought and every action. Schilling's through-line is: *I want to be the best-prepared pitcher, mentally and physically—ever—for every pitch of every game.*

It was not always thus. Schilling is baseball's prodigal son. In his early years, he was an immense talent who wasted his gifts. As his friend George W. Bush is fond of saying, when he was young and irresponsible, he was young and irresponsible.

Raised in a military family, Schilling grew up something of a jester, an undisciplined rogue who delighted but also frustrated and annoyed people who wanted him to do well. Nicknamed "Hoser" in high school, Schilling spent years drifting in the major leagues. He did not know the opposing hitters, did not develop a game plan, did not work hard to perfect his pitches and his motion, did not understand the jobs of his fielders. He was careless and selfish and lazy. He dismissed the advice of more experienced men. Drafted by the Boston Red Sox, he moved to the Baltimore Orioles and then the Houston Astros.

Veteran players and beat reporters mocked and disdained him. In 1990, entering a game for the Orioles as a reliever, he flippantly asked about how to throw to one of the game's best hitters. After Schilling gave up a three-run home run to lose the game, veteran pitcher Joe Price cursed him out in front of teammates. But Price's rant did not change Schilling. Neither did the disdain of his manager, Hall of Famer Frank Robinson, who curtly informed him that he would lose a start unless he cut his long blue-streaked hair and took out his diamond earring.

During the 1991 off-season, Gene Coleman, the training and conditioning coach of the Astros, arranged for Roger Clemens and Schilling to meet as they both worked out at the Astrodome. Schilling had just completed another disappointing season working out of the bullpen, winning only three of eight decisions for the Astros. Clemens lectured the younger pitcher about wasting his physical gifts, using curses to punctuate his remarks.

"He felt at that time that I was someone who was not taking advantage of the gifts that God had given me, that I didn't respect the game the way I should, that I didn't respect my teammates the way I should," Schilling said. "What I thought was going to be kind of a sit-down talk about pitching experience turned out to be an hour-and-a-half butt-chewing from the guy who was in the midst of winning five Cy Youngs.

"When someone of that caliber takes that kind of time and puts that kind of passion into a message, there's obviously something there. And I walked away saying to myself, 'You know, number one, why would he care as much as he did? And number two, if he did care, there must be something there.' I began to turn a corner at that point in my career, both on and off the field. It took time, but no question that it had a huge, huge impact on me."

The Astros traded Schilling to the Phillies before the 1992 season. If Clemens changed Schilling's attitude, a new coach changed his new pitching strategy. "He didn't have the confidence he needed," recalls that coach, Johnny Podres, a World Series star for the Brooklyn and Los Angeles Dodgers in the 1950s and 1960s. "You got to think that with an arm like that and three clubs let him go—and he was working out of *the bullpen*—he should be doing better."

Podres encouraged Schilling to expand his repertoire of pitches. Schilling relied too much on a slider, which hitters could sit on and hit hard.

"I would talk to him, one-on-one, throwing in the bullpen and after those sessions and in the clubhouse. We talked about throwing some cross-seam fastballs. That rising fastball got hitters popping up. And then you can throw some low and away and get them chasing. And then you can use the breaking ball once in a while. And that makes the fastball even better."

◆ ◆ ◆

BEFORE EVERY GAME, Curt Schilling makes a plan. The plan is detailed, down to the pitch, for every situation. Suppose there's a 3–2 count on Derek Jeter with a man on first base? What about a one-ball count against Alfonso Soriano with the bases empty? What if Tino Martinez is hitting with a full count? Schilling not only decides what pitch to throw against different hitters in different situations, but where he wants his fielders to play.

"You work backward from perfection," he says. "You go out thinking perfect game, no-hitter. If you lose those, you go for a shutout. If you lose that, you go for a win."

Between starts, the average dedicated pitcher runs, lifts weights, and listens to discussions of scouting reports. Many pitchers sit in the dugout with the pitching coach and other pitchers to discuss motions, past experiences with hitters, and even the conditions at the field. They confer with their catchers, who will be calling the game.

But Schilling does much more.

"I have never known anybody who prepared like Schill does," manager Bob Brenly says. "I caught and played with some pitchers who spent a lot of time studying advance reports, but Schill was his own advance scout. You know, because of the technology that he made available to himself and the amount of time he spent looking at it. I never played with anybody who had as much attention to detail as Schill did going into a game.

"He watched the CD-ROM, he knew the hitters' weaknesses, he knew what pitches to throw and where [hitters] were likely to hit the ball. So as part of his preparation we talked about positioning our defense with the hitters and how he was going to pitch to them and when you have a pitcher with tremendous command like he does, everything sets up perfectly. We put the guys where we thought they were going to hit the ball, he made the pitch he had to make to force them to hit the ball there, and we made the plays."

After viewing the clips, Schilling decides on pitch sequences to all the hitters—and not just one sequence for every hitter, but different sequences for different situations at different points in the game. With his team behind by one run in the eighth inning, a hitter might swing the bat differently than he would with his team up or down a run in the second inning. Some hitters make adjustments after their first time or two at the plate, and others don't.

Once he knows the opposition, Schilling develops a game plan that works back from the results he wants to the actions he needs to take to achieve those results. It's like having a videotape of the perfect game and then playing it backwards. "When you're on the mound and you're getting ready to throw a pitch and you know the result before it happens, it's a pretty powerful thing," Schilling says. "And it happens to me a lot because I've seen these guys hit off me time and time again, so I know if I make my pitch, I know the ball's going to hit this spot if it gets hit."

Before the game, Schilling meets individually with fielders to tell them where he wants them to play in the field.

"We have a general meeting at the beginning of a three-game series, but if Curt's pitching we have an individual meeting with him the day he's going to pitch," says Matt Williams, the Diamondbacks' third baseman. "It serves two purposes. It serves to confirm his beliefs in what he was trying to do, to positively reinforce his game plan. Secondly, he wants people playing where he wants them to play. He has supreme confidence in his ability to pitch the ball where he wants and getting the hitters to hit the ball where he wants them to hit it. During the game he turns about and looks at the infield, to make sure we were where he wanted us to be. Against the Yankees, in general, Curt's plan was to establish strike one, which is the best pitch in baseball, and then either climb the ladder or descend down the ladder."

To climb the ladder, you throw pitches successively higher and higher; to descend, you throw pitches lower and lower.

"If he was behind in the count he was going to throw his backdoor slider"—a pitch that comes over the plate at the last instant— "against lefthanders, and he had supreme confidence that he could throw that pitch for a strike any time he wanted to. And then he could go back to work."

Schilling's willingness to take responsibility gives his infielders confidence. "He puts out a chart for you: 'Okay, [when Jorge] Posada [hits], I want you playing here for him. For Derek Jeter, I want you to play here,'" first baseman Mark Grace says. "And you just have to do it, and you have to understand that's what he wants. When you ask him, 'Are you sure you want me there?' he takes responsibility. He says, 'If he hits the ball to another spot, it's my fault. I know I can throw the ball anywhere I want to throw it, and that's where he's going to hit the ball if I hit my spot. If I miss my spot and he beats you to your right or your left, that's my fault.' As a fielder, you love playing behind a guy like that, who's never going to blame you for being out of position. He'll always shoulder the blame.

"He'll surprise you. He might have a left-handed pull hitter up, and usually I would be playing close to the line. But he will sometimes have me way off the line, because he's going to pitch him away, away, away."

Teammates chuckle that Schilling prepares too much, makes plans for the obvious. But they acknowledge that even stating the obvious has its value. If you *say* you're going to do something rather than just think it—and tell others—it focuses the mind. And that creates greater confidence.

"Mostly what it does is give him the frame of mind that he knows what he's going to do," notes Grace. "This way, he has complete confidence. That's what it's all about." Second baseman Craig Counsell concurs. "I agree absolutely 100 percent with that," he says.

◆ ◆ ◆

SCHILLING HAS THE CAPACITY to absorb endless streams of data that he studies on video screens and computer printouts and binders three inches thick stuffed with scouting reports.

But there's a difference between information and knowledge. Schilling has knowledge.

Schilling has assembled a "greatest hits" of advice from the game's greatest players—not just pitchers, but any player who achieved extraordinary feats by working hard. Schilling borrows Tom Seaver's drop-and-drive emphasis on pitching with the legs (Seaver dropped so low he got his back knee dirty from scraping the pitcher's mound), Bob Gibson's fast pace (Willie Stargell once remarked that Gibson worked so quickly that you'd think he was double-parked), Roger Clemens's workout ethic (Clemens pushes himself to the point of exhaustion to prepare for game situations when he is drained of energy), Sandy Koufax's smarts and patterns (he could not only throw precise fastballs and curves, but understood a batter's thoughts better than the batter), Johnny Podres's big-game confidence and understanding of mixing pitches (he helped the Brooklyn Dodgers win their only world championship), Tony Gwynn's precision and concentration (he was one of the great virtuosos of athletic control), and Cal Ripken's everyday commitment (he was baseball's ultimate Iron Man, who played in his demanding position for a historic string of 2,632 games).

Like other students of war, Schilling tends to talk in aphorisms. At times he sounds like Sun Tzu or Carl von Clausewitz or his all-time hero, George Patton. *Develop a strategy and work back from strategy to tactics. Apply maximum force at strategic moments. Confuse the opposition. Use tactical retreats to open new possibilities for frontal attacks. Deploy forces in a coordinated way. Allow the general to develop the plan and then take responsibility for its success or failure. Adjust tactics in response to the enemy's actions. Use secret intelligence as a guide to the battlefield.*

◆ ◆ ◆

IN THE TOP half of the fourth inning, Schilling has retired the Yankees without incident. After four innings, the Yankees have sent twelve men to the plate and seen all twelve retired. Only Paul O'Neill has gotten a hit, and he was thrown out trying to stretch a double into a triple.

The Yankees face a quandary as the game progresses. Over the years, the Bronx Bombers have shifted from a pure power game to wearing down the opposition. When a Yankee steps to the plate, he fidgets, moves in and out of the box, takes a lot of pitches and fouls off strikes that are bad pitches to hit. He works the count deep. It's a monotonous way to win but it works.

The Yankees' famous patience at the plate has not been as evident in 2001. Schilling is not letting the Yankees work the count tonight. When the Yankees take the first pitch, it's a strike, so they're behind in the count. The Yankees' aggressiveness has given the advantage to Schilling. He has gotten his outs with minimal effort.

The Yankees have been swinging, hoping to put the ball in play, avoiding falling behind in the count. The Yankees' aggressiveness has given the advantage to Schilling. He has gotten his outs on a minimal number of pitches. Schilling started the six of the first nine Yankee hitters with strikes, and he has the Yankees swinging aggressively early and often—two swinging strikes from Jeter in the first and Martinez in the second, a late first swing from Spencer in the second, one wild swing and two late swings from Clemens in the third. The Yankees are hacking.

"If I'm on, there will be a lot of 0–1, 0–2 counts quickly in the game," Schilling says before the game. "I throw a lot of first-pitch strikes and if they are talking that will work to my advantage. I'm sure they will adjust. I don't imagine they will want to go up and want to be 0–1 or 0–2 just for the sake of taking a pitch. You don't want to adjust before you have to, but you don't want to wait too long."

◆ ◆ ◆

Derek Jeter opens the top of the fourth inning for the Yankees looking all the way on the first pitch. Jeter's body is erect. He leans over to watch the first pitch go low and away for a ball, following the ball from the pitcher's hand into the catcher's glove. He's trying to imprint the ball on his brain, to have instant recall of its spin and location, its speed and movement.

Jeter is ready to swing on the second pitch, but his timing is off. The pitch, a splitter, veers low in the zone. Jeter takes a defensive swing, as if he is feeling for the ball rather than going out to smack it. As he follows through, with his top hand coming off the bat, he holds the follow-through as if feeling for a phantom limb. The swing seems like a practice swing, done for form in the course of feeling out the pitcher and trying to time pitches.

"Curt will run that fastball up in the zone, but the majority of other pitches are down in the dirt," says teammate Randy Johnson. "He can paint both sides of the plate with the fastball, and then drop his splitter in with two strikes. He'll probably throw ten curveballs early in the count, and he throws a slider a lot more to right-handers with runners in scoring position." The slider falls away from right-handed hitters and gets them to lean too far forward—and then they can be beaten with a hard inside pitch.

Jeter's job is to learn how to time Schilling's pitches. Jeter leans in, but as his body folds over the plate his bat stays back. Jeter wants to discover something that he can use on later at bats or pass along to teammates. The pitch is a strike, so the count is 1–2.

Schilling's split fastball—like Clemens's split fastball—is almost impossible to hit. It has the zip of an ordinary fastball, but it's also hard and biting. Because of the angle, it seems to dive away from same-handed hitters.

Schilling plans to go for a strikeout. He disdains the very idea of a "waste" pitch. Even with two strikes on the hitter, why throw the ball away? You have to at least tempt the hitter or play with his mind.

"I've never bought the theory," Schilling says later. "There's no such thing as a wasted pitch. If you're prepared and you know what the hitter's tendencies are and you know what he's thinking, you can make him think different ways. While other people waste a pitch, you can set up an at bat later in the game by making a certain pitch. If you have good stuff, there's no need to waste a pitch. Three pitches can get you an out. That's what you shoot for."

Johnson and Schilling have been talking about pitching since they became part of the same staff a year and a half ago. Johnson has a different take on the value of a waste pitch.

"You don't want to go out and throw a pitch head-high over the middle of the plate," Johnson says. "That serves no purpose. But I wouldn't actually say throwing a ball out of the zone is wasting a pitch. I would call it a setup pitch.

"If I have a batter 0–2 or 1–2 and he's shown me some good swings, naturally I think I need to set up a pitch. If I'm fortunate enough to get him out on that third pitch, that's great. But if I haven't, executing that third pitch so I can set up the next pitch is what I'm trying to do. If I got a hitter 0–2, I may try and throw a fastball down and away to a right-hand hitter; then when the hitter is looking over the plate away, I come back with a slider that starts off all the way through to the plate and breaks in on his back foot. That's setting up a pitch, it's not wasting a pitch."

Grace faced both Schilling and Johnson when he played for the Chicago Cubs. "Curt and Randy—and Roger—they have the ability to make balls look like strikes. They get you to chase high fastballs. Curt can throw splits in the dirt that look like strikes. Randy can throw sliders down and in that are balls, but you get swings. High fastballs, you get swings. They can actually pitch around a guy and get swings. Does that make sense? Even a guy like, say, a Mike Piazza, a Jeff Bagwell, great hitters, he can throw them four straight balls and get an out—get them to ground out or get them to pop-up and get them to strike out. Not many guys can do that consistently—make balls look like strikes. When the pitch comes out of the pitcher's hand, it looks like it's going over the heart of the plate, but then dips low or inside or outside at the last split-second."

Grace continues, "So that's why you rarely see Schilling and others like Randy or Pedro Martinez intentionally walk guys; they'll just say, 'All right, I'll pitch around this guy. That's going to get swings."

Jeter resists chasing an off-speed pitch low over the plate, then taps a ball weakly off the plate. With the count 2–2, Jeter seems readier for the next pitch, a fastball out over the plate. For the first time, Jeter has his balance, shifts his weight well, and extends his arms in a perfect line. But he's still late. He lifts the ball to left field. Danny Bautista takes four steps back for an easy catch.

◆ ◆ ◆

WITH A MAN out in the top of the fourth inning, Paul O'Neill looks at the first pitch outside for a ball. After each pitch, O'Neill steps out of the batter's box for some quick half-swings. O'Neill's intensity clenches his body as he takes his jerking warm-up swings at the plate. After another ball outside, Schilling's next pitch catches the outside corner for a strike. It's a perfect pitch, unhittable, just nicking the back edge of the plate.

Schilling pauses on the mound, collecting his thoughts.

Schilling hits the low-and-outside part of the plate for the second strike, which makes a full count. The next pitch catches the inside part of the plate and O'Neill fouls it down the right side of the field. O'Neill could expect an inside pitch after so many outside pitches, but he can't get the timing right. A curveball falls into the lower-inside part of the plate. O'Neill waves tentatively and gets called out swinging.

O'Neill was expecting heat the whole time at bat and was thrown off by the soft stuff. As he follows through on his swing, O'Neill grimaces, holding his bat out front.

The next batter, Yankee center fielder Bernie Williams, hits left-handed against Schilling. He works the count to 2–2 on an inside-outside-outside-inside sequence. Williams is tempted on one pitch that dives outside the strike zone, but he holds his swing. He fouls another pitch down the first base line. Williams is struggling on every pitch. The pitches are impossible to hit. It's a credit to Williams's patience and concentration that he lasts as long as he does.

With the count even, Schilling handcuffs Williams with a fastball that catches the inside part of the plate, just above the knees. Strike three, inning over.

◆ ◆ ◆

IF EVERY GAME has a star player, most games also have a star pitch—a ball thrown with a spin, angle, location, and movement that immobilizes hitters. In the seventh game of the World Series, the split fastball was that star pitch.

The splitter is a hybrid of a fastball and breaking ball. The "out" pitch for both Curt Schilling and Roger Clemens, the splitter has the tight spin and most of the velocity of a fastball, but it drops hard in the last eight or ten feet.

The pitcher holds the ball tightly between his splayed index and middle fingers, then releases it over the top like a traditional fastball. (A close cousin of the splitter, the forkball, comes out of the pitcher's hand looser and tumbles, rather than spins, to the plate.) The ball moves hard in its early moment of flight but spins so much that it slows down towards home plate. As a result of the late spinning movement, the ball falls at the last moment.

To understand the movement of a splitter, consider the aerodynamic properties of a whole variety of pitches. As the ball moves though space, it creates a low-pressure region behind the ball called a "wake"—similar to the wake of a motorboat or an airplane. The wake actually pulls the ball backwards a little, slowing down its speed. A baseball slows down about 7 miles an hour on the trip from the pitcher's hand to the plate. So if it comes out of a pitcher's hand at a "muzzle speed" of 95 miles an hour, it's going at about 88 miles per hour by the time it reaches the plate.

The movement of air around a baseball works like the aerodynamics of an airplane's wings. "Lift" results when more air rides over the wing's curved top than its flat bottom. Because it has more distance to cover, the air stream on the top of the airfoil has more velocity than the air stream on the bottom. The lesser velocity on the bottom produces more pressure. (If that sounds backwards, think of a clogged pipe, which has lower velocity but greater pressure than an open pipe.) The greater pressure from below gives the wing lift, helping to keep the plane in the air.

Movement through the air creates a thin sheet of air around the baseball called a "boundary layer." Because of the layer's thinness, even small variations in the ball and its movement—its shape and roughness, its spin—produce large effects on the ball's movement. If the ball's 216 stitches extend three millimeters from the surface of the ball, and if the boundary layer is a few millionths of a meter, then the movement of the stitches can produce major effects on the boundary layer—and therefore, the movement of the ball.

The ball's rough surfaces not only cause a ball to dip and bend, but also produce turbulence. Tests at NASA's Ames Research Center in California found a drag of .336 pounds and a lift of .158 pounds (those measurements refer to the amount of force needed to move a one-pound object one foot); if the baseball were smooth like a lacrosse ball, it would have a drag of .292 pounds and a lift of .024 pounds. The ball moves in different ways because of its roughness, which creates a special air system around it.

Suppose a pitcher throws a ball to home plate with backspin. As the ball spins, the ball's stitches pick up air along the bottom of the ball and carry it around the ball to the top. By the time the ball has gone through one spin, the top of the ball has more air than the bottom of the ball. That means that air has more space to travel—and hence greater velocity—on the top of the ball. It's the same dynamic as the airfoil, producing a "lift" on the ball.

All things being equal, the backspin of a fastball gives the ball a bit of a lift, and the topspin of a curveball gives it a bit of a drop.

Exactly how the ball moves on its way to the plate depends on the pitching motion and the angle of the ball's release—whether it's released over the top (like Roger Clemens), on a three-quarters angle (like Curt Schilling or Mariano Rivera), sidearmed (like Randy Johnson), or submarined (like Byung-Hyun Kim). It also depends on where the ball comes out of the hand.

Whatever the mysterious properties of a curveball or a knuckleball, the fastball remains the essential pitch for winning in the major leagues.

"It's power," says Schilling, the military theorist. "Power is something that every human being likes to have in some form. You stand up there and you know you're throwing a fastball. The hitter knows you're throwing a fastball, and the fans know, and you still throw the ball by him? Well, it doesn't feel bad."

Power is even more devastating when combined with deception. Schilling knows that as well as anyone.

"The formula hasn't changed," Schilling says. "Location and change of speeds worked a hundred years ago and they still work today. I don't know anybody that just goes out there and rears back and throws as hard as they can. You have to hit your spots and move the ball around. That's how you get people out. There are times when you can reach back and overthrow a pitch and make a mistake somebody couldn't make at 87 to 88 miles per hour. Yeah, that's kind of a luxury at times. But it's certainly not something you can rely on. I've played with millions of guys that threw hard, but very few succeeded, because most failed to become pitchers."

Chapter Ten

THE SCIENCE OF PITCHING

Roger Clemens works harder in the off-season than he does in the regular season. Using a 7,000-square-foot gym at his home in Houston's Memorial Park—and downtown at the Houstonian Hotel, Club, and Spa—Clemens lifts weights, runs, performs agility exercises, and throws. He trains with Brian McNamee, a former New York City cop who now works as a conditioning coach for the Yankees.

Now thirty-nine years old—ancient by baseball standards, especially for a power pitcher—Clemens drills like he's in football training camp. He drives his body to the point of exhaustion. His logic is simple: workouts need to simulate the toughest game situations. Clemens knows he's going to be standing on the mound on a steamy Sunday afternoon in August, ninety pitches into a close game, sweat pouring off his body, his legs aching—and his motion thrown off-kilter from sheer tiredness. Clemens needs to train for that degree of fatigue when he's working out. Clemens developed this habit of "draining" himself in high school—exercising till he dropped, working out for hours at a time to gain control over his pitches, running hard rather than just jogging.

In their off-season workouts, Clemens and Pettitte pitch off a mound in Clemens's gym, alternately analyzing form and technique and razzing each other like a couple of teenagers. When the Yankees play on the road, Clemens seeks out gyms where he can lift. When the Yankees go to Boston, Clemens goes to Gold's Gym across from Fenway Park, where the regulars know and revere him but treat him like another aging jock who wants to keep the muscles big.

Like the other gym rats, Clemens looks like a bouncer in a bar. He is tall and wide. His face is pudgy and childlike, his hair cut in a crew-cut or arranged in spikes. He wears a five-o'clock shadow and lip balm and eye black. No one ever remembers pitchers wearing eye black before Clemens came around, but it gives him an intimidating look.

Standing on the mound, Clemens peers over his black glove, his eyes glistening. Clemens dominates almost every game, for his six or seven innings, by throwing hard and inside, sometimes up by the shoulders or even the head. Clemens has a nickname for every pitch. He calls the high-inside heat the *bowtie*.

Pitching inside—brushing batters off the plate, punishing a batter for hitting a home run on his next trip to the plate, retaliating for real and imagined crimes on and off the field—has a long and storied heritage in baseball. Old-time hurlers like Don Drysdale, Bob Gibson, and Don Newcombe threw fastballs near the head on a regular basis.

But baseball's culture has softened in the past generation, so buzzing hitters off the plate is not as common as it once was. In an age when pitchers throw harder than ever, only Clemens and Pedro Martinez dare to throw inside and high, so hard, so relentlessly. Most everyone, from the commissioner down to the lowest minor league coach, gets queasy about the danger of injuring or even killing a batter with a fastball against the temple. Only one big-leaguer has ever been killed by a pitch—the Cleveland Indians' Ray Chapman, in 1920, one day after getting beaned by the Yankees' Carl Mays—but other players' careers have been ruined. Tony Conigliaro of the Boston Red Sox saw a bright future end in 1967 when he took a fastball in the eye. Baseball's establishment has ordered umpires to police inside pitching aggressively, issuing quick warnings and follow-up ejections against pitchers that throw too close to the head. Baseball's most thoughtful managers—Joe Torre, Bobby

Cox, Tony La Russa—wince at the thought, but reserve the option to order a pitcher to bean an opposing batter.

"I'm the same guy I always was," Clemens tells writer Pat Jordan, a bonus baby pitcher who flamed out in the minor leagues. "The same pitcher. I'm relentless. I like to pound guys. Challenge power hitters with my fastball. It gets my blood pumping. I want those big hitters to have to make a split-second decision on a 96-mile-an-hour fastball inside at their letters, and they can't. *I want to jiggle their eyeballs.*"

When Clemens throws inside, he follows up with a scowl that dares the batter to make a case of it. "It's part of the game," he says. "It's [the batter's] responsibility to get out of the way."

Yankees manager Joe Torre complained about Clemens's intimidation tactics when Clemens pitched for the Toronto Blue Jays: "Roger Clemens gets away with things that gets other people thrown out of games. As long as the umpires don't do anything, why should he stop?"

The mere thought that Clemens just might throw a 97-mile-an-hour fastball at the head is enough to make most batters tentative at the plate. Hence the bravado about jiggling eyeballs.

But even his college coach, Cliff Gustafson, bristles at his greatest player's willingness to drill hitters high and inside. "He didn't have that reputation when he played for me," he said. "Pitching inside is fine, but knocking down players—I wouldn't allow it. I've never thought that at the amateur level endangering someone's life is appropriate. Not at the professional level either."

"He goes by intimidation," says teammate Derek Jeter. "He's from the same mold as Nolan Ryan—he's older than most guys and he's throwing the ball 95-plus [miles per hour]. He's from the old school, he tries to control the inside part of the plate, he tries to knock you off the plate. I hated to hit against him—I hated it. He used to hit me all the time."

But Clemens does not win because he intimidates batters. He wins because he has the power to burn the ball past even the quickest hitters. That power makes his other pitches—a changeup, a slider, and his famous split-fastball—baffling and intimidating to hitters. When you have just seen a pitch coming in at the eyes at 95 miles per hour, you are going to swing early and lamely at a splitter or a slider low and away.

◆ ◆ ◆

As Clemens takes the mound in the bottom of the fourth inning against the Diamondbacks, he has already thrown sixty pitches.

Since charting pitch counts became part of baseball's standard operating procedure a decade ago, coaches have noted that most pitchers lose their stuff—and run the risk of arm injuries—when they throw the ball more than a hundred times. Fatigue disturbs the sequence of movements in the pitching motion.

A 2001 study by Tricia Murray and colleagues, published in the *American Journal of Sports Medicine,* found that seven out of thirteen key elements of the pitching motion change significantly by the fifth inning—including the shoulder's position in the late cocking phase, the forces exerted by the shoulder and elbow, and the knee's angle at the time of delivery. As the body slows down, so does the ball, by about five miles an hour. Not surprisingly, the risk of injury to the pitcher increases dramatically as the different segments of the motion are disturbed.

In each of his first two playoff starts, Clemens lasted five innings, wearing down as he approached a hundred pitches. Clemens lasted seven innings in Game Three of the World Series, when he gave up one run and struck out nine batters. To pitch much longer than five innings, Clemens needs to get batters out efficiently.

Both Clemens and Schilling have demonstrated an ability to pitch well at all stages of the game. Roger Clemens averaged 109 pitches a game in 2001 to rank third among major-league pitchers, and Schilling averaged 106 to rank eleventh. (The leader in 2001 was Randy Johnson, with 116 per game.) Both pitchers can flag as the game reaches its midpoint, but they also know how to revive themselves as the game goes on. Stats Inc., a private company, has gathered data on how well hitters fared in 2001 at different stages in the game. Probably the best single measure of offensive production is OPS—the sum of a batter's on-base percentage plus slugging percentage. OPS measures a hitter's ability to get on base regularly and to hit for power. Here's how hitters do against Schilling and Clemens at different stages of the game:

PITCH COUNT SCHILLING VS. CLEMENS		
Pitch Count	OPS vs. Schilling	OPS vs. Clemens
1–15	.531	.536
16–30	.762	.721
31–45	.703	.618
46–60	.809	.780
61–75	.622	.687
76–90	.758	.820
91–105	.629	.600
106–120	.707	.851
121–130	.867	.375

Clemens is battling a series of nagging injuries in this final game of the World Series. The Yankees pitcher strained his hamstring in his first playoff game on October 10. It's inevitable that he'll favor the tender right leg, which makes him more tentative when he lifts his left leg and prepares to throw the ball.

Posada is amazed that Clemens pitches the same way, whether he's full of energy or drained, whether he's hale and hearty or ravaged by the flu. "He's a fighter. He never died, never quit, every day, every pitch. It doesn't matter if he's 100 percent or not, he will always give you 100 percent. Every day was the same even though he wasn't feeling the same every day."

◆ ◆ ◆

CLEMENS SHOWS WHAT he means about jiggling eyeballs when Danny Bautista leads off the fourth inning. Bautista, a right-handed hitter who usually sits against right-handed pitchers, has reached base five straight times going back to last night's 15–2 Arizona win. He takes a slightly open stance to see Clemens's pitches better. But it's still hard to see a Clemens fastball up by the eyes.

Clemens throws the first pitch high and inside and Bautista takes it for a ball.

Bautista's strategy against Clemens is to stay back and wait for his pitches rather than attacking them aggressively.

"A pitcher like Clemens, he's going to be jumping," Bautista says. "He's going after you. You stay back and the more you see the ball, the more contact you are going to make. I think 'stay back' to stay in control of my body. I mean, if you're jumping, the ball is going to get to you faster. That's the hard thing for a hitter—to stay comfortable at the plate. That's why they throw fastballs, breaking balls, changeups, to get you out of the [optimal hitting] position."

Bautista wiggles his legs as Clemens goes into his windup, trying to stay alert and flexible for whatever Clemens has to offer. Clemens shakes off catcher Jorge Posada's first signal before agreeing to throw a fastball. Bautista gets ahold of the ball in the upper part of the strike zone and lifts it out to center field. Bernie Williams runs in fifteen steps from his position; Derek Jeter moves back a dozen steps from his shortstop position, gingerly stepping backwards until he hears Williams call him off. Jeter stops and ducks as Williams glides in to make an easy catch.

In this encounter with Clemens, Bautista swings carefully, trying to establish timing against a power pitcher who can also change speeds on his pitches—"pull the string," in the vernacular—or tease and taunt the hitter by throwing the ball softly after sizzling a pitch up by the eyes.

Staying back was not enough this time. But there is a small gain for Bautista: he has observed enough of the Yankees veteran to inform his approach on later at bats.

◆ ◆ ◆

"There's no one like Roger," says Andy Pettitte. "I mean, he's pushing forty and still blowing the ball by hitters. It's ridiculous. The guy is a freak of nature."

As he approaches his fifth decade, Clemens throws as hard as he did when he was a twenty-three-year-old rookie with the Boston Red Sox. Over the years, Clemens has experienced occasional problems with his back and hamstrings. But he has otherwise been healthy for almost two decades. After his rookie season in 1985, Clemens had arthroscopic surgery to repair a small tear in his shoulder and a partial tear of the rotator cuff (the muscles and tendons surrounding the upper-arm bone).

The next year, he dominated baseball with his greatest season ever—winning twenty-four games, striking out 238 batters in 254 innings, and posting a 2.48 earned-run average.

But Clemens's success cannot be explained by saying he's a freak. The answer is much more profound. Medical researchers at the Birmingham campus of the University of Alabama have found that the secret to Roger Clemens's power and longevity can be found in the exquisite perfection of his pitching motion.

To find out why, ask the researchers at the American Sports Medicine Institute, a cutting-edge laboratory affiliated with the Birmingham medical school of the University of Alabama.

Dr. James Andrews, who pioneered Tommy John surgery—the procedure that uses a tendon from the wrist or hamstring to replace a torn ligament in the elbow, a procedure that has saved hundreds of pitching careers—created the institute to study athletic movements with the hope of reducing injuries. Over the years, the ASMI has tested and analyzed more than 900 pitchers.

To collect data, ASMI researchers use video cameras and computer-imaging systems to capture the pitching motions of pitchers from the collegiate level to the major leagues. Pitchers come into the ASMI warehouse, warm up until they're throwing about 80 percent of their normal speed, and then pitch hard off a wooden mound. Before they pitch, fifteen metallic motion sensors the size of marbles are taped to the joints involved in throwing the ball—wrists, elbows, shoulders, hips, knees, ankles. Computer imaging devices pick up the movement of every joint as the pitcher delivers the ball. Those data are converted into stick-figure images on the computer that show the pitcher's twists and turns—and measure every movement in microseconds and degrees. Video cameras also shoot the pitcher on the front, back, and side, recording his movements at a rate of 500 times per second. Computer and video images show precisely every twist and turn, every rate of movement, every relationship between the pitcher's moving parts.

Over the years, the ASMI has identified fifty pitchers with superior form to use as a baseline for assessing other pitchers. The ideal motion puts as little strain as possible on the body and gives the pitcher the power and accuracy he needs to pitch at elite levels. The elite group

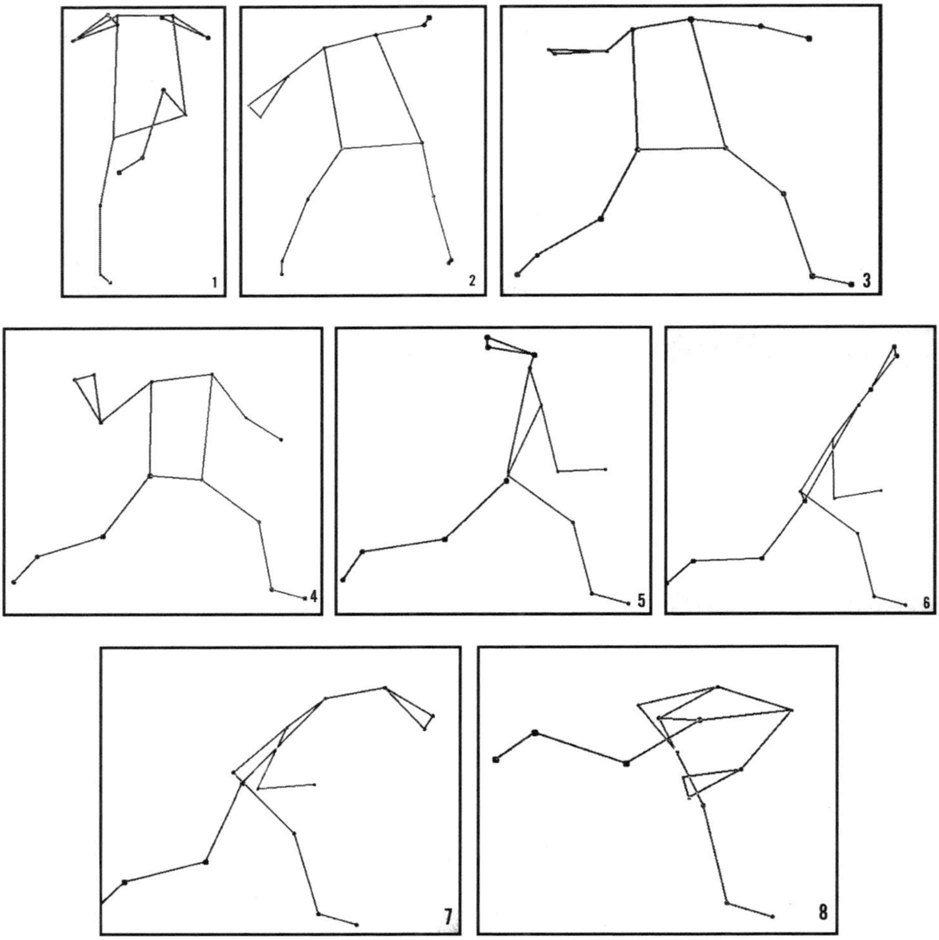

Using video and computer imaging that breaks down pitching motions into as many as 500 images a second, the American Sports Medicine Institute has identified a sequence of movements that make for a strong and safe pitching motion. Scientists at ASMI study the pitching motion by using stick figures derived from computer tracking of fifteen sensors taped to pitchers' joints. A good motion begins with a balanced leg lift (1). The pitcher then swings his arms down and apart while striding forward with the front leg (2), plants his front foot (3), rotates his pelvis and then upper trunk forward while rotating the arm backward (4 and 5), rotates his arm forward and releases the ball (6), and follows through (7 and 8).

(Images courtesy of the American Sports Medicine Institute)

includes Clemens, Barry Zito, Mark Prior, and Jack McDowell. What makes the ASMI scientists sure that these pitchers have such ideal mechanics? To start, they succeed at the highest levels of the game year after year. Second, they have not broken down physically.

Cadaver research supplements the high-speed video analyses. Researchers isolate body parts—shoulders, elbows, wrists—to determine the maximum force that can be applied without breaking. Scientists take the arms of cadavers—the shoulders and elbows and wrists—and use machines to crush them to determine just what levels of force create unbearable strains. Over the years, ASMI's Nigel Zheng and his team of researchers have worked with 500 cadavers to examine the impact of stresses on bones, muscles, ligaments, and tendons.

"There are things you cannot tell with motion analysis," Zheng says. "When a pitcher gets injured, there are very subtle changes in the joints that could come from muscle fatigue or pressure on the joints. The video images give an overall view of what the pitcher does to his body. Cadaver studies enable you to focus on particular stresses on the body."

The cadavers, bodies ranging in age from the twenties to the fifties, are frozen within hours of death and then brought to ASMI in Birmingham. Using existing instruments—like a force probe transducer to measure the effects of local ligament fiber tension and a string gauge to assess the stretching of ligaments—ASMI researchers often design their own laboratory equipment. "You have to build your own equipment, using pulleys and cables and weights. There's no such company that makes the machinery. I wish there was. And it's not like you can sell your equipment to someone else."

◆ ◆ ◆

THE SCIENTISTS AT the American Sports Medicine Institute have concluded that Roger Clemens has such a superior motion that it should become the baseline for good pitching form.

In recent years, a parade of doctors, coaches, and players have come to Birmingham for ASMI's analysis. Major league teams making the pilgrimage to Birmingham include the Boston Red Sox, the New York Mets, the Oakland Athletics, and the Cleveland Indians. When young pitchers ascend the wooden mound in ASMI's motion lab, they are told to do what Roger does.

ASMI has broken down the pitching motion into five critical sets of movements. Together, those movements and phases constitute a "kinetic chain." One moment in the chain sets up the next, which sets up the next, and so on. A pitcher's motion is only as good as the weakest link in the chain. Any flaw reduces the likelihood that the pitcher will throw the ball as hard or as accurately as he can—and, more important to the doctors at ASMI, he increases the chance that he will injure himself.

1. Windup: Leaning on the back leg and lifting the front leg creates a vast supply of potential energy. The higher you lift your front leg, the more energy you create and store for later use. To the naked eye, his leg kick doesn't seem too high—but it is. Slow down the video and you see Clemens lifting his knee up by the letters on his jersey.

When the pitcher lifts his leg to its highest point, he has created the maximum potential energy. It's like lifting a pile of weights. The higher you can lift them, the greater the force when you drop them. This is one reason power pitchers need tree trunks for legs. Without strong legs, a pitcher cannot drive his body forward forcefully.

The high leg kick requires a concerted effort to control the body, keep it balanced. Clemens keeps his body inside an invisible barrel. If he did not keep his arms and legs close to his body, he would disperse his power. Clemens holds his hands in front of his chest. If Clemens were to wave his arms away from his body, he would lose his balance and not be able to gather the energy he needs to hurl the ball forward.

Balance is critical to the rarin'-back phase of the motion. When Clemens lifts his leg, his body is practically vertical, with his knee directly over the heel of his planted foot. It's like a pole is extended straight down his body. Any wobble increases the likelihood that the pitcher will land on the mound milliseconds late or centimeters too far to the right or left. Falling the wrong way could put too much strain on the arm.

"How can you expect a car with a flat tire to drive well?" asks Byung-Hyun Kim, the Diamondbacks' relief ace in 2001.

2. Stride: As he strides toward the plate, Clemens turns his pelvis and then his torso forward at lightening speeds.

The length of the optimal stride ranges from 71 to 80 percent of the pitcher's height. Since Clemens is six feet, four inches tall, he should take a stride forward of fifty-four to sixty inches. The length of the stride depends on a general comfort level, the need to control and balance the body during the motion, and the speed and location of the pitch. Taller pitchers like Randy Johnson work on the lower end of the range to maintain balance and keep the body under control.

Scientists measure the movement of the pelvis and torso in degrees per second. Ideally, the pelvis moves between 550 and 710 degrees per second. That's how scientists measure rotational movement: How many times would a part spin completely around in a second? But, of course, the pelvis turns only about 90 degrees, one-fourth of a complete rotation. So at the rate of 550 to 700 degrees per second, a whole turn of the pelvis takes about one-sixth of second.

Once he has turned his pelvis toward the plate, Clemens and other elite pitchers begin to rotate the upper trunk. The trunk's rotation happens almost twice as fast as the torso rotation—ideally, anywhere from 1,078 to 1,370 degrees per second—which translates to about 90 degrees in about one-sixteenth of a second.

At that moment, Clemens begins to drive his body home. In a split-second, Clemens strides forward, lands on his front leg, turns his pelvis toward the plate, then turns his upper trunk toward the plate.

The stride underscores the importance of the strength of a pitcher's core, the hips and abdomen and chest, which have to power the body around, absorbing the powerful twists and turns of the pitcher's power generation. The pitching shoulder starts to experience some stress at this stage in the motion as well.

When Clemens lands on the mound with his front foot, all of the body's energy shoots like a bolt of lightning down his legs—and then, at the moment of impact, that energy shoots back up the pelvis and torso to the arm as it prepares to release the ball.

3. Arm Cocking: In the moment before the pitcher releases the ball, he cocks his arm to throw behind his back. The arm looks like a slightly bent backwards "L"; he bends his arm, ideally, between 70 and 92 degrees.

As the pitcher's front foot lands, it points toward home plate. If the foot lands too far off an imaginary line between the mound and home plate, the pitcher is liable to lose his balance—and his ability to control the ball.

The shoulder and elbow absorb the most shock in this stage of the motion.

4. Arm Motion

In a blur, the arm straightens out from the "L" position behind his body to a straight position as he releases the ball. This takes about one-thirtieth of a second. Good "arm acceleration" takes place between 2,505 and 3,394 degrees per second—meaning that if the arm were to move for a full second, it would make seven to nine full rotations.

As the arm moves forward, the shoulder acts like a hinge. The arm rotation is three times faster than the arm acceleration—ideally, from 6,912 to 9,836 degrees per second. That translates to anywhere between nineteen and twenty-seven rotations per second. *This is the single most violent act in all of sports.*

The arm and elbow and wrist crack forward like a whip. The pitcher's body is at war with itself. The body's limbs fly away in a circular motion, away from the body—and, at the same time, get pulled in toward the body. One set of forces violently pulls the arm out of the pitcher's socket and another set of forces keeps the shoulders, elbows, and wrists attached. That produces the whip action that all great pitchers require—and it's what creates some crippling injuries.

The stress on the shoulder and elbow continues during this phase.

As Clemens releases the ball, his arm straightens out into a near-perfect line. Now his job is to slow his body down.

After Clemens releases the ball, his torso is almost completely horizontal to the ground and his back leg kicks high in the air. Clemens continues to throw his arm forward after he releases the ball. By the time his trunk is horizontal and his back leg kicks out on a horizontal plane, his pitching hand is inches from the mound, as if he was reaching to grab some dirt.

The shoulder and elbow's outer ligament absorb extraordinary stress at this stage of the motion. As the arm completes its violent motion, the body has to absorb the shock and slow the arm down. The shoulder and elbow experience, at the same time, the push-pull of stretching and compression.

5. Follow-Through: After Clemens releases the ball, with his torso horizontal to the ground, his back leg kicks high in the air. After going horizontal, Clemens lands his right leg on the ground, his body in a crouch facing the plate, ready to field the ball.

◆ ◆ ◆

AFTER DANNY BAUTISTA flies out to Bernie Williams in center field in the bottom of the fourth inning, Mark Grace steps up.

Grace has a fluid swing and a discerning mind. He achieved an obscure but impressive distinction when he became baseball's leader for the decade of the 1990s with 1,745 hits (he also had more doubles, 364, than any other player in that span). Previous decade hit leaders included Robin Yount (1980s), Pete Rose (1970s), Roberto Clemente (1960s), Stan Musial (1950s), Lou Boudreau (1940s), Paul Waner (1930s), Rogers Hornsby (1920s), Ty Cobb (1910s), and Honus Wagner (1900s)—all Hall of Famers except Rose, banned for a betting scandal.

Grace studies scouting reports and watches pitchers intently during games, seeking out hidden patterns on pitches and motions. When pitchers accept the sign from catchers right away, Grace guesses fastball. When pitcher and catcher take a split-second longer to communicate, Grace guesses curveball or an off-speed pitch. Grace has the discipline to avoid chasing bad pitches. Clemens is going to have to bring the ball somewhere near the plate. Grace won't swing at a ball in the dirt, Clemens's out-pitch for most hitters.

"This World Series was the first time I had ever faced him," Grace remembers. "Game Three, where he beat us 2–1, I didn't do anything off of him. Now I know why he's great. You just kind of look for tendencies. But the one thing about great pitchers, they'll keep pitching you a certain way until you adjust. And he was beating me with fastballs away and splits. So the second time I faced him, in Game Seven, I said, 'Okay, I'm going to have to go out there for his fastball away [on the outside part of the plate] or I'm going to have to wait for his split.' And I just decided I was going to try to hit his fastball away. And I got base hits in the second inning and the fourth inning."

Clemens starts Grace outside, and Grace is looking all the way. He's choking up against Clemens, with an inch and a half of bat sticking out from his grip. Clemens also misses outside on the second pitch. Grace might have whacked the ball, driving it the other way, maybe to the left-center field alley. But he lays off. Grace has decided to look over as many pitches as possible.

Grace is creating a mental database of his pitches, their speed, movement location, and, above all, their patterns—up and down, in and out. Grace's soul brother as a hitter is Tony Gwynn of the San Diego Padres, who builds a detailed mental database of pitchers. "You can never get us out the same way twice in a row," Grace says. "It's very rare. If you do, then we tip our caps to you. If you fall into a pattern with us, we're going to whack you."

Clemens throws the next ball high in the strike zone and gets the call from the umpire. Other pitchers don't get that high strike.

Grace shakes his head at Clemens's movement: "The best way I can describe it is, Roger's ball gets halfway there, and then something kicks it in the ass. *Psschw!* And it just splits." The splitter gets its name from the finger grip, but it also describes what happens when the ball reaches the plate. The ball breaks down like a late-breaking curveball, but with much more of the zip of a fastball. "It's got what we call late life," says Grace. "I mean, it's a fastball but it explodes. His fastball's one of those that gets halfway there, looks like something else, and then it's boom! It just gets in on you. So you've got to be really quick.

"Roger's fastball, it's just pure speed. Those guys, the droppers and the drivers, even if they're throwing eighty-eight [miles per hour], it gets on you a little quicker than most eighty-eight pitches. You've just got to lay off the high pitch and get him to throw down in the zone and be quick. And wish yourself luck."

Grace lines the next pitch, a splitter that catches the outside part of the plate, on one hop to Jeter. The shortstop grabs the ball on his right side, like a bullfighter waving a flag. The ball goes off the heel of his glove and skips into left-center field. Jeter runs it down, five steps into the outfield, to hold Grace at first base. Jeter is practically kneeling, facing third base, when he puts his glove on the ball. But the ball bounces higher than he anticipated. Score it a hit.

◆ ◆ ◆

When Cliff Gustafson coached the University of Texas in the College World Series in 1983, his best pitcher was a future major leaguer named Calvin Schiraldi. Schiraldi was named the college pitcher of the year by *Baseball America,* leading the Longhorns to 66–0 season. The second pitcher on the Texas staff was Kirk Killingsworth. And then there was the big kid with the chubby face and chin dimple, whose mother moved to Texas from Ohio after her marriage broke up—the kid who was not known for much of a fastball when he started college baseball at San Jacinto Community College. It was that player—Roger Clemens—who won the clinching game of the Series against Alabama.

Gustafson always knew that Clemens's growing power and control and work ethic made him a better prospect. In the Series finale, with a 4–2 ninth-inning lead, a future major leaguer named Dave Magadan doubled and then scored on a single. Gustafson walked to the mound to take Clemens out. "I got halfway to the mound and he met me there," Gustafson remembers. "He said, 'I'm not coming out of this game—it's *my* game and I'm going to get them.'" Clemens ended the game with a strikeout and two fly balls. "All the great ones have that ability, to get the adrenaline going and then to control the adrenaline. Roger had it that day."

At times in his career, Clemens has let up on his power game, throwing more curveballs and changeups. The changeup floats over the plate as much as fifteen miles an hour slower than a fastball, which makes it a perfect follow-up pitch. But even the best changeup—tantalizing in its laziness, located where the batter cannot reach it—is not worth much without a good fastball. Now he reminds himself regularly that power is what he's all about.

"I'm throwing as hard as I ever have," he told *Texas Monthly* in 2000. "I just need the confidence to race it in there and take my chances. I've been beaten with some poor off-speed [pitches], and that's the kind of thing that'll make you shake your head on the drive back home. I have to remember I'm still a power pitcher, and my fastball is still my best pitch."

◆ ◆ ◆

Pity Damian Miller. With a runner on first, the Diamondbacks catcher, who struck out in the second inning, will try to advance the runner. But he is not going to get any good pitches to hit because Schilling is coming up next. If a good hitter were due up next, Clemens would be determined to keep Miller off base at all costs. He would have to challenge him, maybe throw a fastball over the plate. But he can afford to toy with Miller, throw him junk, force him to swing aggressively.

Miller swings through the first pitch, a fastball moving in on his hands. Posada's glove moves six inches on impact. Miller weakly fouls away the next pitch and then strikes out on a 95-mile-an-hour pitch on the outside part of the plate. The ball moves from slightly off the plate to the outside corner. Clemens badly outmatches Miller.

And now pity Curt Schilling.

Schilling waves at a 95-mile-an-hour fastball from his awkward crouch for strike one. After watching a fastball off the plate, Schilling fouls off the next fastball to the right side and then swings through a high fastball for strike three. Posada has to reach up near the crown of his hat to catch it.

Clemens walks off the mound with eight strikeouts in four innings. His power game prevents the Diamondbacks from scoring, even though they have gotten five base runners—four on hits and one on an error—so far in the game. Power is the pitcher's ultimate trump card.

Yankee Grinding Wins Close Games
Photo courtesy of New York Yankees

In close games, teams search for every edge. Yankees like Tino Martinez earned reputations as "grinders" who could wear down opposing pitchers and control the tempo of the game.

FIFTH INNING

In which the two teams dig in for an extended game of trench warfare, showing how the little things can make a big difference over the course of the game

Chapter Eleven

TRENCH WARFARE

Throughout their three-straight World Championship seasons, the Yankees played a masterful game of wearing down the opposition. Yankee hitters forced opposing pitchers to throw a lot of pitches, tiring them out and seeing everything they had to offer. Curt Schilling was bound to be tired by Game Seven—in fact, after both Games One and Four he told manager Bob Brenly that he might be finished for the year—but he pronounced himself fit to pitch after getting a myofascial massage from the team's physical therapist, Russell Nua.

The Yankees hoped that Schilling might tire and lay the ball over the plate. They also knew that he liked to get ahead in the count, and that he got harder and harder to hit when he was ahead 0–1 or 0–2. So they broke from their customary approach and decided to go after his first and second pitches. The result was that Schilling threw just forty-six pitches in the first four innings, an average of just 3.8 pitches per batter. The way he was going, it looked like Schilling could throw a complete game.

"It's kind of a double-edged sword," says Derek Jeter of the Yankees' celebrated ability to grind down the opposition with long plate appearances. "You want to be patient but you can't be too patient. Because if you're too patient, you're behind in the count all the time. Randy Johnson and Curt Schilling get strikes and then you're 0–2 and you don't know what they're going to throw. You want to be aggressive but you have to be aggressive in the zone."

Yankees outfielder Shane Spencer understands his teammates' desire to swing early, not get behind in the count, but thinks it's a mistake to swing at the first pitch.

"Our guys have not had good success against him. They were wanting to go out and get him early, get a good pitch," he says. "But Schilling's too smart for that. You know he wasn't going to lay a cookie in there. And he pitched just off the plate or up and in. You want guys like Schilling to throw a lot of pitches so he gets less comfortable and starts to make more mistakes. When you've got a guy that's as good as him, and he's throwing one, two, three, four pitches to every hitter, that's it, and we're getting ground balls or pop-ups or striking out on three pitches. We made quick outs."

All was going so well for Schilling. And then Tino Martinez turned his fifth-inning at bat against Schilling into a game of trench warfare.

When the Germans and British dug trenches and set up their fighting units along the Western Front in World War I, the goal was to penetrate the other's territory slowly by wearing them down in a long and bloody war of attrition. The two sides possessed roughly equal strength, and so they remained stuck in the long pits they dug into the earth. At some point, something would happen to give one side an advantage.

The best baseball teams also wait out the other side when things aren't going well, and then exploit the first opportunity to break the stalemate. In 2001, the Yankees won twenty-eight and lost fifteen one-run games; in this World Series, they won all three one-run games, including two dramatic ninth-inning comebacks at Yankee Stadium. They stayed close throughout the game, and then exploited the momentary lapses of their opponents. Even though the Diamondbacks dominated scoring in the World Series, the Yankees could still win their fourth straight championship if they could just keep the game going into the late innings. If they could get ahead in the late innings, they could turn to their unbeatable relief pitcher, Mariano Rivera.

◆ ◆ ◆

WITH THE GAME still scoreless, the Yankees' first baseman, Tino Martinez, steps to the plate in the top of the fifth inning. Martinez wants to start a rally with a hit, but failing that, he wants to wear down Curt Schilling.

Everyone knows that the Yankees will let Martinez go after the season. Martinez has given his best years to the Yankees, but the corporate franchise is always looking for upgrades, and the game's premier power-and-patience player, Jason Giambi of the Oakland Athletics, will be a free agent this winter. Before the season even started, Martinez sold his house in Tenafly, New Jersey.

Since he replaced Don Mattingly at first base, Martinez has become the most consistent Yankee of the period, save Derek Jeter. In the last seven years (1995–2001), Martinez drove in 785 runs, second only to the Houston Astros' Jeff Bagwell, whose 838 runs batted in were the most in the major leagues.

But it was the way Martinez maintained his form that was so impressive. Coming off a poor year in 1999, Martinez worked hard with hitting coach Gary Denbo to get his stroke back. Martinez's approach to training—that year and every year—is to use the off-season to work on his mechanics. He develops the perfect stance and swing and envisions the coming year's pitches and situations. After he develops the mental images and the "body memory" in the off-season, he can forget about mechanics and focus on pitchers and situations during the season. The extra work with Denbo paid off. In 2001, Martinez hit .280 and led the Yankees in home runs with 34 and RBIs with 113.

Martinez has already made World Series history in 2001. After the Diamondbacks scored two runs in the top of the eighth inning of Game Four to take a 3–1 lead, Martinez hit the first pitch he saw from Byung-Hyun Kim over the left-center field wall to tie the game.

In his first at bat of this game, in the second inning, Martinez struck out on split-fastballs. After looking long and hard at the first pitch hitting the outside corner, Martinez failed utterly against two splitters that fell off the table. He's going to have to shorten his swing to get his bat on the ball against Schilling tonight.

◆ ◆ ◆

THE FIRST PITCH to Martinez in the fifth inning is a ball outside, followed by a fastball low, so Martinez gets ahead in the count, 2–0. This is the first time Schilling has fallen behind in the count by more than one pitch.

Working behind in the count is a danger zone for even the best pitchers. On the rare occasions when hitters put the ball into play on an 0–2 count—just sixteen times out of 948 batters in 2001—Schilling yielded eight hits and three home runs.

Analyses by Tendu, a California-based statistics company, underscores the point. Hitters have their best success against Schilling when he gets the ball over the center of the plate between the belt and the knee; about 41 percent of all hits in the Tendu sample (117 of 287) come on pitches in this part of the zone. Overall, hitters bat .326 in this area. Over the plate at the belt, hitters bat .311 against Schilling.

The fastball is Schilling's favorite pitch when he's ahead in the count; he uses it 47 percent of the time (844 of 1,791 times), inducting hitters to swing 54 percent of the time.

The splitter is Schilling's real out pitch, inducing batters to reach out of the strike zone. According to the analysts at Tendu, Schilling uses the splitter 33 percent of the time (586/1,791) when he's ahead in the count; batters swing at 60 percent of those pitches, even though only about half of those are in the strike zone (174/586).

◆ ◆ ◆

At this point in the battle with Martinez, Schilling does not have the luxury of playing his game of fool-the-batter. He needs to get the count even to set up a strikeout, or at least make Martinez start swinging the bat defensively—or, better yet, get Martinez to put the ball in play.

Schilling's performance so far tonight mirrors his performance over the course of the year. For the first 45 pitches of the game in 2001, Schilling's opponents hit .216 (87 for 401 overall). But according to data gathered by Stats Inc., the next fifteen pitches represent Schilling's danger zone: hitters get used to his pitches and make adjustments on their swings. On pitches 46 through 60, opponents hit .309 against Schilling (overall, 46 for 136 with five home runs and seventeen runs batted in).

To counter the batters' growing knowledge, Schilling needs to make adjustments. After he gets over the 46-to-60-pitch hump, Schilling regains mastery of the game. Schilling's opponents hit just .223 against him in the next fifteen pitches (27 for 121). Opponents then settle in to hit .264 (78 for 295) against him from the 76th through the 120th pitch. Schilling threw only fifteen pitches beyond 120 in 2001, yielding only three hits (a .200 average).

◆ ◆ ◆

WITH THE COUNT 2–0, Schilling throws the next pitch on the outside corner for the first strike. Or does he? An overhead replay of the pitch shows the ball missing the corner by six inches or more. It's an important call for Schilling.

Rippley's wide strike zone makes Martinez's defensive batting skills that much more important. Since the umpire is going to give the borderline pitches to Schilling, Martinez cannot wait for the best pitch to smack. He has to swing at everything near the plate. If possible, he needs to foul off enough pitches until he gets something good to hit.

The next pitch proves the point. The pitch is just above the knees on the outside part of the plate. It's a marginal pitch, ball or strike. Martinez pulls it just foul of first base, where Mark Grace fields it a step into foul territory. Schilling has evened the count.

Schilling moves the next pitch inside and low, but it's a ball. Full count.

Another strike and Martinez is out; another ball and he gets a free pass to first base.

On the next pitch, Martinez fouls back a ball over the low part of the plate. Martinez takes a full cut but cannot get all of it. He fouls back the next pitch, too. Schilling put the pitch in the right place—low and inside—but Martinez manages to get a piece of it to stay alive.

Having worked on the inside and low parts of the plate, Schilling decides to go outside and high on the next pitch. It's a high splitter, and Martinez is duly fooled—but he manages to check-swing a ball foul to the right side.

Martinez's plate appearance is turning into a drama of its own: eight pitches, no good wood on the ball, but the kind of patience that might deliver a real opportunity to hit the ball hard.

On the ninth pitch, Schilling gets ready to throw and then pauses, takes the ball out of his glove and looks at it, moving it around his hand for a better grip. Finally he holds the ball for a splitter. He keeps the ball down in his glove as if his hand is a claw. He delivers that pitch low-and-inside—and Martinez fouls the ball yet again with an uppercut swing. The ball bounds down past first base and into short right field off the right-field fence.

Martinez trained for this moment as a thirteen-year-old growing up in Tampa. Every day, he hit balls off a tee into a chain-link fence. His goal was to drive the ball through the fence. He hit balls by the hundreds, until one day he achieved his goal. He still remembers the explosive sound the ball made when it broke through the fence. The drills gave his swing the consistency that has become the envy of other hitters in the major leagues.

On the tenth pitch, Schilling throws the ball over the plate in the lower part of the strike zone. Martinez hits it back behind the plate, toward left side of the diamond.

Schilling is dominant but he has not won this battle yet. It's at bats like this that make him wonder whether he should refine his game of power pitching. He recalls a conversation with baseball's greatest finesse pitcher, Greg Maddux of the Atlanta Braves. "I was talking to Greg Maddux about how he can get seven or eight innings out of eighty pitches. He said to me, 'I can't complain because you throw 95 [miles per hour] and I don't.' He said, 'If I threw 95, I'd throw a lot more pitches too.' The harder you throw, the more foul balls you get."

Finally, a climax: on the eleventh pitch to Martinez, Schilling drills the ball over the plate, low. Martinez gets around on the pitch but lifts the ball to Finley in center field. As if exasperated by the time he has had to wait to field a ball, Finley takes the ball with one hand, then deliberately closes the glove with the other hand.

Jorge Posada looks back at Martinez's at bat as a potential turning point of the game. "It's tough to get a guy out when they foul the ball off," he says. "That's the toughest hitter to get out. He saw a lot of pitches and that helps us later in the game. You never know. The pitcher gets tired and leaves a forkball the middle of the zone and you get a hit and win it. All because he got tired out back in the fifth inning."

"I don't think you're going to get a lot of people going home and putting the tape in the VCR to watch an eight- or ten-pitch at bat," Joe Torre says. "But it's what you have to do to win."

◆ ◆ ◆

GOING DEEP IN the count can exact a big toll on pitchers. After throwing pitch after inconclusive pitch, hurlers can tire out physically and lose their concentration. An eleven-pitch at bat can make the difference between a seven- and an eight-inning game. Randy Johnson knows how a long at bat can shape the course of a game.

"As a pitcher, when you're throwing nine to twelve pitches per inning, it's one thing—you're pitching efficiently, you're getting your team back at the bat, you're getting a rest. But when you throw that many pitches just to one batter—and then if you lose that batter for whatever reason—that can be deflating because of all that effort that you've put forth in trying to get him out. It takes a lot out of you physically to throw that many pitches to one batter, let alone to three batters and get the three outs."

The excitement of a championship game can give the pitcher the adrenaline he needs to work through a long at bat. But reaching back for the something extra, and sustaining it over a long game, requires intense concentration—which itself is psychologically draining.

Long at bats can make the pitcher punch-drunk by the fifth or sixth inning. "It's like boxing," says Rich Donnelly, who has coached for decades and has become one of the premier batting gurus in the game. "You see a guy in the first and second rounds firing punches right and left. By the sixth inning, when they've thrown a hundred and twenty pitches, they're going to get into trouble."

◆ ◆ ◆

THE STRESS AFFECTS the batters too—which is why many hitters do not try to go deep into the count. Fouling off pitches is not just a matter of deciding to do it. Getting just enough wood on the ball to stay alive requires extraordinary athleticism and mental discipline.

Rod Carew, who won seven batting titles over nineteen seasons with the Minnesota Twins and California Angels, says working the count requires a level of confidence and courage that many modern players do not possess. "Guys are afraid to hit with two strikes," says Carew. "That's why they don't work the count more. It's an insecurity thing. They might get that one pitch they can drive, and they're afraid they might not see it again in that at bat. So they want to make sure they take advantage of it."

With the count at two strikes, a batter has to be content with the One-Hand Fred. The hitter has to shorten his swing. You don't get a home run swing. You have to be more relaxed and let the ball hit the bat.

"If a guy's got three or four pitches, you want to figure out when he's most likely to use each one," Carew adds. "As a coach you try to map things out. You try to figure out what he wants to do if it's an 0–2 count, or 1–0, or 2–1. If he goes soft or hard on a particular count, you can start looking for that pitch. It also shows you whatever pitch he's not getting over. Then you have to have discipline and eliminate that pitch from his repertoire. If a guy has a good slider, but he's not getting it over, okay, then you take the slider and wait for a fastball. When he gets behind you know he's going to come with something straight."

The two-strike count produced outs 81.5 percent of the time in 2001. Only one player in baseball hit over .300 with two strikes. The best two-strike hitter in the World Series is Mark Grace, long known for his extraordinary bat control. Grace hit .295 in 176 at bats with two strikes in 2001, second only to Juan Pierre of the Rockies, who hit .335 in 200 at bats. Other players toward the top of the list include Bernie Williams of the Yankees (.250, thirteenth in the majors) and Luis Gonzalez of the Diamondbacks (.241, twenty-second in the majors).

The major leagues' leader in pitches per plate appearance in 2001 was the Diamondbacks' Jay Bell with 4.27. Other leaders included Craig Counsell (twenty-seventh with 3.97), Chuck Knoblauch (thirtieth 3.95), and Jorge Posada (thirty-fifth 3.93).

Forcing the pitcher to put the ball over the plate requires a kind of skill that cannot be taught in spring training, like bunting or hitting the cutoff man.

"It's physical abilities, it's quickness," says Billy Blitzer, who has performed every role of the major league scout from bird dog to postseason advance work. "If you could teach it—how to foul off pitches, how to hit the ball the other way—more players would do it."

Patience requires not just a willingness to hold back on an action, but something more knowing. Patience for the sake of patience, after all, might result in losing a chance to swing at a good pitch.

Michael Mandelbaum, a scholar at Johns Hopkins University and the author of *The Meaning of Sports,* has examined the different skills needed for the major sports and found baseball the most psychologically demanding over the course of the whole game. To bring useful discipline to the plate requires an exquisite combination of mental and physical quickness—over and over again. "Perhaps what is needed in baseball—and in the other sports as well—is judgment, which is related to, but not the same as, patience," Mandelbaum says.

Not swinging the bat can cause its own kind of strain. Batters come to the plate to hit. Holding back on pitches outside the strike zone—especially balls close to the plate—can be a draining process. Barry Bonds, the San Francisco Giants slugger who set a single-season record with seventy-three home runs in 2001, has gotten fewer good pitches to hit than any hitter in baseball history. Bonds so intimidates opposing teams that they refuse to give him any pitches near the plate.

On pitch after pitch, Bonds must restrain himself. On every pitch, Bonds moves into high alert, his attention training on the pitcher's delivery and his body coiling back to move his legs, hip, torso, and hands into motion—and then, in a split-second, the whole system shuts down. It's like a nuclear reactor going on alert, time after time, and then returning its operations to peak levels.

"It's getting a lot harder," Bonds says. "I try to explain to players: it's a lot harder to walk than hit a ground ball and jog back to the dugout. Teams wear me down. I know they do it intentionally. It's not something you want to do for 162 games, or 140-some that I played in. You need discipline to do that, or you need a manager to give you a day or two off."

The strain of a long at bat depends on the situation and the character and physical makeup of both the hitter and pitcher.

"Nobody can relate to a walk like Barry Bonds," broadcaster Tim McCarver says. Every year, it seems, Bonds breaks his own record for most walks in a season. In 2004, Bonds would set the unfathomable record of 232 walks in 617 plate appearances—meaning that he was not allowed to hit 38 percent of the time.

"What Tino did was important but I'm not sure it was as much of a strain or that it did all that much to wear down Schilling," McCarver says. "It was a real defensive at bat. Schilling was in charge. And Schilling is such a strong physical specimen. All pitchers are different, and the strength of even the same pitcher's arm and body varies from game to game. Schilling and Clemens can be different from Schilling and Clemens of a different day. On this day, Schilling was very strong."

In a scoreless game, in a battle of trench warfare, every at bat can make a difference.

◆ ◆ ◆

WITH ONE OUT in the top of the fifth inning, Jorge Posada wants to follow Tino Martinez's example and force Curt Schilling to throw a lot of pitches. But Schilling will not let him do it.

With Posada standing off the plate, Schilling works the outside part of the plate. Two identical pitches off the plate produce different calls—first a ball, then a strike. Schilling asks Rippley if the first pitch was outside. Rippley nods yes.

Posada fouls the next pitch off in the dirt. Schilling has Posada where he wants him. Now Schilling wants to get Posada to chase another ball. He throws another pitch low-and-inside, but Posada lays off and it's now 2–2. Having run the balls in and low on Posada, Schilling now gets a waist-high pitch on the outside corner for a called strike three.

The right-handed Shane Spencer looks at three balls—all good pitcher's pitches, out of reach of the hitter, all tempting—before swinging at a pitch running in on him. The pitch is out of the strike zone, but Spencer swings anyway and lifts the ball to short center field. Second baseman Craig Counsell moves back to make an easy catch.

Should he have been swinging on 3–0? It's the kind of thing Torre looks for when deciding what to do with his platoon outfielder. Swinging on that 3–0 pitch does not endear him to Torre.

Schilling has now faced the minimum fifteen batters in this game. But so much can change. The big question is whether Martinez's eleven-pitch at bat will cost Schilling the physical stamina and concentration he needs later in the game.

◆ ◆ ◆

ROGER CLEMENS HAS already thrown a lot of pitches—seventy-five over the first four innings—and needs to conserve his strength for tough situations. He has not thrown a complete game since May 28, 2000, when he lost a 2–0 duel against the Boston Red Sox ace Pedro Martinez at Yankee Stadium.

Shortstop Tony Womack leads off the home fifth inning for the Diamondbacks with the game still scoreless. Clemens mixes hard and soft stuff—first throwing a floater up and outside for a ball, then a fastball over the plate, then a floater outside, and then a fastball up and outside. Trying to get Clemens to throw more, Womack is taking all the way on the next pitch, a fastball that catches the outside part of the plate.

It's the perfect setup to come inside with a hard fastball, which is just what Clemens does. Womack grounds to second baseman Soriano for the first out of the inning.

Womack was trying to answer Tino Martinez's long at bat—and get Clemens out of the game before the eighth inning.

"Our guys knew Clemens well," says manager Bob Brenly. "If you could run up a pitch count, we can get him out of the ballgame. And the way he started that ballgame, that's all we were thinking about, was to find a way to get him out of here."

◆ ◆ ◆

WITH ONE OUT in the bottom of the fifth inning, Craig Counsell bounces a low-and-outside fastball over Clemens's timed leap. Leaping for the ball, Clemens concentrates completely as he extends his glove hand straight up. Clemens and the ball make an inverted exclamation mark. Clemens comes down hard on his damaged hamstring and tumbles forward.

The ball bounces twice in front of second base, where Jeter takes the ball in front of Soriano and throws Counsell out at first base. Jeter is closer to first base than Soriano when he grabs the ball. On a rush play, infielders often grab the ball with a bare hand. But that would not work on this play. Jeter would lose the flow of the play—and might bobble the ball.

By keeping his weight low, Jeter maintains a balance. He achieves the equivalent of making a "set" throw while on the move. Cutting across the infield, he has the momentum to throw to first base. By staying low, folding his head and hands in toward his torso as he grabs the ball, Jeter maintains his balance as he charges forward. Like a passenger in a moving train, Jeter manages to stay balanced and even still while moving forward on the ball.

Jeter takes his time throwing the ball, realizing that Counsell doesn't have time to beat a clean play. Jeter flips the ball sidearmed, a bullet to first base. After the play, Jeter keeps running, limping as he slows down.

◆ ◆ ◆

ON THE NEXT play, Alfonso Soriano shows just how hard it can be for even the most athletic players to handle a simple ground ball.

On a 1–2 count, Luis Gonzalez slaps an outside fastball to Soriano. Backing off the ball, as if his legs are pulled back by a magnet, the Yankees' second baseman bobbles the ball and can't recover quick enough to get the runner.

After starting his career at shortstop, Soriano now likes playing second base and wants to make his career there. But he frustrates his manager and teammates with his mental lapses. He's not always ready for a play and he rushes his movements when he catches the ball or throws to first base. He can do anything on the field, but he doesn't always have the mental focus to make all the basic plays consistently. It's not that he doesn't work on his game. Yankees coach Willie Randolph, a former second baseman, hits hundreds of grounders to Soriano before games.

For Soriano to reach his potential, someone like Randolph or veteran infielder Luis Sojo needs to teach him how to study the game on every pitch, stay in the moment, never allow his attention to wander. Soriano is smart, hardworking, and athletic, but he is not always intent on the field.

"He's like that colt trying to stand up for the first time," says Charley Steiner, an analyst with ESPN. "He struggles to do the basic things. But he can be awesome too. He can make a remarkable play. It's when he's got time to think that he's not always sure if he should move in or back up."

Matt Williams has a chance to do his job—knock in runs—with a base runner and two outs in the bottom of the fifth inning. The veteran third baseman takes a long swing, an obvious power swing, but he fouls it for the first strike. Williams gets the fat part of the bat on the ball, but he's late; he would have powered that ball out of the stadium in his younger days.

The fielders are positioned deep to prevent a ball going in the gap between them.

Williams bounces a ball to Jeter at short, who tosses to Soriano for a force play at second base just ahead of Gonzalez's slide.

The game has passed its middle point. Both teams not only fail to score, but can't even put together a rally. The most important moment of the game offensively has been Tino Martinez's ability to get Curt Schilling to throw eleven pitches. But the bats of both teams—even the Diamondbacks, who exploded for fifteen runs the night before—remain silent.

Chapter Twelve

MANAGING THE GAME

Obscure characters stand in the background of every great organization. For brief moments, these characters make decisions that can shape the organization for years. One such figure is a lifelong public relations man who convinced the Yankees' principal owner, George M. Steinbrenner III, to hire Joe Torre as manager.

Arthur Richman, who takes the greatest pride in his membership in the St. Louis Browns Hall of Fame, typifies baseball's old-school system of networking. Play "Six Degrees of Separation" with him and you make connections to everyone who has mattered in baseball and politics in the twentieth century. Just one or two degrees away are Babe Ruth and Shoeless Joe Jackson in baseball and Mao Zedong and Winston Churchill in politics. One of his favorites was Richard Nixon, whom Richman occasionally chauffeured home to Saddle River, New Jersey, after Mets games.

Richman's baseball career began at the age of twelve when he befriended Harlond Clift, the Browns' third baseman, and started traveling with the team. Since then he has made a career out of schmoozing and boozing and hanging around Major League Baseball players.

After working for twenty years as a writer for the New York *Daily Mirror,* Richman became promotions manager and traveling secretary for the Mets in 1965. He worked for the Mets for twenty-five years. Then he moved to the Bronx to work for Steinbrenner.

Over the years, Steinbrenner has relied on an ever-changing claque of advisors. In 1996, when Steinbrenner forced out Buck Showalter as manager, he turned to Richman to find a replacement. Richman came up with a final list of four men with managerial experience—Tony La Russa, Davey Johnson, Sparky Anderson, and Torre. All but Torre either had offers with better salaries or geographic limitations.

"Joe Torre was one of the best men at my wedding—I had ten best men, all baseball people—and I roomed with him for five years when he managed the Mets and I was the traveling secretary, so we were pretty close. He was out in Cincinnati, where his wife came from, and I said, 'Would you like to manage the Yankees, Joe?' and he said, 'Are you crazy? Of course I would.' He had turned down the general manager's job earlier. I said, 'All right, I'm going to speak to Steinbrenner, I think I've got you the job at $500,000 to start with.'

"We brought in Joe and the press conference and the media crucified Steinbrenner and the New York *Daily News* had a great big headline: 'CLUELESS JOE.' And the paper said [he was] the worst manager in baseball. Has he really won anything? And Steinbrenner came in one evening and said 'What did you do to me?' and I said, 'If you're unhappy about it, fire me.' And he said, 'Okay, I'll think about it.' I always liked Joe and he got along well with the ballplayers. I had a lot of guys I could choose from but I thought being that he was from New York, maybe he would get along. Now he's up for the Hall of Fame."

For a brief period when Richman was in Steinbrenner's inner circle, he had the power to hire the man in the dugout. He made a gut decision, based more on friendship than a business plan. It was typical of the old way of running a baseball team.

Visit Richman in his office at Yankee Stadium and you take a tour of baseball history, with some side trips through American history. The walls are covered with pictures of Richman with baseball's all-time greatest players. The faded photographs show the march of progress from Ty Cobb and Shoeless Joe Jackson to Joe DiMaggio and Don

Larsen, from Willie Mays and Hank Aaron to Tom Seaver and Roger Clemens. Other photographs show him with Richard Nixon, Ronald Reagan, George W. Bush, and George H.W. Bush.

Richman is more of a people person than a baseball person, but with him that's a distinction without a difference. Baseball is people to Richman. He's a baseball Zelig, the person who has nudged baseball history by spending time in the company of the men who played the game.

In 1956, Richman played a direct hand in the greatest single feat in World Series history. Yankees' manager Casey Stengel told Richman that he planned to start Don Larsen in Game Five of the Series—and to make sure Larsen limited his drinking the night before the game. In Game Two of the Series, a hungover Larsen lasted only one and two-thirds innings, yielding four runs, in the Brooklyn Dodgers' 13–8 victory.

Now, with the Series tied at two games apiece, Stengel needed Larsen to control his drinking and pitch a decent game. Always more prolific as a drinker than a pitcher, Larsen won just three of twenty-four decisions for the Baltimore Orioles in 1954. Despite his greater success with the Yankees—he won twenty games and lost seven in two years—Stengel worried that he would not be ready for his next start.

"We went out for our usual drinks and I said, 'Tonight you've got to behave yourself. You could only have three or four drinks because you're pitching tomorrow.' He got bombed in the second game of the World Series that year. He said, 'How do you know?' I said, 'Casey told me.' So we had three or four drinks and I said, 'You have to get home at a Christian hour tonight,' and I got him in a cab at 11:15 or so to go to the Concourse Plaza where all the Yankees lived. And he said, 'Can I at least have a pizza?' and I said all right. We had a pizza and I took him up to his room."

The next day, Larson gave the greatest performance in World Series history. He pitched a perfect game against the Dodgers.

Almost four decades later, this nebbish baseball lifer hired Joe Torre. The modern Yankees dynasty was born.

◆ ◆ ◆

"A BASEBALL TEAM wears its manager as a man wears a suit," says Bill James, the author of the only comprehensive study of managers. "A suit that looks good on Al Pacino might not look quite the same on you. A light green pinstripe that looks sensational on Demi Moore would look ridiculous on me."

Finding the right fit is a tricky proposition because the character of a team changes every year. Younger teams often need a gruff taskmaster like Dallas Green, the drill sergeant who led the Philadelphia Phillies to a World Championship in 1980. A stern disciplinarian creates a sense of purpose and order after a loose players' manager, but over time his martial ways start to grate on the players. Older teams require less direction. Veteran ballplayers, when they have developed good routines for performing well, need to be left alone. That is, until the clubhouse gets so atomized that the players cease to perform as a team.

Most managers only succeed for two or three years, then fall out of sync with their players. Teams usually succeed when they alternate tough guys with pussycats.

Economists Kenneth Chapman and Lawrence Southwick, looking at a century's worth of data on managerial longevity, support James's thesis about the fit between the manager and the team. Writing in the *American Economic Review,* Chapman and Southwick find that managers face an increasing hazard of losing their jobs over their first three years on the job. Tensions between managers and disagreements inevitably accumulate about how the team should operate.

But if they last, managers become more secure after three years. The ones who survive, by design or accident, fit the evolving culture of the organization. Once the manager lasts as long as three years, he has an opportunity to shape the organization to match his personality.

When Bob Brenly called his first team meeting as manager of the Arizona Diamondbacks in spring training in 2001, he knew every player in the room. He had played with Matt Williams on the San Francisco Giants and he broadcast Diamondbacks games since their first year in 1998. He knew the former manager, Buck Showalter, liked him and respected him. But he also thought the Diamondbacks were ready for a looser rein than Showalter held.

Showalter had joined the Diamondbacks three years before they played their first game. The franchise was awarded in June 1995 and would not start play until April 1998. Showalter had the opportunity to build a franchise from scratch and he went about his business deliberately. He had a hand in the design of the stadium and the uniforms, helped to create the five-year plan to bring the team to respectability, identified the kind of players he wanted owner Jerry Colangelo to sign, oversaw the analysis of players the team might get in the special expansion draft. He scripted an exact system of training and evaluating players.

When the Diamondbacks finally came together for their first spring training in 1998, they found a strict workout schedule that supported a broader organizational plan. Showalter wanted a disciplined bunch of warriors playing in a system. Everyone up and down the organization would know the team's way of doing business and their own responsibilities within that system. Showalter was one part World War II General George Patton and one part business management guru Tom Peters.

Matt Williams, an original member of the Diamondbacks, appreciated Showalter's approach. "You have to be prepared," Williams says. "You can't let yourself relax because you never know what's going to happen, so you might as well make sure you're comfortable doing it. Buck was notorious for it—getting us out there every day, which I loved. Buck didn't have all those rules for the sake of rules. He had to establish some rules because he was the manager of an expansion team with a lot of kids and he had to do that to make sure we were on the right path."

By the 2000 season, the rules started to grate. The Diamondbacks had a collection of veteran players who had each developed his own routine to get ready for games. Mark Grace and Matt Williams showed up early and worked in the batting cage and infield. Randy Johnson and Curt Schilling followed deliberate four-day routines—running, light weights, studying videos and stats, meeting with coaches and teammates—to get ready to pitch on the fifth day. Steve Finley followed his new age training regimen. Craig Counsell worked on his stance and fielding. Mike Morgan worked with physical therapist Russell Nua to keep energy in his aging body. Luis Gonzalez saved his swings for the game rather than exhausting himself in batting practice.

In his first meeting with the players, Brenly announced that Showalter's structured regime was over. To demonstrate the point, he picked up a copy of Showalter's organizational plan and hurled it into a garbage can. Then he took a napkin and wrote two rules on it: *(1) Show up on time, ready to play. (2) Play hard.*

Buck Showalter bristles at the suggestion that he ran too tight a ship with a restrictive rule book. "First of all," he says, "it wasn't a rule book. It was an organizational plan. We started that organization from scratch and needed to have a plan to create a winner. That's what that book was—not a rule book."

But perceptions are everything to a group of twenty-five men who must live together for eight months a year. If Showalter's regime seemed too regimented to a critical mass of players, that's all that mattered. And Brenly's more relaxed approach made the players loose.

"B.B. came along and let you come to the park at five and take just a few swings because you're tired or it was August," Williams says.

It was precisely because Williams and his teammates already wanted to work hard that rules mandating such work were unnecessary.

"The bunch of guys we had were all mostly veterans and they knew what needed to get done," says utility infielder Greg Colbrunn. "That [spring training] meeting had a big effect on us, but for the most part we also had a bunch of veterans that knew how to play the game. And you had that special feeling from day one."

As the Diamondbacks marched to the World Series, veteran players competed with each other to show who could work harder. By the World Series, players were willing to sacrifice almost anything to win. This was going to be the last chance for Mark Grace, Jay Bell, and Mike Morgan. It might be the last chance for others as well. The Diamondbacks were built to win now, and it was going to take all twenty-five players to do the job.

◆ ◆ ◆

JOE TORRE, MEANWHILE, was on the verge of winning his fourth consecutive World Championship with the Yankees. The Yankees' principal owner, George Steinbrenner, has always spent lavishly to bring some of the game's best players to the Bronx. But money could not guarantee success, as the Yankees discovered in the years before Torre's arrival in 1996.

The Yankees won under Torre because he set strict standards for the team—from behavior in the clubhouse to execution of plays on the field—and eliminated the players who would not play by his rules.

Torre embodies both major types of manager—the coddler and the stern disciplinarian. Torre makes players know they are respected and even loved. In his folksy gatherings with media in the Yankee dugout before games, Torre praises the integrity and decency of even the most ornery players.

"But," says TV broadcaster Tim McCarver, "don't misunderstand all that classy sense of humor, that coddling demeanor, for weakness. Don't mistake anything he does for weakness." Torre draws a line for his players. *Do whatever you want on your time, but follow these rules—or else.* Any breach of his few rules results in banishment. The list of players that Torre has exiled—Hideo Nomo, Charlie Hayes, Ruben Sierra, Kenny Rogers, David Wells, Rubin Rivera—serves as a warning to all the millionaires who come to the Yankee clubhouse for the first time.

Torre is, in short, a coddling capo—an unusual hybrid personality that is essential for success over a long period of time.

◆ ◆ ◆

THE INFLUENCE OF a manager extends beyond his management of the players in the clubhouse. Decisions about game strategy—pitching changes, hit-and-run plays, sacrifice bunts and steal plays, positioning fielders, pinch hitters—can win or lose five or six games a year.

Like all modern managers, Bob Brenly and Joe Torre immerse themselves in videos and statistical data. The Yankees use the most extensive team of advance scouts in the game to prepare for important series—against, say, their bitter rivals from Boston—as well as all postseason opponents. The scouts produce three-inch-thick books, filled with detailed reports on every player on an opposition team. The reports tell how well players hit, run, throw, field, run the bases, position themselves in the field, steal bases, bunt—with even more detailed information on their hitting and pitching patterns. Brenly and Torre and their coaching staffs break down the data and feed the useful morsels to pitchers and hitters.

Brenly and Torre follow traditional on-field strategy. Both like to bunt. Both embrace the growing specialization of pitchers. Both like to make late-game defensive replacements. Both also have club rosters filled with veterans, and they're content to let them play the game without interference.

How successful is their field strategy? Bill James and other statisticians have devised a formula—which they call the Pythagorean method—to estimate how many games a team should expect to win, given how many runs they score and how many runs they allow. When a team gets more than its expected number of wins, the manager deserves credit for at least some of them. Over baseball history, only twenty-two teams have exceeded their Pythagorean win totals by at least eight. The biggest overachievers were the 1974 San Diego Padres and 1984 New York Mets, who each won twelve more games than expected. The 1970 Cincinnati Reds won eleven more games than projected, and the 1963 Houston Colt .45s, 1997 San Francisco Giants, and 1998 Kansas City Royals each won ten more than projected. Five teams won nine more games than projected and eleven teams won eight more than projected. That's out of 1,970 total teams playing over more than a century.

And the performances of Joe Torre and Bob Brenly? The Yankees won 95 games under Torre when the Pythagorean formula would have predicted 90.68 wins. The Diamondbacks won 92 games under Brenly when the Pythagorean formula would have predicted 96.14. So on the field at least, Torre gets credit for winning four-plus extra games, while Brenly is responsible for losing four-plus games.

◆ ◆ ◆

Bob Brenly and Joe Torre will have plenty of decisions in the next few innings. How long can Schilling and Clemens last? Who do you call on in relief? Do you get Randy Johnson in the game the day after he starts? Do you ask Mariano Rivera to throw two innings—or come in before the Yankees get a lead? Do you make all the righty-lefty switches? Do you play cautious defense in the late innings, positioning the corner infielders by the line to guard against doubles down the lines? Do you move infielders in when the opposition gets a runner on third base with fewer than two outs? Do you use the sacrifice bunt? Do you dare to steal a base? Do you follow what the statistics say or do you go by guts? Do you call on the old pros to deliver or give bit players a chance to shine?

Managing a baseball team is often compared to playing chess. Each side makes decisions based on a logic that changes pitch by pitch and batter by batter. Those decisions require anticipation of what the other side might do as a countermove. The number of decisions a manager can make over the course of a game is infinite. The manager makes his decisions partly on the basis of hard knowledge—like the statistics that have become a central part of the game—but he also relies on intuition. A manager absorbs all kinds of soft data, from the body language of a struggling pitcher to the heaviness of the stadium air, to understand numbers in the context of a game's subtle unfolding.

The chess master Garry Kasparov could have been talking for Joe Torre or Bob Brenly when he told *Harvard Business Review:* "Even at the highest levels it is impossible to calculate very far out.... Inevitably you reach a point where you've got to navigate by using your imagination and feelings rather than your intellect or logic. At that moment, you're playing with your gut."

Whatever the manager's brains and the player's skills, luck will always play a major role in baseball. For the first time, scholars are now studying the dimensions of luck with surprising findings. Luck might seem the ultimate random phenomenon. But a ten-year study has found that people make their own luck with the way they prepare and react to changing circumstances in their lives.

Lucky people, says Richard Wiseman, a British psychologist, "Are skilled at creating and noticing chance opportunities, make fortuitous decisions by listening to their intuition, create self-fulfilling prophesies via positive expectations, and adopt a resilient attitude that transforms bad luck into good." A good baseball manager creates luck by anticipating events that probably won't happen—just in case. Players create luck when they respond decisively to new opportunities that unfold on the field.

Maybe, just maybe, the manager's oft-derided "hunch" play—the decision to use a certain player based on some rough calculation of the look in the player's eyes, the game's tempo and hidden logic, and a raw feeling about the game's atmospherics—has a deserving place in the game after all.

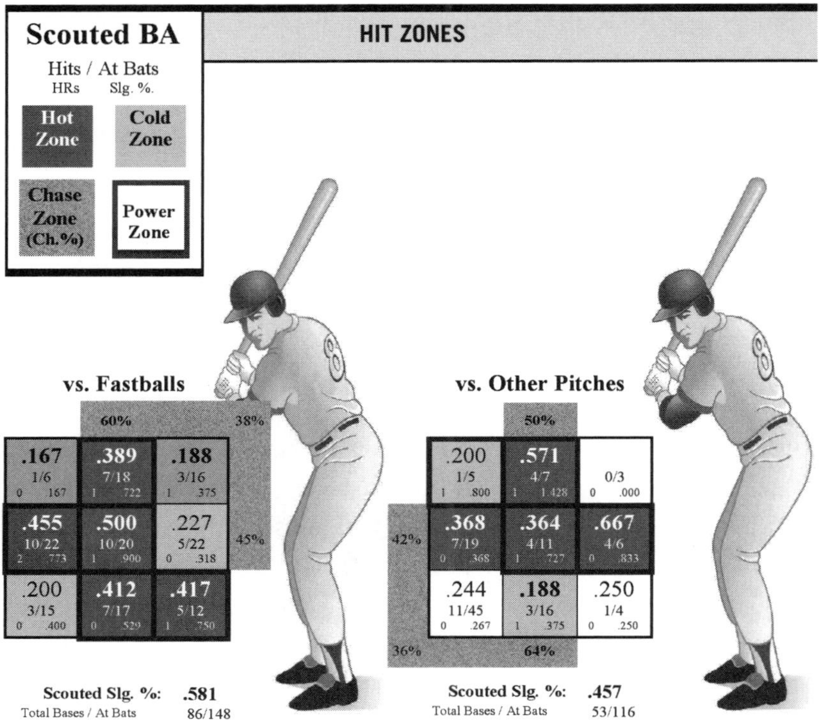

In the last generation, statistics have driven every decision in baseball, from low-level scouting and player development to preparation for the World Series. Inside Edge, a private scouting company, develops hitting charts—like this graphic of Danny Bautista's hitting zones—to show how hitters perform against different pitches in different locations.

SIXTH INNING

In which one team finally gets on the scoreboard—and the sport's statistics revolution provides revealing clues for every pitch and hit of the game

Chapter Thirteen

THE NUMBERS GAME

AT THE DAWN of the twenty-first century, baseball is awash in numbers.

Baseball people have always loved numbers. Players and fans can recite endless numbers about famous and obscure players and teams, and some numbers hold mythic significance: 755 (career home runs, by Henry Aaron); .406 (the last .400 season, by Ted Williams); 2,632 (most consecutive games played, by Cal Ripken); 4,256 (most career hits, by Pete Rose); 511 (the most career wins, by Cy Young); and 61 (most home runs in a season, in the pre-steroids era, by Roger Maris).

Baseball is, in fact, the most statistical of all games because it can be broken down into separate pieces. On every play, players make discrete actions on the ball—pitching, swinging, catching, throwing—separated in time and space from teammates and opponents. In other team sports, it's not so easy to disentangle players and plays to count who is responsible for what actions. Football is a game of power and patterns, each play requiring the simultaneous action of several different players. Sure, it's possible to count yardage and tackles and sacks, but football entails essentially group acts. Basketball and hockey are even more fluid games, more contests of coordination and tempo than series of discrete acts.

But for almost a century, the passion for statistics was restricted to the flat numbers found on the back of bubble-gum cards: W, L, SO, BB, ERA, HR, RBI, AVG.

Sabermetrics has changed all that. Sabermetrics is the neologism created by joining the acronym for the American Society for American Baseball Research (SABR) with the Greek word for measure (*metron*).

Sabermetrics has challenged the conventional wisdom on every issue of importance to the game of baseball. What's the best lineup? Should a batter sacrifice? Should a runner attempt a steal? How long should a pitcher stay in a game? Which pitcher should be used against a batter? What's the out-pitch for a certain hitter? Is a walk as good as a hit? How much do strikeouts matter—for pitchers *and* hitters? Where should the fielders position themselves? What's the best configuration of a ballpark?

Sabermetrics has two key elements: gathering the data and analyzing the data. Historically, statistics are gathered when the game's official scorekeepers record the events of the game: innings pitched, strikeouts, walks, groundouts, pop-ups; at bats, walks, hits, runs batted in, runs scored; chances, assists, putouts, errors.

With the proliferation of satellite television and personal computers, most of baseball's thirty franchises and a half-dozen private companies now gather information on every single event that takes place in a game—every pitch (by type, speed, location, and hitter response), where every ball hit is batted into play, every fielding attempt, every move by a base runner.

Vast databases now provide information on everything that happens in a game—not just the end results, but also the particular qualities and consequences of each player's actions, and inactions, on the field.

If knowledge is power, then secret knowledge is secret power. In recent years, as the playoffs and World Series have become a mini-season of up to nineteen games, baseball has become a battle of intelligence systems. The Yankees and Diamondbacks have deployed unprecedented platoons of scouts to gather inside data on each other, which they then used to develop strategy for the World Series. Preparation-obsessed players like Curt Schilling develop their own game plans with vast video libraries that document each pitch involving every player in the game.

But gathering data is just the beginning. Sabermetricians have devised a sweeping new array of statistics to determine what players and which actions produce the greatest impact on the game. This alphabet soup of statistical measures and formulae—OPS (on-base plus slugging average), ERP (estimated runs produced), LWTS (linear weights system), TA (total average), EQU (equivalency average), and DIPS (defense independent pitching statistics), for example—provide analyses of what happens on the field in new, quantifiable ways.

Baseball uses three levels of statistics. The simplest kind of statistic is the tally: How many hits, home runs, wins, strikeouts, errors, et cetera, can be attributed to a player or team? The second is a rate: How many runs per nine innings does a pitcher yield? What is a player's batting average or fielding percentage? The final kind of number—wholly a creation of the new age of statistics—weighs all measures to account for the different circumstances (different ballparks, defensive support, eras) in which a player or team is acting.

New statistics have provided a fresh approach to evaluating talent, building teams, and developing game strategy. Numbers provide the fodder to challenge traditional strategy for starting pitchers, relievers, fielding, positioning, intentional walks, stealing, sacrifice bunts, and just about everything else. The new knowledge about baseball is publicly available to all comers on Internet sites and in books the size of the big-city telephone directories.

Once resisted by baseball traditionalists, exotic statistics now guide every decision in the game.

◆ ◆ ◆

THE GAME REMAINED scoreless when Alfonso Soriano started the sixth inning for the Yankees by striking out on five pitches.

After jamming Soriano on the first pitch, getting him to foul off a fastball on his hands, Schilling threw the next two pitches off the plate. Soriano took a ball low and away, then a knee-high pitch just off the plate. Then he uppercut an inside fastball foul. Finally, Schilling went outside again, getting Soriano to reach, unsuccessfully, for a sizzling fastball.

Statistics gathered by Tendu, a California company, show that Soriano is one of the more aggressive hitters in the game. Soriano swings at only 34 percent of first pitches, but then he swings at almost everything. He swings at about 60 percent of 1–0, 2–0, 0–1, and 0–2 pitches. He is even more aggressive when the count is even, swinging at 65 percent of 1–1 pitches and 77 percent of 2–2 pitches, 62 percent of 2–1 pitches, 68 percent of 3–1 pitches. The only pitch Soriano lays off is the 3–0 pitch, but that doesn't matter because he hardly ever gets one.

Soriano hits best right away (.459 on the 0–0 count) and when he gets ahead by a couple pitches to force the pitcher to throw strikes (.423 on 2–0 and .455 on 3–1). He is a poor hitter when he's behind in the count, especially on 0–2 (.164) and 1–2 (.178).

Soriano's fortunes turn on what happens with the 1–1 count (when he hits .359). Whether the count goes to 2–1 or 1–2 creates a 254-point swing in batting average (.432 versus .178). He hits .334 on fastballs and .257 on non-fastballs.

Had enough statistics on Soriano's proclivities at the plate? The most lethal pitch for Soriano is the split-fastball from a right-handed pitcher. Soriano hits only .179 on that pitch. Schilling knows it, too. If he can set up Soriano, he can strike him out on a low-and-away splitter.

◆ ◆ ◆

THE SECOND BATTER, Scott Brosius, strikes out on three pitches. Brosius swings late and fouls the first pitch behind the plate. Then a changeup baffles him; he swings weakly through a ball over the center of the plate, as if in slow motion. Then, on a fastball in the dirt off the plate, he starts to swing, tries to check his swing, but goes around anyway, weakly. Schilling plays a mean sadist against Brosius, mercilessly teasing and embarrassing him.

On a one-ball count, Roger Clemens puts his bat out and lifts a weak pop fly to Danny Bautista in left field to end the Yankees' turn at bat.

◆ ◆ ◆

AFTER SIX INNINGS, Schilling has faced the minimum number of batters. Eighteen batters have come up to the plate and eighteen batters have walked back to the dugout. Only Paul O'Neill has reached base, and he was thrown out trying to stretch a double into a triple, way back in the first inning.

Using data on the Yankees' hitters from the 2001 season, mathematician Doug Drinen of the University of the South in Sewanee, Tennessee, calculated the odds against an average pitcher facing the minimum eighteen batters in the first six innings to be 1,080 to 1. Adding Schilling's superb statistics to his calculations, Drinen figures that odds against Schilling facing the minimum number of Yankees through six innings were 259 to 1.

Schilling has now thrown just seventy-six pitches, fifty of them strikes. Not until the fifth inning did all three Yankee batters show the discipline to avoid swinging at the first pitch—and two of them struck out on a total of nine pitches.

Another statistic underscores Schilling's dominance: the strikeout-to-walk ratio. Right now, Schilling's ratio is 8 to 1. Over the course of the season, he struck out 7.5 batters for every batter he walked (293 strikeouts and 39 walks over 256.66 innings). Schilling's teammate Randy Johnson was also masterful, with a ratio of 5.23 to 1 (372 strikeouts and 71 walks in 249 innings). Through the sixth inning, Schilling has struck out 55 batters and walked just 6 in 47 innings of work in the playoffs and World Series—a postseason strikeout-to-walk ratio of 7.83 to 1.

◆ ◆ ◆

AT AN ADVANCED age for pitchers—he will turn thirty-five later in the month—Schilling can go deep into games with harder stuff than any modern pitcher besides Hall of Famer Nolan Ryan and his teammate Randy Johnson. What gives Schilling such endurance? How can he be strong at such an advanced age? Training and conditioning tell part of the story. His near-perfect pitching form tells another part of the story.

But a third part of the story is less obvious. Schilling's struggles as a young man—his immaturity, his failure to establish himself as an effective starter—gave him the time he needed to develop a strong and durable arm. Schilling did not throw 100 innings until 1992, his fourth year in the major leagues. By that time, he was physically ready to pitch well over 200 innings a year without overwhelming strain on his arm.

Throughout history, pitchers who have pitched few innings early in their career have developed the strength to pitch into their late thirties and early forties. Exhibit A is Warren Spahn, who missed three seasons to military service before the age of twenty-five—and who won twenty-three games at the age of forty-two and pitched 197 innings at age forty-four. Exhibit B is Nolan Ryan, who pitched an average of just over 100 innings in his first five years. Maybe more important, Ryan faced an average of just twenty-six batters in his first seven pro seasons. Ryan's arm never failed him. He pitched until he was forty-six years old.

"The average male may stop growing when he is sixteen or seventeen," Arthur Pappas, the team doctor for the Boston Red Sox, told *Sports Illustrated* in 1989. "But there's a continued development of joint cartilage that goes on beyond that. There's no question that there's a certain connection between the number of pitches thrown [early in a pitcher's career] and later pitching problems. A young pitcher's tissues are still developing, and he's not yet throwing with the control that a more mature pitcher has. So he can throw his shoulder muscles out of balance."

Weariness makes it hard for the pitcher to maintain good form. Even minor mechanical flaws—striding too soon or too late, bringing that hand back too far, turning the hips and torso a little slower—put too much strain on the hips, back, shoulder, and elbow.

Using data from the 1997 *Sporting News Baseball Register,* Lee Sinins and Will Carroll analyzed the careers of 135 pitchers who threw 175 innings in a year before the age of twenty-two. A vast majority of the pitchers who pitched so many innings suffered significant injuries. Forty-four of them—about a third—experienced injuries with a serious and direct impact on their careers. Another eighteen (about 13 percent) experienced a less dramatic but still direct negative impact from pitching too many innings at a young age. Thirty-eight pitchers (about 28 percent) had middling careers that could be attributed to overwork.

Only seventeen of the pitchers in the sample of 135 pitchers enjoyed significant success over their careers.

◆ ◆ ◆

In the bottom of the sixth inning of a scoreless game, Steve Finley smacks a soft line drive into center field for a single. The Diamondbacks' center fielder is looking all the way on the first pitch, which Clemens overthrew high. The 1–0 count is advantageous to Finley—and dangerous for Clemens. Opponents batted .360 against Clemens after he fell behind on the first pitch. Fortunately for Clemens, he does not fall behind very often on his first pitch. In 227 at bats recorded by Tendu, a private statistics company, Clemens fell behind only fifty times.

On the second pitch, Clemens throws the ball over the middle of the plate. Finley extends his arms and drives the ball up the middle for a clean hit. After five innings, Finley has became the first leadoff man from either team to reach base in the game.

Finley turns into the pitch like a dancer turning a partner, softly but crisply, following through on his swing with both hands. Unlike his late-blooming teammate Luis Gonzalez, Finley actually opens his stance as he swings, his bat still poised behind his hands as the ball moves over the plate.

It's not where Clemens wants the pitch. Catcher Jorge Posada's glove waits on the outside part of the plate as the ball arrives. The bat whips out from behind Finley's hands; the fat part of the bat hits the ball and goes into center field for a clean single.

Down in the count, Clemens knew he had to throw the ball over the plate. He cannot afford to get behind in the count 2–0. In 2001, hitters got hits on twelve of twenty-five times they put the ball in play on a 2–0 count—good for an average of .480. What's remarkable about that statistic, more than the high average, is that it did not happen very often. Of the 833 times that batters put the ball in play in 2001, it happened on a 2–0 count only twenty-five times—or about 3 percent of the time. Even more impressive, batters put the ball into play on a 3–0 count only two times—less than one-fourth of 1 percent of all pitches.

The 1–0 pitch is so important because it represents the hitter's best chance to put Clemens in a bad position by either swinging at a ball over the plate or by reaching the advantageous position of a 2–0 count. On a 2–0 count, the hitter can be much more selective. The hitter can watch borderline pitches—the splitter low and away, the fastball up and inside—rather than defensively swinging at them.

Spray charts show that Finley, a left-handed batter, hits the ball to all fields at the BOB. Finley hit eight singles down the right field line and eight singles off the left field line. Eighteen of his singles were to center and right-center field. Finley beat out four infield grounders to the left side of the diamond and seven grounders to the right side of the diamond. He went with the extreme parts of the diamond for his doubles at the BOB—hitting four down the left field line and five down the right field line, with another three somewhere in the great expanses of center field. Finley's two triples at the BOB were hit to the deepest part of center field. He pulled the ball for home run power, hitting all seven home runs at home to the right side of center field.

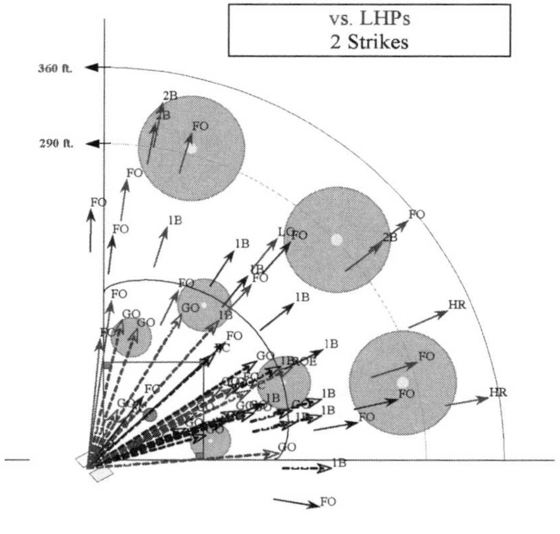

Spray charts—like this report on Steve Finley—help to position the defense.

Chart courtesy of Inside Edge

Instantly after Finley's hit—like automatic computer trading on Wall Street—Joe Torre orders Ramiro Mendoza to start warming up in the bullpen. In the seventh game of the World Series, Torre will not hesitate to replace a tiring pitcher.

Like Clemens, Mendoza is a right-handed pitcher, but he has a quicker move to first base. Mendoza would bring a different look to the game. The Diamondbacks are getting used to Clemens.

Mendoza would be the perfect counterpoint to Clemens. Clemens throws a mix of hard fastballs (up and in) and darting splitters (down and away). Mendoza throws a steady stream of sinkerballs, down in the strike zone, which induce batters to hit ground balls. Mendoza has thrown two and one-third innings in the series so far, yielding one hit and striking out one batter. His role would be to retire the next batter or two and hold the runner on base.

With Finley dancing around first base, Clemens tosses softly to first baseman Tino Martinez. Clemens's goal is not to pick off Finley but to keep him close to first base. Then Finley can't get a good jump if Bautista hits the ball. Holding back a runner a few steps can be the difference in whether he goes from first to third on a single or scores on a double.

Chapter Fourteen

STRATEGY OF SCORING

With Steve Finley on first base and no outs, the Diamondbacks' Danny Bautista steps up to the plate—and the strategic maneuverings of the managers begin in earnest.

The immediate question is whether the Diamondbacks' left fielder will execute a sacrifice bunt to move Finley to second base.

Bautista turns toward third base to study the signs from coach Eddie Rodriguez. He turns quickly toward the plate, knowing what manager Bob Brenly has ordered him to do.

The Yankees look for cues. But Bautista betrays nothing. His face is intent but blank.

Born in Santo Domingo in the Dominican Republic, Bautista's molasses-brown skin is accented by a small mustache. Bautista is one of the game's small men—five feet, eleven inches, 170 pounds. He's a matchstick man, his long stirrups exaggerating the thinness of his legs. He still has the slender build that once caused a dozen scouts to reject him in tryouts as a teenager.

Bautista does not usually play against right-handed pitchers. Bautista and Reggie Sanders platoon in right field. But Bautista got three hits in Game Six, so Brenly has decided to keep him in the lineup.

Bautista taps the plate with his bat, stares out at the mound as Clemens prepares to throw. Bautista takes a slightly open stance. He grips the bat softly, holding the bat's barrel behind his helmet. He's loose. As Clemens moves into his motion, Bautista knows Clemens will probably throw to first base to try to pick off Finley.

Brenly's first instinct is to order Bautista to bunt to move Finley into scoring position. Bautista sacrificed three times in 2001. One run could win the game. Brenly at first decides to order the bunt—and then changes his mind.

"I'm going to give him one whack at it," Brenly tells Bob Melvin, his bench coach.

By showing a willingness to bunt, Brenly gets Clemens to throw the ball up in the strike zone, a hard pitch to bunt. Bautista can hit *that* pitch. As Bautista waits for Clemens's pitch, he strums his fingers on the bat handle. He's loose and ready for whatever Clemens has to offer.

◆ ◆ ◆

A CENTERPIECE OF baseball strategy throughout the ages is to sacrifice a runner to second base in a close game. Getting the runner into scoring position—where he can score on a single—reduces the task of the hitter.

The appeal of the sacrifice goes beyond generating runs. The sacrifice bunt is part of baseball's moral appeal: *Work hard, contribute to the team, play a role, be selfless, give yourself up for the greater good.*

But the sacrifice is a losing strategy, at least when considering statistical probabilities. Bunting a runner to second base reduces a team's chances to score a run. Look at a simple matrix of game situations and the statistical chances of scoring a run for each. Baseball Prospectus, a website devoted to baseball statistics and analysis, has calculated the probabilities of scoring in different situations for the 2001 season.

Runners	No outs	One out	Two outs
No runners	.5346	.2877	.1160
Runner on first base	.9227	.5536	.2445
Runner on second base	1.1629	.7026	.3480
Runners on first and second base	1.5204	.9001	.4334
Runner on third base	1.5192	.9790	.3627
Runners on first and third bases	1.8436	1.2664	.5094
Runners on second and third bases	2.0391	1.4179	.5953
Bases loaded	2.3427	1.5867	.7938

Each of the chart's cells shows the number of runs a team can expect to score for each of the twenty-four situations a team might have in an inning. Statheads refer to these numbers as expected future runs, or EFR. The situation of runner on first base with no outs can be expected to produce .9227 runs, while a runner on second base with one out has an EFR of only .7026. It's easier to move a runner a longer distance with fewer outs than a shorter distance with one out.

◆ ◆ ◆

BRENLY CAN MAKE another strategic move to get Steve Finley to second base—tell Finley to steal the base.

Finley is a speedy man, whether on the base paths or scampering about the outfield. A successful steal means you don't give up an out to advance a runner. Getting something for nothing makes sense for the team at bat, right? Why not try? At different periods in baseball history—like the 1970s and 1980s, when speedsters like Lou Brock, Joe Morgan, and Rickey Henderson made baserunning the centerpiece of offensive strategy—the manager would have told Finley to steal second base.

But it doesn't make much sense to attempt a steal. Statistical analysis shows that you should steal only *if you have a success rate of about 70 or 75 percent.* How do we know this? Pete Palmer, one of the trailblazing figures in modern statistical analysis, devised a formula for determining the break-even point for stealing. The formula plugs in numbers for the team's expected runs using different strategies—not attempting a steal, successfully stealing a base, and failing in an attempt to steal a base.

Here's Palmer's formula:

$$\frac{(\text{SP EFR}-\text{FS EFR})}{(\text{SP EFR}-\text{FS EFR}) + (\text{SS EFR}-\text{SP EFR})}$$

SP EFR represents the expected runs for not attempting a steal ("standing pat"), FS EFR represents a failed steal attempt ("failed steal"), and SS EFR stands for a successful steal attempt ("successful steal").

Using Baseball Prospectus figures for 2001, the break-even point for stolen-base attempts with a man on first and no outs is (.815–.239) / (1.051–.239), which equals .709—meaning that base runners have to be successful 70 percent of the time to score as many runs as they would standing pat. With a man on first and one out, the break-even point is about 75 percent.

In recent years, the steal has declined in importance. Managers have looked at the stats, but they also pay attention to the dynamics of the game situation. The Diamondbacks' Tony Womack, himself a base-stealing threat, explains: "Pitchers are quicker. Catchers are getting stronger. The managers are trying to control the game—a lot more throw-overs, a lot more pitchouts. They're slowing the game down a lot."

Finley is probably not a good enough base stealer to justify an attempt. Finley stole eleven bases in 2001 and got caught seven times, a success rate of only 61 percent. Earlier in his career, Finley attempting a steal might have made more sense. Over his career, Finley has stolen 256 bases in 346 attempts, a success rate of 74 percent. Finley does not get the explosive jump on the base paths that he once did. So Brenly should probably try to let Bautista, Grace, and Miller get Finley home rather than trying to get him to second base first.

◆ ◆ ◆

EVEN IF A sacrifice or steal don't make sense statistically, *feigning* a sacrifice or a steal is another matter. If Clemens *thinks* a sacrifice or a steal is possible, he might get distracted from the business at hand—getting the hitter out.

In the analysis of Texas A&M economist Theodore L. Turocy, the mere possibility of a stolen base creates a "game of inspection" on the field.

"In the game, the defense chooses between 'inspecting,' which gives the defense a positive probability to successfully stop the stolen base play, and not inspecting, in which case the stolen base play, if attempted, is successful for the offense." Having to inspect the base runner reduces the pitcher's ability to be sharp on the mound. The infielders are placed in the same position as guards at a factory: if they fear someone will steal something from the loading dock in the back, they are distracted from their duty to keep watch over the front door.

Texas A&M's Turocy has proved statistically what baseball people have long seen with their own eyes: hitters perform better when a potential base stealer dances off first base. A hitter's OPS—the sum of a player's on-base percentage and slugging percentage—increases when a known base-stealing threat occupies the bases. When the bases are occupied by a known base stealer (someone who attempts steals at least 20 percent of the time), the hitter's median OPS increases 132 points. With an occasional base stealer (someone who steals up to 20 percent of the time), the OPS increases 42 points. With a runner who never attempts a stolen base, the OPS remains the same.

Finley isn't going to try to steal. But he's ready to run—and distract Clemens as much as possible.

Clemens decides to throw to first not just to keep Finley close, but to see whether Bautista shows whether he will bunt or swing away. Will Bautista square his body toward the pitcher and hold the fat part of his bat to bunt? Or will be keep his stance?

Of course, Bautista could feign bunt as Clemens throws to first base, and then swing away when he actually gets a pitch to hit. Or vice versa. Who knows what information the pickoff throw really provides?

Clemens makes the throw to first base. Finley is back easily. Bautista betrays nothing.

◆ ◆ ◆

WITH A RUNNER on first base and no outs in the home half of the sixth inning, the first pitch to Bautista could provide the hinge to the game.

A switch hitter, Bautista is willing to swing at first pitches. In 2001, the pitcher threw strikes to Bautista on about 61 percent of his first pitches, according to data gathered by Stats Inc. It makes sense to swing at first pitches thrown by Clemens, since he rarely falls behind and is not going to hurl anything good to hit when he is ahead in the count. When he gets ahead in the count, Clemens is going to offer either an unhittable splitter away or an unhittable fastball up in the eyes.

Bautista's spray chart shows a classic all-fields hitter. In 2001 at the BOB, he hit six doubles—one down the left field line, another down the right field line, and four clustered toward the middle of the outfield. Bautista also scattered his singles evenly across the field. Those patterns hold for all the other stadiums where the Diamondbacks played in 2001. You field Bautista straightaway, knowing that he can hit the ball anywhere, anytime. Clemens has moved the ball around on Bautista so far—pitching him inside-away-away-low-low-inside in the second inning and inside-high in the fourth.

Bautista's hitter profile is like the map of a gentrifying urban neighborhood—danger zones right next to safe areas.

Bautista does not hit well on high pitches over the right and left squares of the top row—but he hits very well on pitches thrown to the square in between. On fastballs, Bautista hits .167 on pitches on the upper-outside part of the strike zone and .188 against pitches on the upper-inside part of the zone. But when the pitch drifts over to the middle of the upper part of the zone, Bautista hits well: .389 on fastball and .571 against all pitches. To get Bautista out, pitchers need to hit the corners up in the strike zone, but they don't dare miss and let the ball drift over the middle.

Clemens has had mixed success against Bautista. In the second inning, Clemens worked hard to pitch around Bautista's hot zones and walked him on six pitches. The first pitch came to the inside part of the plate, where Bautista hits .267. The next pitches were away-over, away-low, over-low, up and in. In attempting to avoid Bautista's hot zones, Clemens walked him. In the fourth inning, Clemens missed high on his first pitch before getting Bautista on a soft fly ball to center field.

As the first pitch of the at bat comes out of Clemens's hand, Bautista coils his body back. He commits himself to swing as the ball is two-thirds of the way along its fifty-five-foot journey from the pitcher's hand to home plate. It's a good pitch to hit—in fact, the best hitter's pitch of the night from Clemens. The ball, a straight fastball, crosses the plate at Bautista's letters.

If Bautista bunts, Clemens wants to get the pitch high and inside. If the pitch has enough zip, Bautista will pop it in the air for an easy out.

But the bunt play is off. Bautista hits the pitch on the fat part of the bat. The ball rockets on a line between Bernie Williams in center field and Shane Spencer in left field.

The possibility of a bunt play put Bautista in a good position to get a good pitch over the plate. "Danny has trouble with pitches inside, and obviously they were pitching him inside, inside, inside," says catcher Jorge Posada. "And he made a little adjustment and bailed out, tried to get into the bucket so he could get to pitches inside. And this pitch was a little more over the plate, and he got to us."

Williams and Spencer sprint across the outfield grass toward the ball. Williams gets there first. The ball bounces four times before hitting the wall just to the left of the 413-foot sign in left-center field.

Bautista has at least a double, and the fleet Steve Finley glides around third base to score. The Diamondbacks take the lead. It's now Diamondbacks 1, Yankees 0.

◆ ◆ ◆

BAUTISTA'S BIG HIT seems to confirm the hoariest truism of baseball's conventional wisdom: *When you're hot, you're hot.*

Bautista has been getting more than his share of hits in the World Series. Going into tonight's game, Bautista has six hits in eleven at bats; last night, in the Diamondbacks' 15–2 romp, he had three hits in four at bats with five runs batted in.

"When you're seeing the ball well, you stay real focused and you stay back very good," Bautista says. "You got more chance to see it. I was seeing the ball good then."

All season long, Bob Brenly put Reggie Sanders in the lineup against right-handed batters. But Brenly gave Bautista the start against Clemens. "The alternative was sitting a guy who had five runs batted in," Brenly said before the game. You have to play a hitter when he's hot.

Managers usually make decisions about platoon outfielders on the basis of handedness: Righties hit against lefties, and vice versa. Jay Bell and Craig Counsell shared time at second base on this basis until the end of the year. According to the revealing OPS statistics, Bell hit slightly better against righties than lefties (.774 to .681), while Counsell did much better against lefties (.831 to .689).

Brenly is starting Bautista based on his gut sense that Bautista is hot. When players perform well, they report that they are in a special zone, seeing and feeling the ball better, capable of hitting with little effort. When they are in a slump, they cannot hit anything.

But in fact analyses of hitting patterns show that hits are distributed randomly. Players do get hits in bunches. But those bunches happen not because of a keener eye during good times but because—to be Zen about it—the balls fall when they fall and get caught when they get caught. The physicist Richard A. Muller used a random generator to show how a .333 hitter's hits might be distributed over 300 at bats.

O H O H O O O O O O O O H O O O H O O O O O H O H O H O H O O O O O H O O O
O O H H O O H H H O O O O H O O H O O O H O O O H O O H O O O O H O O O O O
O H O H O O O O H H O H O H O O O O O H O H O H O O O H H O O H O O H H O O
O O O O O O H O O O O O O H O O H O O O O H O O O H O O O O H O H O O H O O
H H O H O O O H O H O O H O O O H H H O H O H O O O H O O H O H H H O H H O
H O H O O O O H H H H O O H O O O H O H O O H O O O H O H O O O O O H H O H
O O H H H H O O O O O H H O H O H O O O O O O H O O H H O O O O O O H O H H
H O H O O H O O O O O O O H O O O O O H H O O H O H O H O H O H O O

Hits cluster to produce the appearance of hot and cold streaks—eight outs in a row here, eight hits in ten at bats there. But in fact the batter's one hits in three at bats are randomly dispersed.

Research on the greatest baseball feats of all time—as well as the great failures—show that even the most extraordinary feats fall within the bounds of randomness. A five-game winning streak, a four-for-four game, a ten-strikeout pitching performance, a home run in the bottom of the ninth inning—all occur because the player or the team has a certain level of mastery that plays out over time. If you're a .300 hitter, you're going to get thirty hits every 100 at bats, one way or another. Getting hot represents nothing more than the random clustering of these hits, within a player's basic level of skill.

The only notable exception to this truth of "patterned chance" is Joe DiMaggio's fifty-six-game hitting streak in 1941. Edward Purcell, a Nobel laureate in physics, calculated that for a hitting streak of even fifty games to occur within the bounds of randomness, the ranks of history's players would have to include four lifetime .400 hitters or fifty-two lifetime .350 hitters. But over the course of baseball history, not even a single player has hit over .400 and only three hitters have hit over .350 in their entire careers. DiMaggio's streak might be the most impressive single-season accomplishment in sports history. The likelihood of his streak ever occurring is less than one in a million.

◆ ◆ ◆

WHEN DANNY BAUTISTA hits the ball past Bernie Williams in center field, he has one thought in his mind: Triple.

Williams crouches down by the outfield wall to field the ball with his right hand. As he rears back to throw the ball, he stands up, his legs spread evenly. He throws the ball like a pitcher, completing his follow-through on his front foot.

The throw comes into the cutoff man, Derek Jeter, in the air. Jeter stands in a direct line between Williams and third baseman Scott Brosius. Jeter faces the outfield as he leaps into the air, his right leg lifted and softly bent, his left leg dangling behind. As he catches the ball, Jeter twists his body toward third base, moves his glove and hand down to his waist to switch the ball to his throwing hand, lands back on his right foot, and lifts his left leg like a pitcher kicking into his motion. A split-second later, Jeter has rocked forward, his front leg landing like a pitcher completing his motion, as Jeter whips his right arm forward.

Jeter's play looks like it takes place in one motion, but really it is a carefully calibrated set of discrete actions, each done to perfection.

By the time Bautista goes airborne for his slide, the ball has caught up with him in the race for third base. Brosius has the ball when Bautista is still five feet from the bag. Brosius has plenty of time to put down the tag. Bautista tries to slip his right hand past Brosius's tag, but he can't do it. Jeter's throw travels on a perfect arc to the outfield side of third base. Brosius has planted his feet three feet apart.

He grabs the high throw, and in one motion swipes down hard at Bautista, who slides headfirst into the base. Bautista is out easily.

Concerned about jamming his hand into the bag, Bautista lifts his hand over the bag and then tags the bag. That microsecond of caution gives Brosius an extra microsecond to find Bautista and slap down the tag.

The play keeps the Yankees in the game. If Bautista makes it safely to third base, the Diamondbacks can put together a big inning.

Jeter is nonchalant about the play. "You gotta hurry and you don't have time to plant," he says. "I started my motion when I was catching it. I just had to throw it as fast as I could and get it close to the bag. I just had to get rid of it. The throw was high but it was good enough for Scott."

Ironically, the Diamondbacks might have been better off if either Finley or Bautista were slower base runners. If Finley had been slower, he might at least have drawn a throw at home plate—or caused Jeter, the relay man, to pause to check out the play at the plate before turning his attention to Bautista. If Finley had drawn a throw to the plate, Bautista might have made it safely to third. If Bautista had been slower—if he had been Matt Williams, for example—he would have been satisfied with a stand-up double.

"That could have been a game-transforming play," broadcaster Tim McCarver says, looking back on the play three years later. "If Bautista only gets a single or makes it to third safely, it could have led to getting a pinch hitter for Schilling. If you don't have a fast runner, it could have turned out to be the makings of a big inning. It's part of the delicious minutiae of baseball—except that it's not minutiae, it's huge in the context of the game. Single events can turn out to have a huge—huge—impact on the course of a game. That was one of them."

◆ ◆ ◆

BAUTISTA'S FAILED effort to reach third base underscores the unintended consequences of baseball's ballpark revolution.

In an effort to evoke small ballparks of yesteryear like Ebbets Field and Fenway Park—and to make it easier to hit home runs—major-league franchises have built stadiums with smaller outfield dimensions.

Old-timey stadiums giveth, and old-timey stadiums taketh. Smaller ballpark dimensions have resulted in the near extinction of one of the most exciting plays in the game—the triple. In 2001, Cristian Guzman of the Minnesota Twins led the major leagues with fourteen triples. In the days of Ty Cobb and Babe Ruth, it was not uncommon for players to get more than twenty triples in a shorter season. In the first two decades of the twentieth century, one out of eighteen hits were triples; by the 1980s, triples were one of forty-three hits.

The demise of the triple is not just a matter of ballpark dimensions. It's also a matter of attitude. "The offensive strategy of big hits, not 'small ball,' make a double as good as a triple for most teams and innings of offense," says Bob Bluthardt, the head of the ballparks committee for the Society for American Baseball Research. Get a man on second and the next bopper will bring him in. Getting ninety feet closer to home doesn't add that much to the offense. That's the mentality of the modern power game, anyway.

Broadcaster Tim McCarver agrees that the demise of the triple is as much about baserunning as ballpark dimensions. "Guys aren't running out of the batter's box fast enough. Some hitters, when they get on, think their job is done, but it's just beginning. Just look at the way some of them run to first, guys like Juan Gonzalez or Ruben Sierra, after hitting the ball in the gap. You should go *through* the bag, but they go *to* the bag."

Bautista is at least trying to become the first player in the 2001 World Series—after 482 trips to the plate by both teams—to hit a triple. He fails, but give him credit for forcing the Yankees to execute all the plays.

◆ ◆ ◆

BAUTISTA'S DECISION TO slide head-first probably hurts his effort. Researchers have found that head-first slides not only pose greater danger of injury—jammed hands, shoulders, and elbows—but might even take longer.

The logic of the head-first slide is that it maintains the runner's counterclockwise movement and helps him get to the base quicker; the feet-first slider has to turn his body and almost stop in mid-motion like a cartoon character before making a descent to the base.

A 1984 study by Richard Corzatt and colleagues, published in the *American Journal of Sports Medicine,* breaks the slide into four phases—sprint, attainment of sliding position, airborne, and landing. In the first phase, the body leans forward 70 degrees. As the runner gets ready to slide—about fifteen feet from the base—the head-first player maintains this forward motion, while the feet-first player needs to lean back while getting ready to put his feet forward. This moment of pause, called the "relaxing phase," logically figures to slow down the feet-first player. Head-first sliding means no pause in the movement toward the base, which could mean a quicker trip to the base. The head-first slider also distributes the shock of the slide over a greater part of his body, making the landing less of a jolt. Corzatt *et al* take no position on which slide is best, but the research offers tantalizing data that seem to favor the belly-floppers.

But a later study published in the same journal questions the advantages of the head-first slide. The 2002 study by Steven Kane and colleagues found that runners actually get to the base faster with the feet-first slide and risk less damaging injuries. Using high-speed photography of 180 slides by amateur and professional players, Kane *et al* speculate that the superior forward movement of the head-first slide is countered by other factors.

The researchers observe: "The surface area of the chest, abdomen, anterior legs, and knees, which contact the base path in a head-first slide, is much greater than that of the buttock and posterior thigh that contact the base path in the feet-first slide. This increase in surface areas likely results in a greater amount of friction in the ground and the athlete in the last several feet of the head-first slide and may reduce the slider's speed."

Videos show that most head-first sliders hesitate momentarily before going airborne. Kane *et al* write: "This leads us to believe that the fear of diving onto a relatively hard surface with one's chest and abdomen is difficult to overcome, and the resultant hesitation may result in a loss of forward momentum."

Broadcaster Tim McCarver frowns when he sees Bautista flop into third base.

"The hands are the foremost body parts," he says later. "They should be protected like a pianist's. There are so many injuries. It's epidemic, really. Not only serious injuries, but curtailing the day-to-day-ness of players. It's not the tag [that causes injuries], it's the bag that does the damage because the bag doesn't move. A sprained thumb doesn't sound like much, but you got to cradle the bat with your fingers. You could damage toes and heels and limp your way to the plate. Sliding with the legs is not only quicker but also has much more authority and power. The real insanity comes when guys try to dive into catchers."

Manager Bob Brenly accepts the head-first slide even though he knows its dangers.

"It's obviously very dangerous. But it's a dramatic way of showing the guy's hustling. It shows he's willing to throw his body down on the ground for the good of the ball club. In Danny's case, his adrenaline, his emotions, got the better of him. He looked like Superman flying in." Because of the danger of jamming fingers, head-first sliders hook their hands around the bag. But it's not easy to use finesse in the midst of a violent movement.

"I still think there's a place for it in the game," says Brenly. "Anybody who was a big fan of baseball through the seventies and the eighties has a vivid picture of Pete Rose flying through the air, with his helmet coming off, and the front of the uniform covered with mud and dirt. And that's what a ballplayer's supposed to look like."

Many organizations have begun to teach younger players to go feet-first in the minor leagues. No one should ever slide head first, McCarver says with authority. Was it okay for the original masters, Pete Rose and Rickey Henderson? "Yeah," he says after a pause. "But there's only one Leonard Bernstein. There's only one Pavarotti. No one else should try."

◆ ◆ ◆

BAUTISTA'S FAILED EFFORT to stretch his double into a triple leaves the bases empty in the bottom of the sixth inning. Mark Grace grounds out to Alfonso Soriano on a 1–1 pitch, and then Damian Miller goes down on five pitches—a called strike up in the zone, a fastball that he swings through, a ball bounced in the dirt beyond Posada's reach, a foul, another foul, and a high-outside fastball that Miller chases.

◆ ◆ ◆

AT THE HEART of the statistics revolution is a basic truth that somehow eluded baseball people for generations: to judge players and strategy, assess how well they help to produce or prevent runs.

The most conventional measure of hitting excellence is batting average, calculated by dividing the number of hits by the number of official at bats. The most common measures of power hitting are home runs and runs batted in. The most common measure of pitching performance is earned-run average, the average number of runs scored by the opposition per nine innings. Other common measures of pitching performance include wins and saves.

These sacred statistics say little about the actual production or prevention of runs. A hitter's batting average, for example, treats all hits equally, even though a home run is better than a triple, which is better than a double, which is better than a single. Getting a hit is always better than making an out, so in some rough way, a batting average measures success. But that doesn't tell how the hit contributed to scoring a run. Home runs tell more, but not much. As a raw number, a player's home run total does not reveal anything about his *rate* of success or his overall *impact*. Runs batted in say more about the overall impact—they show the batter's ability to move his teammates around the bases—but the RBI statistic is a raw number that depends as much on situations (how many runners are on base when the hitter comes to the plate?) as the player's overall ability.

Earned-run average is probably the best traditional measure of pitching because it indicates a pitcher's rate of success in preventing runs. Bob Gibson's league-leading ERA of 1.12 in 1968 is clearly superior to Randy Johnson's 2.49 in 2001. But wait—maybe not. The pitchers competed in different worlds. Gibson played in an age of low-scoring games, when big stadiums, high mounds, generous strike zones, and conservative offensive strategies favored pitchers; Johnson plays in an age of offensive dominance, when almost every aspect of the game favors hitters. But the problem with ERA goes beyond baseball's shift from a defensive to an offensive game. ERA does not consider the impact of a team's defense on ERA. One team might have a diamond full of defensive wizards, who range far and wide to catch balls batted all over the field—while another team might field players with little ability to catch anything hit far from their set positions.

Wins and losses and saves reveal even less about a pitcher's performance. A starter gets a win when he pitches at least five innings and leaves the game with a lead that his team keeps. But a pitcher also gets a win for recording a single out when the team comes from behind to win the game in the next half inning. A pitcher can even get the win if he enters the game in relief with his team in the lead, blows the lead, and then watches as his team takes back the lead in the next inning. Pitchers can get wins if they perform magnificently—or terribly—over anywhere from one out to nine or even more innings. The save statistic also provides little information. While some relievers labor hard to protect a perilous lead, others simply enter a game well under control and record a few easy outs.

Only by understanding the real value of different events can statistics be created that make smart judgments about players and strategy. One good place to start is to understand how each kind of event changes the likelihood of winning the game. Consider the following:

Event	Change in win probability
Walk	.0281
Hit by pitch	.0284
Single	.0418
Double	.0646
Triple	.0948
Home run	.1217
Strikeout	-.0276
Groundout	-.0220
Fly out	-.0248
Ground into double play	-.0753

Source: Jahn K. Hakes and Raymond D. Sauer, "An Economic Evaluation of the *Moneyball* Hypothesis," unpublished paper, Department of Economics, Clemson University, 2004.

Putting together a winning team depends not so much on getting superstar players who can do it all—the classic "five-tool" players—as assembling a roster full of players who, together, can do the most positive things and avoid doing the most negative things. Every contribution and every mistake matters.

◆ ◆ ◆

IN THE WORLD of baseball statistics, few concepts have surprised the cognoscenti's understanding more than DIPS. The *New York Times* says the statistic is "an idea so radical that it defies belief."

DIPS stands for Defense Independent Pitching Statistics. DIPS begins by separating all of the outcomes of plate appearances into two categories. The first category, called "Defense Independent," consists of events beyond the control of fielders—strikeouts, walks, hit batsmen, and home runs. The second category, "Defense Dependent," includes all of the events that require fielders to act—hits, ground balls, fly balls, sacrifice bunts, sacrifice flies.

What DIPS seems to reveal is that almost anything can happen when batters put the ball into play—that is, when there is a "defense-dependent" play. It almost doesn't matter whether a pitcher is great, mediocre, or poor. The pitcher cannot control whether infielders scoop up ground balls or outfielders chase down fly balls. When the batter gets his bat on the ball, he has as good a chance of getting a hit whether he's facing a stud like Randy Johnson or a dud like Scott Karl.

Long-established baseball wisdom holds that the best pitchers induce hitters to hit weak grounders and pop-ups that their fielders can handle with ease. But the DIPS analysis suggests that such an approach in fact subjects the pitcher to the fickle finger of fate.

Since grounders and pop-ups can be so random, the pitcher needs to do two things to control his destiny. First, he needs to prevent batters from putting the ball into play—to avoid the chanciness of fielders handling grounders and pop flies. The more strikeouts a pitcher gets, the less room there is for fielders to let a grounder get by or a pop to fall in. Second, the pitcher needs to avoid giving up walks.

It's all about power and control. The great pitchers—like the Diamondbacks' Curt Schilling and Randy Johnson and the Yankees' Roger Clemens and Mariano Rivera—all prove the point.

The mind behind DIPS belongs to Voros McCracken, a former paralegal and researcher with the Internet site www.baseballprimer.com. Looking at pitching statistics for a three-year period, McCracken discovered that what happens to batted balls depends on little more than "random chance." Sometimes fielders convert the batted balls into outs, and sometimes they don't.

From McCracken comes the following bombshell: "There is little if any difference among major-league pitchers in their ability to prevent hits on balls hit in the field of play."

McCracken's most telling numbers focus on opponents' batting averages when balls are put into play. Opponents bat .301 against Johnson when they hit the ball into fair territory, .295 against Schilling, and .293 against Clemens. Other pitchers have gotten luckier. Batters hit just .234 against Mark Buehrle of the White Sox, .237 against Joe Mays of Minnesota, .242 against A.J. Burnett of Florida, and .247 against Robert Person of Philadelphia when they put the ball into play. These pitchers get more help from their fielders than Johnson, Schilling, and Clemens.

From game to game, month to month, and year to year, a pitcher's success varies dramatically when batters put the ball into play. Control pitchers like Greg Maddux or Derek Lowe can perform just as well from one game to the next, forcing hitters to weak ground balls—but they get dramatically different results. Sometimes the fielders convert the balls into outs, and sometimes they don't.

If DIPS makes pitching seem like a crapshoot, that's only partly right. Pitchers have limited means of controlling the game—by striking out hitters and yielding as few walks, hit batsmen, and home runs as possible.

When hitters put the ball into play, they don't fare any better or worse against a poor pitcher like Scott Karl than they do against a master like Randy Johnson. The difference is that hitters make contact a lot less against Johnson. "Randy Johnson gives up fewer hits than Scott Karl. That's not because batters hit the ball harder off Karl than Johnson, but *because they hit the ball more often off Karl than Johnson.*" Johnson's ability to strike out opponents with few walks enables him to dominate the opposition—and minimize the role of chance in the game. In 2001, Johnson set a little-noticed but telling record: he struck out an average of 13.44 batters per nine innings. Tellingly, Johnson has had five of the top ten best seasons in baseball history for strikeouts per nine innings.

McCracken's analysis holds lessons for hitters as well as pitchers. Every Little League coach tells youngsters to put the bat on the ball, knowing that younger players have a hard time consistently fielding and throwing the ball. But DIPS shows that the advice holds for the major league level as well. Any time a batter hits the ball—*weakly or well*—anything can happen depending on a combination of the team's defensive skills, how smart they position themselves in the field, and (gasp) luck.

But wait. Can it really be true that whether batted balls produce hits or outs is a matter of *random chance*?

McCracken's claims inspired a creative response by Tom Tippett, a researcher for the website Diamond Mind Baseball. Tippett looked at every pitching performance since 1913—the first year for which adequate data became available—and found that pitchers have a significant effect on when a batter puts the ball into play. Even accounting for the impact of ballparks and team defense, better pitchers get more outs on batted balls—consistently—than less capable pitchers.

Tippett calculated the number of batted balls that are converted into outs, relative to the league and team averages, over many pitchers' careers. The leaders in this group included Walter Johnson, Tom Seaver, Catfish Hunter, Warren Spahn, Ferguson Jenkins, Grover Cleveland Alexander, Phil Niekro, and Jim Palmer—all Hall of Fame members. Great pitchers, then, can get outs by getting hitters to put the ball into play. But with the exception of the knuckleballer Niekro, these pitchers also succeeded by overwhelming hitters.

Even if Tippett wins the argument, McCracken still offers two important lessons for building pitching staffs. Power and control do more to make a great pitcher great than anything else. The more a pitcher can keep the ball out of play, the more he can prevent random events from beating him.

Chapter Fifteen

THE NEXT GENERATION

When they are not bewildering and angering baseball traditionalists, baseball's new generation of statistical analysts are dreaming up the next generation of databases, software systems, and team-building applications.

Detractors to the Statistics Revolution say that the data contained in hitting and pitching charts can be faulty. "You want me to trust what some college kid is seeing in a game—and make decisions on the basis of those stats?" Buck Showalter, a key figure in the construction of both the Yankees and Diamondbacks, asks incredulously. "There are so many things that they don't see right in front of them and there are so many things that can't be found in any statistic anywhere." Now the manager of the Texas Rangers, Showalter turns to his pitching coach, Orel Hershiser, and asks: "How many times do we turn to each other in the dugout every game and point out the things that happen that aren't going to be found in any statistics? Five? Six? More?" Hershiser nods in agreement.

Showalter's right. Individual franchises and for-profit companies have used a wide range of systems to track pitches and hits. The statistics they gather are uneven and unreliable. The people hired to watch satellite feeds of baseball games and chart pitches, for the most part, have not been trained in how to watch games. Many don't know the difference between a splitter and a forkball, a fastball and a cutter, a changeup and a slow curve. And when they do, they do not get good views of pitches. Seeing where the ball crosses the strike zone can be difficult because of the odd angles of the plate from center field cameras and the tendency of broadcasters to cut from image to image, especially late in close games. When the ball is hit, the TV rarely shows the whole field, so determining the zone where the ball falls can be difficult.

Ron Antinoja of Tendu has improved the quality of data by training his workers to watch games more carefully. Antinoja has developed briefing papers on pitchers that guide game charters what to look for—for example, Schilling drops his hand this way on a splitter and that way on a fastball, or Clemens follows through on a fastball this way and a changeup that way. Tendu provides charters with a long list of cues for pitchers and hitters, telltale signs about what the two sides of the duel are trying to do. Antinoja also instituted a system of quality control to assess whether the games were charted correctly.

Antinoja has lobbied officials from Major League Baseball to invest in a reliable system of tracking plays on the field, which he estimates would cost one million dollars a year. The officials blanched at the price tag—about the salary of a backup infielder—but Antinoja argues that good data requires an on-ground operation as smart and diligent as the nuclear power emergency systems he once designed. "Garbage in, garbage out," he says.

Regardless of the skepticism of Showalter and others, more data *do* tell more than fewer data. You just have to put the numbers into context.

As the quality of data improve, statistical analysis will reveal more than just the abilities of players in different situations and the unfolding logic of a game. Data will produce useful information about a player's mechanics—how he throws a pitch, swings the bat, runs the bases, fields and throws the ball. Data will provide three-dimensional analyses of every action to take place on the field, not just blunt numbers about the outcomes of those actions.

Baseball statistics have moved through two phases so far. Version 1.0 was the primitive stage, in which data amounted to little more than the information collected in score sheets and box scores. Version 2.0 marked a major advance, as statisticians used the power of video and the PC to gather more data and crunch it in new ways.

Version 3.0 will use computer-tracking systems to gather data on everything that happens on the field—with greater precision—in real time.

Baseball has already begun electronic analysis of pitch locations. In 2003, cameras mounted in a handful of stadiums monitored the ball-strike calls of umpires. The QuesTec Umpire Information System gives baseball officials objective data to make judgments about the accuracy of umpires' calls. In the future, Major League Baseball will place cameras all over the stadium to record the movement of every ball from the pitcher's hand to the plate, from the hitter's bat to the field, from one fielder to another. "A good system will be able to tell you every pitch perfectly—what kind of pitch, how fast it went, where it went in the strike zone," says Antinoja. Such raw data can be spliced and diced in countless ways.

Even more revealing, cameras might soon record the movements of the players' bodies, yielding data on every step and twist, catch and throw, swing and hit. Such three-dimensional modeling will start in isolated research centers like the American Sports Medicine Institute, but it will be carried over to training camps and stadiums when the price of the technology inevitably falls and the data that are gathered can be put into a database and manipulated in useful ways.

As technologies improve, data could track how much exertion a pitcher puts on his shoulder or when fatigue upsets his pitching motion. Cameras can record how base runners start and stop as they dance off first base in anticipation of stealing second base. Computers can track every pitch thrown in the bullpen.

Computerizing equipment could produce other kinds of data useful for understanding medical issues as well as effective mechanics for hitting, running, throwing, and catching. Football programs at major colleges like Virginia Tech and Oklahoma already use specially equipped helmets to record the location, direction, and magnitude of blows to the head on every play. Helmets are outfitted with a Head Impact Telemetry System—a pad equipped with a microprocessor and radio transmitter, which instantly databases every blow to the head and even delivers a warning to coaches when the force of a blow reaches a certain severity.

Equipment of all kinds—gloves, bats, spikes, and uniforms—will get fitted with sensors that record data and send alerts to players and coaches. Major universities, the military, and the garment industry already have invested millions in the development of "smart clothing" that monitors a baby's sleep, adjusts the level of heat on the body, and even fights germs. Why not outfit baseball players in smart uniforms to assess their bodies' movements?

Proliferating data will produce ever-more measures of player abilities and tendencies. Rather than being satisfied with data about righties versus lefties, the next generation can track high-fastball pitchers against low-changeup hitters, old soft-tossers against aggressive hackers, inside-pitching intimidators versus crafty low-and-away tossers, players with big looping swings versus those with compact cuts. All these data could be cross-referenced in countless ways—age, handedness, ballpark, month, weather conditions, time of game, and more.

The biggest challenge of the Statistical Revolution is to make sensible use of data. Coaches and players feel overwhelmed by the sheer volume of information. Matt Williams worked with an analyst to study videos and statistics but ended up cluttering his mind and losing his focus. He stopped trying.

"He got all my at bats on a CD-ROM and broke down all my at bats against certain pitchers and then gave me printouts about how this guy's gotten me out or how I've had success," the Diamondbacks' third baseman recalls. "The reports would show tendencies: Here's what he's going to give you if you have an 0–0 count and you're leading off the inning. If you've got guys on base, here's how he's approached you and here's why he's had success. It's a fantastic way for some people who are more cerebral about it, but I confused myself. I found myself standing up there thinking, 'Okay, if I have a guy on second base, what does the chart say about what I should look for?' I was walking up to the box and simply forgetting what I was there for: see the ball, get a good pitch, and hit it hard. I was thinking about whether the first pitch was going to be a curveball and letting my pitch go by. I was not being as aggressive as I know I need to be."

To be useful, data must somehow fit with the user's intellectual capacity—the coach's understanding of game situations or the trainer's work to condition the body to throw, hit, catch, and run. Data need to fit into templates that different minds can grasp.

Antinoja, the founder of Tendu, uses the same philosophy for organizing baseball numbers that he used to develop emergency management systems for nuclear power plants and control systems for satellites: provide as much data as possible, in as many formats as possible, but then allow the user to make the real decisions about what matters.

"When a nuclear power plant is in an upset condition," Antinoja says, "bells and horns are going off and human operators look back and forth [at computer screens with data about plant operations] and what they have in their minds are all these patterns. Subconsciously they associate lights with different challenges and information." Baseball people also need a high volume of data. Speaking of his computerized data, Antinoja says: "My screens tend to be a little noisy. The situations we are talking about are complex and we want to look deep into the situation."

With constantly shifting sets of complex data, people look for patterns they can understand.

To the monitors of a nuclear power plant, the primary goal is to ensure as much predictability—as little surprise and excitement—as possible. Will statistics take the surprise and excitement out of baseball? The answer is yes if the fans and analysts get stuck in the strange warp of fantasy baseball, where ersatz managers select ersatz teams to play ersatz seasons, losing consciousness of the real game as they spend hours in the glow of computer screens.

But for the people who actually spend time on the field or in the stands, statistics will always play a secondary role.

"Human beings are better at thinking about these problems than any computer can be," Antinoja says. "It's just very difficult to make calculations. I would never want to close the loop at a nuclear power plant. [Workers who monitor plants need to] see the things that are going wrong and [get] access to information to make the right decisions. They need to use the computer to look at everything that's happening and then make their own judgments. Brains are phenomenal at making judgments. Let humans do the concluding with the facts presented by the computer. That is a combination that is better than anything that artificial intelligence can do. We allow the human to click for things and let him know what he needs to know to make the best decisions."

Statistics will never offer more than data, which real-live humans need to use cleverly and wisely. Knowledgeable use of data could produce leaps in understanding. "Real-life epiphanies are small advances produced by intensive immersion in the subject matter and obsessive high-level rumination," says Steven Pinker, one of the world's foremost authorities on cognition.

But only real baseball people will ever understand the sensation of a high-inside fastball or what to do when a 240-pound granite base runner storms into second base to break up a double play. Sophisticated number-crunching will never help a player perform the simple tasks of swinging a bat or turning a pivot.

"It's the easy problems that are hard," Pinker says.

Photos Courtesy of Arizona Diamondbacks & New York Yankees

Brenly vs. Torre

The Arizona Diamondbacks and New York Yankees were both veteran ballclubs that needed little day-to-day managing. Bob Brenly and Joe Torre excelled in providing a good working environment, with clear expectations and faith in their entire cast of characters.

SEVENTH INNING

In which the virtues of veterans—deep knowledge of the game, emotional intelligence, and mental toughness—find expression

Chapter Sixteen

VIRTUES OF VETERANS

The 2001 World Series provided a showcase for some of the game's most revered veteran players.

Veterans are different. Just by surviving in the game for ten, twelve, or more years, they have demonstrated an ability to keep their bodies strong and resilient. They have gained experience they can apply consciously and subconsciously in everything they do. Every microscopic movement—every pitcher's release point, every shortstop's feint toward the middle of the diamond, every outfielder's pickup and throw from the wall—gets burned into the veteran's mind and body.

Most important of all, veteran players learn to control their attitudes about what happens on the field. A player survives long enough to become a veteran because of his ability to modulate the giddiness of success, the anxiety and confusion of a slump, the anger of a bad call. Controlling feelings—maintaining an intensity of feeling without letting that intensity take on its own life—is the essence of the veteran player.

Paul O'Neill has become the symbol of the Yankees' veteran savvy in their three consecutive championship seasons. The son of a minor league player named Chick O'Neill—the older O'Neill's chances to make it to the majors ended in a paratrooper accident in World War II—O'Neill carries intensity with him wherever he goes. Tall and angular, he looks like a particularly intense version of the Man in the Yellow Hat, the guardian of the children's book character Curious George.

Three nights earlier, when the thirty-eight-year-old Paul O'Neill jogged off the field at Yankee Stadium for the last time in the eighth inning, the stands rocked in rhythmic chants: *"Paul Oh-Neill! Paul Oh-Neill! Paul Oh-Neill!"* The Yankees' left fielder ran with his head down, avoiding eye contact with 56,000 fans in the stands as he approached the dugout along the first base line. Finally, he looked up, tugged the bill of his hat twice, and then went into the dugout.

Just how intense is Paul O'Neill as a ballplayer? The standard stories show him slamming his bat down after a strikeout or a weak pop fly, beating the water cooler in the dugout after a close play on the base paths, and screaming at an umpire on a disputed call. When he argues a call and the umpire barks back, O'Neill seethes for hours afterward until he has burned off his excess fuel. After striking out, his teammates hear him scolding himself as he returns to right field: *Keep back! Don't rush the swing! Look for the right pitch! Keep your shoulders in!*

His teammate Mike Stanton says: "He plays on emotion. Not everyone does. Some guys, like Mike Mussina for instance, like to take emotion out of the equation. But Paul is a guy who is never going to be satisfied. He's a perfectionist. And you never reach perfection in this game, so that's what still drives him."

"If he hits a single he is not happy. He wanted a double," says broadcaster Tim McCarver. "If he hits a double he is not happy. He wanted a triple. If he hits a triple he is not happy. He wanted a home run. And if he hits a home run, it didn't go far enough."

McCarver sees a hairline separating constructive and destructive anger. "Anger can fuel success or it can be destructive. It depends on what motivates you. I would rather see a young player animated by whatever [motivations] than seeing someone with lethargy. There are some players that when they lose or don't get a hit, just say, 'Oh, well. If it comes, it comes.'"

It helps to have foil, a coach or a teammate who can moderate or channel the intensity. McCarver laughs when he thinks of O'Neill's foil: "When O'Neill doesn't get a hit one game, his whole thing is, 'I'm quitting. I can't hit any more.' Don Zimmer is from Cincinnati, where O'Neill's from too. He used to say, 'Paul, I have a buddy in Cincinnati with a construction job. I can get you a job with just a quick phone call.' It was perfect. O'Neill would laugh and he would be on track...."

"O'Neill was intense," Jeter says, looking back. "O'Neill never could figure out how he could hit a ball hard and make an out."

"What you have to know is that his temper is never directed toward anyone else," says scout Billy Blitzer. "He explodes. But he never shows anyone up. He is trying to get himself to focus and execute right."

O'Neill's anger and intensity have not always been appreciated by managers and teammates. When he played for the Reds, he and his manager, Lou Piniella, clashed regularly. Piniella has been known for his own volatility throughout his long career as a player and a manager. It's not the temper that irked Piniella, but what the manager perceived to be selfishness. Even when the team scored, O'Neill would be angry when he failed at the plate. Exasperated, Piniella scoffed: *Is the game about you or the team?* O'Neill and Piniella differed about how to harness O'Neill's talent. The Reds wanted O'Neill to hit more home runs and accept a decline in his batting average. O'Neill resisted the push and his statistics suffered in all categories. The Reds management's belief that O'Neill was self-centered, not just volatile, led to his trade to the Yankees.

Over the years, Piniella has changed his mind about O'Neill's temper. When he managed the Seattle Mariners and O'Neill played for the Yankees, Piniella admired O'Neill's long throws from right field, his ability and willingness to take an extra base, his ability to fight off pitch after pitch and tire the pitcher.

Paul O'Neill's sister Molly, a food critic for the *New York Times,* says Paul "has been playing baseball as if his life depended on it since he was two years old. He had to. His four older brothers would have used him as a base if he hadn't learned how to swing a bat." Even though he was a runt, he did not yield on the field. After he broke an ankle in Little League, he played with a cast on his foot. Paul's competition with his brothers created a burning desire to achieve, Molly says. "Paul had a sense of injustice early on. He criminalized his individual tormentors." As the younger kid in a family of athletes, O'Neill regularly lost in head-to-head contests—and fought to get better and even the score. "If an older brother was in the process of winning, he was 'lucky.' If he won, he had 'cheated,' and Paul would follow the winner around with challenges for rematches phrased in a sportsmanlike manner: 'What's the matter, cheater? Afraid you won't get lucky again?'"

O'Neill is not a Hall of Fame player. Occasionally O'Neill hit for a high average—he led the league with a .359 average in 1994—but he finished with a .288 average over his seventeen-year career. He had doubles power but never hit more than twenty-eight home runs a season, averaging just under seventeen a year. The most stolen bases he had was twenty-two—and that was in his final season of 2001, when he missed a month and ran the bases with his smarts more than his legs.

In his nine years with the Yankees, he was exactly the player the team needed to win championships. Like Yankees from Babe Ruth to Reggie Jackson, he benefited from a short right field fence and a lineup of solid stars. O'Neill epitomized the Yankees' grinding approach of the late 1990s and early 2000s. The Yankees had a large stable of thoroughbreds like Derek Jeter, Roger Clemens, and Mariano Rivera. But in the reign of Joe Torre, the Yankees excelled because they took a veteran, disciplined approach to the game.

To outfielder Shane Spencer, players like O'Neill molded the team by providing a constant source of focus and tension. Nothing was good enough—not a four-for-four day at the plate, not an assist from the right-field corner, not an 8–2 Yankees' win—if something somewhere went wrong. He not only practiced swings in the outfield, but also getting a jump on the ball and releasing the ball. "Watching him, his work ethic, in the outfield taught me a lot," Spencer says. "He wasn't the fastest guy, but he worked hard and practiced. In my Christmas card I sent him, I said, 'Thank you for making me a better player.' He just had the drive. He wanted to be the best he could every day, and he worked at it. He worked on hitting all the time. He worked on his outfield. He worked on throwing the ball. He didn't get rid of the ball quick, but he was very accurate."

◆ ◆ ◆

O'Neill bats with a man on base and no outs in the top of the seventh inning. Knowing that Schilling is beating the Yankees with first-pitch strikes, O'Neill hits the first pitch—an outside fastball—into center field for a quick single. It's his second hit of the night. Steve Finley considers a shoestring play but puts on the brakes at the last moment, content to block the ball instead and keep runners at first and second base.

◆ ◆ ◆

Rick Downs, the Yankees hitting coach, sums up Paul O'Neill's famous temper this way: "Believe it or not, he knows when to go ballistic. It helps him be a better hitter. He has a great ability to swing at his pitch. He doesn't let circumstances dictate how he performs. He knows when to let it go, and then he turns the page. Next time up he's forgotten and he's ready to perform."

If Downs is right, O'Neill might be one of the healthiest players in the game psychologically.

Psychology has always operated at the margin in baseball and other sports. The ethos of toughness that pervades sports is so powerful that there is often little room for consideration of fear and longing, of how childhood influences made the man. Athletes often get frozen into the selves they created when they enjoyed their first successes back in Little League or high school. The demands of the profession can be so narrow that the player does not have an opportunity to understand the context of his special talent. Even acknowledging a need for help threatens to undermine the very qualities that bring the athlete success in the first place—single-minded determination, discipline to improve skills, confidence in the face of defeat.

But with the investment of hundreds of millions of dollars in teams, and with success so uncertain, many teams have taken to using psychological testing and counseling to make sure they get and keep the kinds of players who can succeed in the unreality of professional sports.

Working with the pitching guru Tom House—the former pitcher who has played a significant role in Randy Johnson's maturation—a sports psychology consultant named Matt Mitchell has developed one system for assessing and improving an athlete's psychological capacity.

The Athletic Desire Index assesses players along seven dimensions—internal motivation ("How much does the athlete want to sacrifice to be a winner?"), drive ("Does the athlete respond positively to competition?"), mental toughness ("Can the athlete accept strong criticism without being hurt?"), emotional management ("Is the athlete not easily depressed or frustrated by bad breaks or mistakes?"), self-confidence ("Does the athlete make decisions confidently?"), determination ("Is the athlete willing to persevere in the face of adversity?"), and self-responsibility ("Does the athlete accept criticism and blame even when it is not deserved?").

Originally devised to help teams improve decisions about drafting and signing players, the ADI can also be used to guide young players as they grow into the greater responsibilities and challenges of elite competition.

Testing of athletes has shown that psychological traits determine success more than other factors. By the time baseball players reach the upper levels of the minor leagues, the differences in their raw physical talent are slim. The players with the strong psychological tools are usually the ones that succeed. A psychological survey of players from the Houston Astros organization, conducted by Ronald Smith and Donald Christensen of the University of Washington, correctly predicted fully 73 percent of all players' ability to advance to higher levels of the system.

"Psychological skills are relatively independent of the physical skills, and both are significant related to the performance and survival in professional baseball," Smith and Christensen wrote in the *Journal of Sport and Exercise Psychology* in 1995. In fact, the psychological skills determined as much about the success of a player as his physical abilities to hit a baseball—about 20 percent each, according to the analysts. The importance of psychology is even greater for pitchers, affecting a pitcher's earned-run average more decisively than physical skills.

Inside that academic paper lies one of the most powerful secrets in the multi-billion-dollar baseball industry. Like professionals in other fields, the distribution of talent falls inside a bell curve. A few elite players stand apart from the thousands of players who toil in the five levels of professional baseball, from the Rookie League to the majors. On the other end of the curve, a more sizable group has no chance whatsoever of making it to the majors; they're baseball's version of cannon fodder, filling rosters so the real prospects have foils for their advance. In the middle lies a vast population of might-make-its.

"A very small percentage of the players in the big leagues actually are much better than everyone else, and deserve to be paid the millions," Paul DePodesta, the young general manager of the Los Angeles Dodgers, tells author Michael Lewis in the *New York Times Magazine*. "A slightly larger percentage of players are actually *worse* than players who are stuck in the minors." Lesser players often make it to the majors—and survive—because they put the best possible frame around their abilities. They do what's expected and become known quantities. They fit in. They don't get too up in good times or too down in bad times. They do what they're told—swing for the fences, specialize in the bullpen, or change hitting or pitching mechanics—as if it's part of an unerring canon.

Working with athletes poses unusual challenges. "Athletes are not usually the brightest of the bright," Matt Miller says. "They're going to ask you, 'What does my mother have to do with it?'"

Miller has developed a battery of ninety-seven simple questions to develop an athlete's profile and a system of follow-up exercises to help the athlete improve his ability to manage his feelings and focus his attention on what matters. The most important sign of an athlete's emotional stability, Miller says, is the ability to laugh at the absurdity of what they do for a living. "You have to be able to get them to laugh at their situation. It's a tremendous ice-breaker. It diverts them from their pain."

The ultimate goal is for the athlete to have "emotional ownership" of what he does.

The stars of the World Series can claim such emotional ownership. The leading players in the game—Curt Schilling and Randy Johnson, Roger Clemens and Mariano Rivera, Derek Jeter and Jorge Posada, Mark Grace and Matt Williams, Steve Finley and Craig Counsell—are known as much for their mental approach to the game as their skills on the field.

Players like Paul O'Neill operate on a sharp edge. Anger is a central part of the game because it focuses their attention. The question is where the anger will be directed. Will the anger become a source of motivation, a tool to sharpen focus on what matters? Or will it be a distraction, a reason to doubt and displace blame and responsibility?

His coaches and teammates judge Paul O'Neill on the basis of his need to assume responsibility for what he does—and more important, the ability to leave bad stuff behind.

In his retirement, O'Neill has shown a less competitive side of his personality. Charley Steiner, an ESPN analyst who became a play-by-play announcer for the Yankees in 2002, got to know O'Neill the player and O'Neill the color commentator.

"Paul is two entirely different guys. He's a remarkably thoughtful guy, fun to talk to about all kinds of things. He's as relaxed as an announcer as he was intense as a player."

But the competitive juices will always flow in the O'Neill family. His brother Robert, who manages his business affairs, blurts out during one telephone conversation: "You know, he should be the Yankees' manager—I mean, once Torre leaves. He should have that job. He wants it. He's the one who should have it."

◆ ◆ ◆

DEREK JETER—WHO opened the seventh inning by lining a 1–0 fastball into left field for a single—epitomizes both the intensity and even temper needed to succeed on the field.

Jeter cares. He tenses up when told about the statistical analyses of his fielding. He firmly disagrees with criticisms about his positioning on the field. He bristles when people suggest that he change positions—to third base, maybe, or to center field.

But Jeter's intensity is cool. On the field, he loses sight of all the distractions of the circus atmosphere of Yankee Stadium and his celebrity lifestyle in New York.

During the last six years, when the Yankees have won four championships, Jeter has become a symbol of the team's success and style. Jeter stands six feet, three inches, and he weighs 200 pounds. Just a generation before, shortstops were little men prized for their ability to dart around the infield. Postwar shortstops were not all runts like Fred Patek (148 pounds) but were not usually much bigger than Pee Wee Reese

(175 pounds). The traditional shortstop possessed speed, scrappiness, and smarts—but not much strength. Jeter is part of the golden age of shortstops that also features perennial MVP candidates Alex Rodriguez and Nomar Garciaparra and Miguel Tejada and Omar Vizquel. Jeter has power and explosiveness and swagger—and a seemingly innate sense of how plays unfold on the field.

Setting himself in the box, he holds his right hand back toward the umpire as if to freeze the action. The gesture, really nothing more than a bodily tick, seems a classic sign of Yankee arrogance: *The game begins when I'm ready.* And in fact, no matter what other high-priced talent takes the field for New York, the game begins and ends with Jeter.

Hollywood as it sounds, Jeter was born to be a Yankee. Jeter is the greatest shortstop—the most important player on the team—for the greatest franchise in all of sports.

As a kid growing up in Kalamazoo, Michigan, Jeter's father took him to Tiger Stadium in Detroit to see the Bronx Bombers. He was a good student—he had a 3.82 grade-point average in high school—and wanted a college education. The University of Michigan recruited him and he enrolled in Ann Arbor, but the Yankees signed him as their top draft pick in 1992 before the Wolverines had a chance to put him on the field. In 1996, he became the first rookie to play shortstop for the Yankees since Tom Tresh in 1962, winning Rookie of the Year Award. That year the Yankees won their first world championship of the modern dynasty.

It almost seemed like winning was too easy for Jeter. He is a five-tool player—he can hit, hit with power, run, field, and throw—but lots of five-tool players never reach their potential. But Jeter works hard. He lifts weights and studies the game, does the drills, blocks out the noise of fame in the city, and listens when wiser men talk. He's a celebrity seen around town with supermodels, but his focus on the field is total. He comes from the Midwest, but his good looks epitomize the New York melting pot: his father is black and his mother is white. He is amused when people try to guess his race.

But it's Jeter's cool intensity that impresses insiders. His manager, Joe Torre, found a quintessentially Jeter moment during one of the Yankees' rare losing streaks. "During our bad streak he always had this gleam in his eye, like this is the day we're going to break out of this," Torre recalls. "There was never any doubt in this kid. I saw that from 1996, the first time I met him."

◆ ◆ ◆

THE YANKEES HAVE their first legitimate threat of the game in the top of the seventh inning. Two good base runners, Derek Jeter and Paul O'Neill, are on base with no outs. And now Bernie Williams—who has not hit well in the World Series so far—steps up to the plate.

The Yankees' center fielder has been something of an enigma in his career. He is not as graceful as Joe DiMaggio, not as muscled and powerful as Mickey Mantle, but he is their true heir in center field because he claimed the position as his own. Unlike other occupants of center field, Williams is not plagued by expectations.

At times, Williams has appeared to be fragile. In his younger days, he was nicknamed Bambi for his doe-in-the-headlights look at a time of crisis. When he came up to the Yankees in 1991, he was not so sure of himself—and, for some reason that remains a mystery, he was subject to the vicious taunts of his teammate Mel Hall. Yankees officials were so scared Hall's jockeying would break Williams that they threatened to trade Hall if he did not stop.

The late David Riesman, a theorist of social psychology, identified two kinds of people—the "other-directed" person who seeks attention and energy from interactions with others, and the "inner-directed" person who lives according to his own rhythms and ideals. Williams doesn't look outside for a model of how to live his life, but finds how to live by looking inside himself. When the Yankees take batting practice, Williams often stands alone. He moves slowly across the Yankees clubhouse and speaks softly with just a few players as he gets ready for a game. When he is in the clubhouse, Williams sits in his corner locker, away from the busyness of the place, and strums his guitar alongside a boom box that softly plays jazz. He's a classically trained musician whose first CD, *The Journey Within*, will win some critical praise. He is asked whether he takes the field with the rhythms of jazz in his head.

"No," he says softly. "What I hear is silence. Silence. Nothing else is around when I'm at the plate."

His friend Gerald Williams says, "He tries to slow everything down so he can interpret everything properly and never lets emotion overtake him in any given situation. He tries to think as rationally as possible." Joe Torre compares Bernie Williams to tennis legend Arthur Ashe—coolly intense, driven by his own standards and his own desire for achievement.

Listen to how Williams describes his approach to hitting: "A swing is a very personal thing." Other people's approaches, in other words, do not matter. "A lot has to do with attitude." It's all about who you are as an individual, and your ability to focus on the job at hand. "Some players hack hard all the time. Some cut down on their swing with two strikes. Myself, I like to react to the ball." The drama of hitting is man against ball, not man against himself or even man against man.

His Zen approach removes the tendency to take things personally. "Unless I know the pitcher, I like to keep my swing under control." You have to control what you can control, not guess too much, not care about the mysterious thoughts of your opponent. "It's always a battle to get your mechanics right. Having that perfect swing is a good goal. If your mechanics are right, you don't have to think about it before the game. You can concentrate on the pitcher and react to the pitch." By getting mechanics right before a game, you can avoid cluttering your mind during a game. "Practice is when you think about your elbow and shoulder and not going under the ball. Hopefully you practice good enough so when you get into a game your mechanics are right."

There's not a lot that the Yankees' center fielder does with great sparkle. He plays shallow in center field not because he's great at ranging back but because his arm is weak and he needs an extra step or two on throws home or to the bases. He runs fast but sometimes misreads the ball coming off the bat. As a base runner, he has not shown great instincts either stealing bases or going from first to third on a hit. He gets a late jump and sometimes doesn't reach his stride as a runner until it's too late.

But in an organization known for headlines and controversy, Williams dazzles slowly.

Williams compensates for his shortcomings. He approaches manager Joe Torre in the dugout during a game for advice about a fielding or baserunning play. "He's a straight shooter, an honest guy who gives you an honest opinion," Williams says of Torre. "It's not like he has to prove anything. He has been through everything."

Whatever his shortcomings, Bernie Williams has lasted long enough to reach statistical milestones—hits, home runs, doubles, runs batted in—that rank him among the top ten of Yankees, along with immortals Babe Ruth, Joe DiMaggio, and Mickey Mantle. He is also among the top two or three Yankee players in a number of categories for postseason play. He won the league batting title in 1998 when he hit .339 and two years later had career highs in home runs with 30 and runs batted in with 121.

In many ways, the Yankee that Bernie Williams most resembles in Elliott Maddox, the mild-mannered player who took away the center field position from Bobby Murcer in the 1970s. Murcer was supposed to be the second coming of Mickey Mantle, and manager Bill Virdon's decision to use Maddox caused a stir. But Maddox delivered consistency, both offensively and defensively, for two years. The difference is that Williams has lasted for almost a decade. Williams is not spectacular. But his unflappable character frees the manager to deal with the temper tantrums and tabloid bombshells and salary disputes swirling around other players.

After three foul balls—a fastball hit back to the left side, another fastball into the dirt toward first base, and a foul off the catcher's mitt on a 97-mile-an-hour fastball that Schilling threw for a strikeout—Williams hits a ground ball to Grace a third of the way between first and second base. Grace throws to Tony Womack at second base for the force play.

The key pitch in this sequence came when Schilling gunned for a strikeout on an 0–2 pitch. Schilling got the fastball on the outside of the plate but Williams managed to get wood on the ball. The pitch, a straight fastball, lacked the bite of other Schilling offerings. A strikeout would have held the runners back and kept the hobbled Jeter and the aging O'Neill clogging the bases.

The Yankees now have runners on first and third with one out.

◆ ◆ ◆

FOR THE FIRST time all game, Arizona has a crisis to manage in the seventh inning. Bob Brenly walks to the mound to talk with Curt Schilling. The Diamondbacks have Mike Morgan and Miguel Batista warming up in the bullpen. Schilling hasn't yielded any hard hits but he might be tiring. Brenly asks Damian Miller, his catcher, if Schilling has lost any speed on his fastball or bite on his splitter. Miller says no. Schilling says he is feeling fine.

Schilling wants to pitch a complete game. As a young pitcher with the Philadelphia Phillies, he had already grown to disdain the modern practice of pulling a pitcher after six or seven innings. And he hates the new term "quality start," which means any game in which the pitcher gives up three runs or fewer over six innings.

"I approach the game as mine," Schilling says. "With pitch counts and all the junk that comes with being a young pitcher in the '90s, it's not something a lot of teams are interested in pushing their kids to do. They don't care to have them learn what it's like to get a guy out for a fourth time without your good stuff. I've run into a lot more guys who get pulled out after six with a smile on their face than guys who are angry at being pulled after six." Even in a World Series game, with all pitchers available to throw, Schilling wants to pitch a complete game.

◆ ◆ ◆

WITH DEREK JETER dancing off third base and Bernie Williams on first, Tino Martinez comes up with a chance to tie the game with a fly ball or single.

After taking a borderline pitch high for a strike, the Yankees' first baseman whacks a fastball on the outside corner to right field to tie the game. Schilling has been going outside a lot this game and Martinez was probably expecting it. The ball had less pop on it too, making it easier for Martinez to extend his arms and get the fat part of the bat on the ball. Jeter scores easily.

Diamondbacks 1, Yankees 1.

Bernie Williams stops at second base as Danny Bautista backs up on the ball in right field. Should Williams have tried to go to third? Should he challenge Bautista when he is not charging the ball? Maybe and maybe not. The rap on Williams is that he doesn't have the right instincts on this play. But he also does not run his team into mistakes.

The inning soon yawns to a close. Jorge Posada pops up on the second pitch. And after two foul balls put him behind in the count 0–2, Shane Spencer hits an outside curveball to Steve Finley in right-center field.

◆ ◆ ◆

PART OF A WINNING team's makeup is having an expectation of winning. The Yankees do not build their team to make the playoffs. They know that they will make the playoffs, every single year. They build the team to succeed in the mini-season after the season.

Like all Yankees, Shane Spencer has a completely relaxed attitude about playing in the big game.

"I really think that when the playoffs come, I don't think there is any nervousness," the outfielder says. "I never was. I loved it. I just thought it was the greatest thing in the world. You know, you're going against the best pitchers in baseball, and they're supposed to get you out, so if you get out, it's not a big deal, you know? If you get a hit, it's even greater. So, it's a great experience. You could get two hits in the whole Series, but make two great defensive plays, or you move a guy over with a ground ball, and everybody goes crazy. You just throw the stats out of the book. It's just an amazing experience. And I've been fortunate to be in four in a row with the Yankees."

Spencer knows how lucky he is to avoid the fate of some of the great ones—like Ernie Banks of the Cubs—who never played an inning of postseason baseball. "You know, you hear about these guys that have played fifteen years and never been to the playoffs—so many of them. I knew I was spoiled. It was just a great time and great place. We had a tight bunch. We had some veterans that had been at other teams that came together at the same time. And then we had young players that all came up in the minor league for the Yankees. And when you come to a game, you just feel like you're going to win. You're not going to win every day. You know that. But we felt like, if it was the fifth or sixth inning and it was one-run game either way, we felt like we were going to win every day."

Spencer experiences an ease, a comfort, that other players cannot imagine. Matt Williams of the Diamondbacks shakes his head when told of Spencer's nonchalance. He's been to the World Series just once before and is too nervous to imagine living in Spencer's pinstriped idyll.

"Between you and me, that's BS," he says. "Everybody's got butterflies, every single time at bat. If you don't there's something wrong with you. Before every game, you have butterflies in your stomach, spring training game, intrasquad games. There's a difference between fear and adrenaline, there's a difference between fear and anxiety, being excited and being afraid. But if you learn how to use that anxiety to your advantage—being excited about the place you're at—I'm sorry, I had butterflies every game I ever played. But all it is is adrenaline, it's the release of your adrenal glands, and it's a good thing. It makes you know you're excited about what's happening. Shane might not have been nervous, but I had butterflies, I was excited with every at bat and every pitch."

Mark Grace is nervous too, but he's too excited to notice. Remembering where he came from keeps Grace focused on the game.

The Diamondbacks' first baseman remembers playing two years in the minor leagues, eating bad fast food and sleeping in bad hotels and traveling on cramped buses with a bunch of players who did not have the drive or athleticism or intelligence to make it to the major leagues. He wanted out. "That'll toughen you up," he says. "It'll make you appreciate the big leagues. When I got called up, my triple-A manager, Pete McCannon, said, 'Hey kid, you're going to the big leagues. Do me a favor—I don't ever want to see you again.' And I never played another minor league game after that."

Chapter Seventeen

SPECIALIZATION

Before every game, Joe Torre sits in the Yankees' dugout to take questions from the media. Other managers sit behind their desk in their office in the clubhouse. But the media crush before Yankee games—even mid-season games against bottom-feeders like the Tampa Bay Devil Rays—is too big for that. So Torre takes a seat in the dugout, waits for reporters to make a semi-circle around him, and takes questions. Torre answers each question patiently and calmly, like a grandfather telling a young boy how to bait a hook. The questions get repeated over and over, but Torre puts together a fresh response for every question. He pauses before answering some questions, raising an eyebrow, as if he has never heard the question put quite *that* way before. When he exhausts his supply of fresh responses, he gently prefaces his comments with, "Like I said before..."

Ever since the Yankees began their modern dynasty in 1996, one of Torre's "like I said before" statements concerns relief pitching.

Torre regularly extols the virtues of having a closer like Mariano Rivera. In baseball's modern parlance and practice, the closer is the relief pitcher whose sole job is to record the game's last outs to clinch a victory.

"When you have someone like Mo, you make it a seven- or eight-inning game," Torre says, in one of his dugout sessions. "If you have the right setup man, you can shorten the length of a game to six innings. It's automatic. You get a lead after six or seven innings, and you have a win."

Baseball's orthodoxy at the turn of the century includes the following: When ahead in the seventh or eighth inning, remove the starting pitcher in favor of a "setup man," then bring in the closer for the ninth inning. In the Yankees' first of four recent championships, the Yankees used Rivera as their setup man and John Wetteland as their closer. Upon Wetteland's departure after that season, the Yankees have rotated a series of setup men—Mike Stanton, Jeff Nelson, Ramiro Mendoza, and a cast of a dozen more—and turned the game over to Rivera in the ninth.

Joe Torre—and every other manager in baseball—accepts this approach and applies it with diligence. Torre is one of the rare managers who uses his closer more than one inning, especially in the playoffs and World Series. But he embraces specialization.

◆ ◆ ◆

A SUDDEN ATMOSPHERIC change comes to the Bank One Ballpark in the seventh inning. For innings now, a gentle breeze has touched the field of play. Now, all of a sudden, the wind picks up and brings dirt and dust from outside the stadium to inside the bowl of the stadium. Players and coaches and umpires stagger, wiping the dirt out of their eyes and lips and ears.

Steve Rippley, the home plate umpire, confers with Commissioner Bud Selig and other major league officials about closing the BOB's roof to keep out the desert elements. But the arguments against closing the roof prevail. With the roof closed, the dirt and dust would stay in the stadium and then get pushed around by the stadium's massive air-conditioning system.

When the roof is open the ball carries better, so hitters have a slight advantage. Randy Johnson has complained when hitters have launched the ball with the roof open. Coming off the mound after yielding a critical home run, Johnson could be seen mouthing: "Close the roof."

Joe Torre and Bob Brenly might want to consider bringing in a ground ball pitcher if they are concerned about a fly ball getting out of the ballpark. Most power pitchers are also fly ball pitchers. It's an exquisite tradeoff. The potential for getting lots of strikeouts—keeping the ball out of play—has to be considered against the possibility of a fly ball getting atmospheric assistance out of the park.

For now, Selig decides to keep the stadium's roof open.

Soon, an eerie rain arrives, as if sent to wash the field. After an inning, the winds die down and the rain stops.

◆ ◆ ◆

THE AUTOMATIC MOVE for Bob Brenly in the bottom of the seventh inning would be to get a pinch-hitter to bat for Curt Schilling. Schilling has thrown more than ninety pitches tonight—on just three days of rest, for his second straight start—and he doesn't have the power or control that he showed earlier in the game.

Brenly would accomplish two goals with a pinch hitter: he would get a strong situational hitter at the plate, and he would bring in a new pitcher with a fresh arm. In the eighth inning, the Yankees will bat two right-handed hitters—Alfonso Soriano and Scott Brosius—and then use a pinch hitter in the pitcher's spot in the batting order. If they replace Schilling, the Diamondbacks would probably bring in a right-handed pitcher like Miguel Batista or Mike Morgan to face the first two hitters. Byung-Hyun Kim is also right-handed, but Brenly is reluctant to bring him in after meltdowns in Games Four and Five in New York. The Diamondbacks would probably bring in a left-handed pitcher after that, since Torre would send a left-handed pinch hitter—most likely, David Justice—to hit for the pitcher's spot in the lineup.

But that's getting ahead of the game.

Schilling tells Brenly he wants to stay in. Brenly agrees. Brenly's logic is simple: the Seventh Game of the World Series is a different game. Your toughest pitcher can summon strength when he needs to. Schilling at 70 or 80 percent strength is better than any reliever at full strength.

So Schilling bats.

Facing Clemens, Schilling looks the way hitters look when they're facing *him*—weak and unsure, lucky to catch a ball or two in between the strikes. Schilling waves at the first pitch for a strike and fouls a high pitch back on a check swing. Schilling can't get around on the fastball. After a couple of balls—Clemens was throwing waste pitches—Clemens gets Schilling to strike out looking as a fastball whizzes by him on the outside corner of the plate. Schilling drags his bat back to the dugout.

The next batter, shortstop Tony Womack, takes a fastball for a strike and then swings and misses on an outside-low splitter. Ahead by two strikes, Clemens tries to get Womack to swing at a bad pitch. The next pitch is high and outside; then Clemens throws the ball knee-high and outside. After a couple of foul balls, Womack slaps the ball past a diving Alfonso Soriano into right field.

More than the hit—Womack slapped a good pitch on the outside corner—it is Womack's ability to force Clemens to throw seven pitches that spells the end for Clemens. Joe Torre senses that Clemens is losing his edge. Torre replaces his starter after 114 pitches.

◆ ◆ ◆

THE LATEST BASEBALL specialist to get popular recognition for his niche is the setup man—the pitcher who performs before the closer.

The Yankees' Mike Stanton, brought in to relieve Clemens, is the quintessential setup man.

The southpaw is strong and durable. He doesn't need glory. He can pitch day after day, in any situation—starting an inning, with runners on base, for one to six batters.

Stanton used to share setup duties with Jeff Nelson. Stanton pitched against left-handed hitters, and Nelson pitched against right-handed batters. With Nelson's departure, Stanton now pitches against all comers. In 2001, he pitched in seventy-six games. Stanton's ability to hold the opposition in the seventh and eighth innings created a clean environment for Mariano Rivera, the team's celebrated closer, to enter the game with a one to three-run Yankees lead, no base runners and no outs, in the ninth inning.

Years ago, setup men were lumped in with a larger group called middle relievers—a collection of lesser pitchers who weren't good enough for either starting or closing roles. But in the last generation, baseball has embraced specialized players, including setup men. Every team has its right- and left-handed pinch hitters, pinch runners, late-inning defensive players, and relief pitchers with tightly scripted roles. And now every team has its starters, long relievers, mop-up men, setup men, right-handed specialists, left-handed specialists, and closers. Pitching roles have become so strictly defined that the size of pitching staffs has increased from as few as eight pitchers to as many as thirteen.

As Bill James explains in his seminal *Historical Baseball Abstract,* specialization of relief pitching took place in stages. In baseball's early years, starting pitchers were expected to pitch complete games, so the role of relievers was an afterthought. From the 1930s to 1950s, relievers entered the game only when the starter faltered, and then they pitched as long as they could. Starting in the 1950s, managers identified a relief ace and used him when the starter struggled in a tight game—when the score was tied or the team was one or two runs ahead or behind. The relief ace was the toughest of the team's pitchers, often brought in to rescue the team from imminent danger.

The turning point in the use of relievers occurred in 1960 when a Chicago sports writer named Jerome Holtzman invented the "save" statistic. The save was intended to acknowledge the contributions of a relief pitcher who did not earn a win but contributed significantly to a win in a game's late innings. In the 1960s, managers began using ace relievers not just when the starter faltered, but when a fresh arm might be considered preferable. Starting in the 1970s, managers began to use ace relievers only in "save situations," when the reliever could get official credit for closing the game. The 1970s was the heyday of ace relievers, then known as "firemen" for their ability to extinguish rallies late in the game. Relief pitchers like Mike Marshall, Rollie Fingers, Bruce Sutter, Goose Gossage, and Sparky Lyle won acclaim for their ability to utterly dominate the late innings of games. These pitchers often entered the game in the seventh or eighth inning and stayed for two or three tough innings—often several days in a row. As a result, many experienced serious arm injuries.

To limit the stress on the arms of closers, managers resolved to restrict their closers' workload. Most famously, Oakland Athletics manager Tony La Russa limited his relief ace, Dennis Eckersley, to one-inning save situations—the ninth inning of games in which the A's led by one to three runs. Eckersley and other closers of this period (like Robb Nen, John Franco, Tom Henke, Jeff Reardon, and Lee Smith) pitched only when they would qualify for a save, usually just in the ninth inning. Even if the game's toughest challenge occurred in earlier innings, with the team tied or behind by a run or two, the closer never entered the game at that earlier stage. Oddly, the team's less capable pitchers took on those tough assignments.

As the closer's role narrowed, many managers began to identify other pitchers on the staff who could "set up" the closer with a strong one or two innings before the ninth inning. When John Wetteland was saving games for the Yankees, Joe Torre used Mariano Rivera to set him up. When Rivera was promoted to the role of closer in 1997, the Yankees turned to Mike Stanton and Jeff Nelson.

All season, Stanton helped the Yankees hold the opposition before a well-rested Mariano Rivera closed the game in the ninth inning. Stanton is not Rivera's equal, but he has the temperament and durability needed to hold the opposition before the closer enters the game. Torre rewarded Stanton for his tough pitching by picking him and Jeff Nelson for the All-Star Game that summer—the first time middle relievers had ever been so honored.

Statistics tell the story of pitching specialization. The number of complete games has declined from over forty per team to under ten from 1969 to 2001. The number of pitchers each team uses increased from 1.6 to 2.5 a game from 1969 to 1997. If trends continue—and they probably will—teams will soon use an average of four pitchers a game.

◆ ◆ ◆

How far can baseball go with specialization? A generation ago, Charles O. Finley had an idea for a specialist for situations like this.

Finley, the maverick owner of the Oakland Athletics dynasty of the 1970s, wanted to pep up the game by using world-class athletes for specific situations. An early proponent of the designated hitter rule, which, starting in 1973, gave teams the option of replacing the poor-hitting pitcher in the lineup with a slugger, Finley lobbied for a designated runner rule, too. Why not let a speedy runner replace a slow runner on the bases? Finley actually hired a world-class sprinter named Herb Washington to pinch-run for the A's in 1974 and 1975. Washington never batted, but played in 105 games, stealing thirty-one bases and scoring thirty-three runs.

Despite his speed, though, Washington was not a great base runner. He got caught stealing seventeen times. To excel in one aspect of baseball, it's useful to have a deep knowledge—burned into the memory and muscles—of the peculiar game of baseball.

Tony Womack is not a world-class sprinter, but he's a good baseball player. But Mike Stanton is too good—too skilled at stilling even the best base runners—for Womack to steal second base.

With a 1–1 count and three pickoff attempts, Womack breaks for second. The Diamondbacks' shortstop is flat-footed as he gets his jump. He doesn't even break until Stanton has thrown the pitch. Counsell swings right through a high fastball. Posada gets the ball and double-clutches, but still has time to throw Womack out.

Jeter takes the throw in front of second base, with Womack six or seven feet from the base. Womack slides right into the throw. Jeter spins around when making the tag, turns toward the umpire for the call, and pumps his right hand in a microsecond celebration.

Now with the runner erased, Counsell pops the ball to Tino Martinez, who grabs the ball twenty feet into foul territory. The Diamondbacks' rally is over. After seven innings, the score remains tied, 1 to 1.

Mariano Rivera, a native of Panama, was part of the transformation of baseball from the national pastime to a global enterprise.

Photo courtesy of New York Yankees

EIGHTH INNING

In which the game's greatest new source of talent—Latin America—provides the World Series finale with a clutch home run and devastating pitching to give one team the decided advantage

Chapter Eighteen

GOING GLOBAL

As Alfonso Soriano leads off the eighth inning against Curt Schilling—smacking his bubble gum, his body rubbery and loose, his wide eyes scanning the scene—he knows he has reached baseball's greatest stage. The Yankees' rookie is fully aware that Curt Schilling has prepared for him by looking at video clips of his turns at the plate. He knows Schilling has worked out a sequence of pitches to throw. Schilling will throw the rookie pitches low and away and then come inside and bust his hands. He'll throw heat and then hope to get Soriano to swing through a floater.

Of all the players in the game, Soriano cares the least about baseball's chessboard strategies. He is going to the plate to swing wherever the ball is pitched—up or down, in or out, heat or off-speed stuff. He will chase any pitch, and he will hit it hard, like Yogi Berra in the 1950s or Manny Sanguillen in the 1970s.

Soriano flashes a smile instantly, even when he's trying to maintain the Yankees' trademark cool.

This six-foot-one-inch, 180-pound youngster carries a thirty-five-inch, thirty-three-ounce bat, one of the heaviest in the game. Other players, from the most lithe to the most muscle-bound, use light bats with thin handles. The smaller bats give hitters a greater velocity; the barrel of the bat comes around like the end of a whip.

Soriano says he uses the heavier bat to control his swing. "When I have a light bat I can't stay back, and that's the only way you can see the ball," he says. "I swing too quick with a lighter bat. I have strong wrists, so I can get around on the ball with a heavier bat. It makes me take longer and see the ball better. With a heavy bat, I drop my bat on the ball. I'm not rushing. I have more time." He holds the bat away from his body to extend his arms when he swings.

When Soriano swings, old-timers gasp at the resemblance to Hank Aaron, with his strong forearms and quick wrists. Jim Kaat, one of baseball's best pitchers in the Aaron years and now a Yankees broadcaster, says: "I cannot *believe* how much they resemble each other. They called Hank the Hammer because he just dropped his bat on the ball, and that's the way with Sori. He's got that whippet-like strength just like Aaron. He isn't as disciplined or as cool and relaxed. But his body type and his quick wrists still remind me of Hank. He comes down on the ball like a hammer."

◆ ◆ ◆

SORIANO IS PART of a global revolution in baseball—and all of sports—at the turn of the century. In 2001, 25.3 percent of the players on the thirty major-league rosters came from foreign countries and almost half of the minor-league players came from foreign countries. For two straight years, the Rookies of the Year for both leagues came from foreign countries, two each from Japan and two from the Dominican Republic. Foreign dominance of the game has become an established fact.

The global revolution has become so powerful that Major League Baseball is developing plans for a World Cup tournament in baseball similar to the soccer tournament that grips the attention of the world every four years. The first tournament will take place in March 2006.

Soriano came to the game from San Pedro de Macoris in the Dominican Republic. As a youngster, he played as soon as he got out of school until sundown, first in the pickup games in the dusty fields of the impoverished island country, then in the "academies" operated by Major League Baseball franchises from the United States and Japan. As a sixteen-year-old in 1994, Soriano attended the camp of the Hiroshima Carp and signed a contract to play in Japan. He wanted to play in the United States, but Japan was a chance to go pro, so he took it.

He hated his two years in Japan, when he was captive to a team that signed him for a relative pittance. But the grim discipline and the drills, which started at nine in the morning and ended at dusk, hard-wired his brain to swing a bat. His mother urged him to stay at home during one visit when he showed her his blood-blistered hands. But if his performance in Japan's Eastern League was only average—he hit .214 the first year, .252 the second—he improved constantly. He learned the game and increased his athletic ability. He even cut his time in the sixty-yard dash from 7.4 seconds to 6.5 seconds.

Years later, Soriano credits the Japanese drilling for making his hands strong. Hideki Matsui, one of Japan's best players, says Soriano was lucky to land with the Carp. "They were very well known to have a lot of practice—more than most other teams," says Matsui, a superstar with the Yomiuri Giants. "Being in that environment was a plus for him, including the wrists. All teams are different, everybody's different from different cultures, so I don't think there's one way. But Soriano ended up with the best team for him."

Before long, Soriano and the Carp clashed over his salary—the Carp paid him $40,000 a year, while the average foreign-born players earned $220,000—and whether he was legally bound to remain with the Carp. After threats and lawsuits, Soriano exploited a loophole in his contract and found his way to the U.S. To get out of Japan, he "retired," like Hideo Nomo had done a few years before to slip out of his Japanese obligations.

Speaking Spanish and Japanese—which he picked up watching movies on TV—he began his American journey.

With raw athleticism, Soriano succeeds without completely learning the fundamentals. He will swing at almost anything. Over his young major-league career, he has averaged just 3.88 pitches per at bat. He almost never draws a walk. In 666 plate appearances, he has walked only 30 times—less than 5 percent of the time. In 2001, his rookie year with the Yankees, Soriano struck out 125 times in 574 at bats and walked only 29 times. But at the same time, he hit eighteen home runs and stole forty-three bases—the most potent combination of speed and power for a rookie since Tommie Agee hit twenty-two homers and stole forty-four bases for the Chicago White Sox in 1966.

Soriano's play for the Yankees in 2001 almost didn't happen. It took a breakdown by Chuck Knoblauch for Soriano to get his chance. Over a two-year period, Knoblauch had lost his ability to throw the ball. Once one of the game's best infielders, Knoblauch woke up one day unable to throw the ball to his target at first base. When Soriano starred in spring training in 2001, Joe Torre moved Knoblauch to left field, where the plays are fewer and simpler. He gave Soriano a chance to play second base every day.

◆ ◆ ◆

NOT THAT IT matters much to him, but Soriano quickly falls behind in the count, 0–2. The first pitch catches the low-outside part of the plate. On the next pitch, Soriano swings under a low splitter. Soriano is completely fooled on that pitch. He lets go of the bat and steps over the plate on the follow-through.

Schilling has a chance for a strikeout and he throws a near-perfect pitch, low and outside. But the Yankee second baseman stays alive by swatting the ball foul. Schilling changes the tempo and throws the next pitch high and outside, and Soriano's loose swing catches up to that one, too. Barely. He fouls the fastball off to the left side.

Schilling is throwing good pitches but Soriano is hanging in there, looking for the right pitch to drive somewhere. Schilling's moving his pitches a little higher each time—climbing the ladder, to use the parlance of the game. Soriano is loose, with his rubber band of a body twisting around and snapping free on the follow-through. "He's not afraid to fail," says teammate Derek Jeter, who has been one of his mentors in his rookie year. "That's a quality to have, especially when you play the game, because you're going to fail. He's not afraid. If he makes a mistake, he gets right back at it."

Schilling is still ahead in the count and only needs a strike to retire Soriano. Soriano popped out on a low-outside pitch in the third inning and struck out on an outside fastball in the sixth. With his penchant for chasing bad pitches, Soriano sometimes makes life easy for a savvy pitcher.

Damian Miller calls for a fastball up and away. The catcher wants to keep climbing the ladder. But Schilling shakes him off. "In my mind I was two pitches away from going to that pitch," he says after the game. "And I felt like if I made a good split [fastball] pitch right there and bounced it, I would get a swing and a miss."

Schilling throws the next pitch low. The pitch starts high but veers down and away.

Foremost in Soriano's mind is his desire to avoid striking out. "At that time I had two strikes and I could do nothing except try to make contact. I know that he doesn't want to throw nothing over the plate—I know that he wants to throw it high, outside, down. He throws a nasty splitter; it looks like a fastball and at the last minute it goes down. I want to put the ball in play. With two strikes, there's not too much I can do with it. I've got to inside-out the ball to make contact because I don't want to strike out.

"Always my first two swings are different from the last one because you have to shorten down the swing and be more patient. On Number Three, I have to be more selective and have more concentration on the pitch." Soriano cannot be selective—he doesn't know how yet—but he *can* shorten his swing and gain some control over the bat. "I put my bat down and hit it like a golf ball, like a drive," he says.

Miller's glove waits in the dirt for the ball. The ball arrives near Soriano's shins when he swings.

Soriano reaches out and golfs the ball with an extreme uppercut to deep right field. His left leg twists, with a hitch, before shifting into the ball to whack it. As he hits the ball, his bat is a perfect extension of his arms, which themselves are extended directly out of his body.

The ball sails about twenty rows into the bleachers for a home run. The Yankees now lead, 2–1.

◆ ◆ ◆

Mark Grace, the Diamondbacks' first baseman, watches in wonder as the ball sails fifteen rows into the seats. "It's a great pitch, a split low and away. And he goes down and hit a one-iron out of the ballpark. I'm thinking, how the f— did he do that? You know, not only that, but now we're in the eighth inning, and we just got it stuck up our ass. And Schilling's like, 'That was my best split of the night, and he knocked it fifteen rows deep.' Tip your cap to that kid."

McCarver agrees Schilling threw a perfect pitch—for almost any other batter besides Soriano. "Pitchers will throw a pitch that to any other hitter is the right one. Yet with Soriano, it's a different story. From a pitcher's and a catcher's standpoint, you just don't believe it. It blows the mind when you consider the perfect location of that pitch."

Watching the ball disappear into the seats from his position at third base, Matt Williams is amazed. "I can't believe he hit that pitch," he says. "But he's so strong. He just One-Hand Fredded it. Some guys hit home runs with two strikes because they just flick that bat and that's what he did. He didn't take a big ol' swing at it. He was fooled. But he's surprisingly strong for a wiry kid."

"His body is all about explosiveness," says Jeff Mangold, the Yankees' strength and conditioning coach. "He has an unbelievable amount of fast-twitch muscle fiber, and his muscles are very long, but powerful."

Soriano raises his right fist in triumph as he rounds the bases. If there is such a thing as shy cockiness, Soriano exudes it.

With the Yankees now ahead 2–1, Schilling looks confused as he walks around the mound. He turns away from Soriano as he rounds the bases.

◆ ◆ ◆

SORIANO SAYS HE would not be able to hit the same home run again. He has discovered his hitting zone, and that low-outside splitter is far outside the zone.

"At that moment, I didn't know what pitches I like because it was my first year in the big leagues," Soriano says. "I just wanted to make contact. He threw a nasty splitter and I put my bat to the ball and hit a homer. Now that I have some time in the big leagues I know that I wait for a ball in the middle. I didn't know what my good pitches were in that game. Now I know what pitch I like—I like it in the middle, and in the inside, and up. I didn't have a lot of experience to know what pitches I like."

◆ ◆ ◆

ALFONSO SORIANO, DANNY BAUTISTA, and Miguel Batista of the Dominican Republic, Mariano Rivera of Panama, Luis Sojo of Venezuela, Orlando Hernandez of Cuba, and Byung-Hyun Kim of South Korea are part of the international revolution in baseball. All are now playing in the World Series.

The stories of the foreign players are all different, and they're all the same. Virtually all of the players come from poor cities and towns. Their parents toil at menial labor, often working two or more jobs at a time. Because of limited opportunity for school and work—and recreation—they play baseball twelve months a year. They know the odds against making the major leagues are long, but they also know someone who knew someone who knew someone who made it, so it gives them hope. Often, they are the lucky one in a family of athletes—the one who got a chance to play because the other siblings work. They don't have any real equipment and they play on dusty, rocky fields. They're good enough to attract the attention of one of the dozens of scouts roaming the countryside looking for cheap talent. No matter how great their athleticism, their skills are rough. And they are naïve and susceptible to manipulation and disappointment.

Baseball in Latin America, to some skeptics' eyes, looks a lot like previous episodes of American colonialism. This time, the resource is not slaves, sugar, mining, oil, drugs, or tourism, but ballplayers. The U.S. and Japanese leagues have transformed once-independent leagues and turned the Dominican Republic into a farm system for the major leagues. The American teams chew up players by the hundreds, while a relative handful realize their dreams of playing Major League Baseball.

Foreign players have helped to fill a void left by young Americans, whose attention has been diverted by TV and video games, football and basketball, the ennui of affluence and the distractions of modern society.

"The kids here are never going to have the education they need to be a professional doctor or a professional engineer or anything else," says Epy Guerrero, supervisor of international scouting for the Milwaukee Brewers. "They know their only chance is baseball."

Teams cannot sign players until they are sixteen years and nine months old. But agents can sign them any time, and some pre-teens have deals with agents. "For most Dominicans, baseball isn't just everything, it's the only thing," says Omar Minaya, an executive with the New York Mets and later the Montreal Expos.

Poverty and unorganized games, played in empty lots and streets, give an advantage to many players from Cuba, the Dominican Republic, and other Third World countries. Baseball is purer in those countries. The game is stripped to its essentials. Nigel Zheng, a researcher at the American Sports Medicine Institute and a native of China, is not at all surprised that even slight pitchers throw harder than Americans, who enjoy all of the advantages of nutrition and modern training methods.

"They listen to their body," Zheng says. "When their arm is tired they stop throwing, and when it feels better they start throwing again. In the United States, with Little League and other organized leagues, pitchers are so concerned about winning and pleasing their coaches and parents that they don't stop when they should stop. They don't know how to listen to their body."

The recruitment of foreign players began in earnest when baseball's have-not franchises—the teams lacking the resources of affluent organizations like the Yankees and Dodgers—went south in search of cheap talent. The first teams to seek out Latin talent aggressively were the Toronto Blue Jays and Montreal Expos. By covering the territory before anyone else, they were able to sign whatever players they wanted. They enjoyed what economists call a "positional advantage," the edge that comes from being the first to adopt an innovation.

But in recent years, the rich teams have used their wealth to dominate the scramble for players in Latin America and Asia.

A loophole in baseball's amateur draft gives the powerful teams an opportunity to control global talent. The draft was created in 1965 to distribute talent fairly to all major league teams. Every year, all of the nation's amateur high school and college players are put on a long list, and major league organizations take turns in picking them—with the previous year's worst team selecting first, the second-worst team second, and so on. Teams that draft players have the exclusive rights to sign that player for a year. The draft has done more to equalize talent than anything else in baseball history.

But non-Americans are not subject to the draft. Amateur players from outside the U.S. are all free agents, at liberty to negotiate with whatever team they want. Gene Orza, the counsel to the Major League Baseball Players Association, states: "You have a situation now where a player who lives in Texas has less rights than a player born in Italy." Sandy Alderson, Major League Baseball's vice president for baseball operations, agrees: "In order for the draft to work as it should work, to make the best players available to the weakest teams, it needs to be universal. That's true in all other sports."

Teams with extensive scouting and recruitment systems—and the most ready cash to sign top-flight players—enjoy an advantage over the rest. The Yankees now dominate the international market. "Internationally they're pretty much the only team that doesn't have a budget," says Joe Kehoskie, an agent for several foreign-born players. "If they see somebody they like, they just sign him. When the Yankees' scouts drive up to a tryout camp in their Yankee polo shorts, there's a wave of dread that just comes over the other major league teams. You can almost feel it when they come in." Gordon Blakeley, the Yankees' director of international scouting, states the obvious: "We're not really worried about anybody else. We know that if we want a player, we can usually sign him."

Internationalization came late to baseball. Even though Jackie Robinson broke the color line in 1947, few teams had more than two or three players of color until the late 1960s. It was at that time that Latin players like Roberto Clemente and Rico Carty came to the majors. American baseball has tapped the Asian market tentatively, first going after pitchers like Hideo Nomo and Hideki Irabu and later position players like Ichiro Suzuki and Hideki Matsui.

Baseball is just part of a broader trend toward internationalization in professional sports. The National Basketball Association now reaches 750 million households in 212 countries in forty-two languages;

sixty-five players from thirty-five countries play in the NBA. Yao Ming, the Chinese star for the Houston Rockets, has prompted fourteen separate outlets to cover his games on Chinese television. The National Football League's Super Bowl plays to an audience of 800 million.

◆ ◆ ◆

THE GREATEST SEEDBED for baseball—anywhere on earth—is the city of San Pedro de Macoris, Dominican Republic, about forty-five miles west of the national capital of Santo Domingo. The city of 212,000 developed around the sugar industry in the years after World War I. With broad European settlement, the town developed a decidedly international flavor with a renowned university, Universidad Central del Este. The city is now part of an industrial-free zone, but free trade has not changed the basic fact of life—that young people have few options for economic security or even survival.

With limited opportunities for schooling and work, baseball becomes the community's focal point. Kids leave school before they are teenagers to take menial jobs like selling fish or shining shoes. And they play baseball. All over town, kids throw balls against concrete walls, catch it with milk cartons, and hit with broom handles—not that different from stickball played on the streets of New York from the 1930s to the 1960s.

The Dominican Republic has 1,600 players under contract with the major league systems. From 1933 to 2001, thirty-nine players born in the Dominican Republic were All-Stars—thirteen of them from San Pedro de Macoris. Dominicans have been some of the great players of all time—the Alou brothers and their offspring, Juan Marichal, Rico Carty, Pedro Guerrero, George Bell, Joaquin Andujar, Julio Franco, Sammy Sosa, Bartolo Colon, Manny Ramirez, Pedro Martinez.

Players sign for a few hundred or a few thousand dollars to play for the academies. Players usually sign when they're sixteen years old and play for three years. At the academies, the players rise at seven in the morning, eat, work out, start playing games at ten-thirty, then do more conditioning and play more games later in the day.

Critics have agitated for reform of the academies, saying that they exploit illiterate and impressionable boys and their families with little chance of success. The Washington lawyer Brendan Sullivan—a former pitcher for the San Diego Padres—says the academies deliver little more than rank exploitation.

"Sure, they were thrilled to have gone from dirt lots in the Dominican to playing in a U.S. stadium before fans and getting paychecks every two weeks," Sullivan says. "But once a team decides that a Dominican won't make it to the big leagues, he is discarded as an unprofitable resource. That's true for U.S. players, but at least they have a high school diploma, and often college, and thus have fall-back skills. Most Dominicans don't. They go home to the poverty they came from or try to eke out an existence at menial labor in the States, with nothing left over except tales of their playing days and chasing the dream."

Milton Jamail, who teaches Latin American Studies at the University of Texas, has been interviewing players south of the border for almost three decades. He knows about the rough ride that Latinos face, but does not fault the academies. He acknowledges Sullivan's point—that many academy players have no real chance to play professionally. "But that's also what happens with U.S. players," he says. "You draft someone in the eighteenth round and they almost never make it to the major leagues. They're there to play the guys who have a chance, and then they're let go." A profession with long odds is not inherently exploitive. Even a sliver of a chance is enough to give a youngster hope, to instill habits of hard work and focus.

"These kids are so young, and they're dealing with everything that has to do with adolescence," says Jamail. "It's incredible to me that they have this much discipline. The fact that these kids have a focus allows them to transcend some things."

Chapter Nineteen

STRIVING

Danny Bautista tells a typical story of how the poverty of the Caribbean has produced a wealth of baseball talent.

Bautista remembers playing baseball in his native Dominican Republic with balls made of socks stuffed with rocks and other hard materials, gloves fashioned out of Parmalat milk cartons, and bats carved out of tree limbs. Baseball was the center of Bautista's life, but it was no guarantee. Like getting up every morning to help his father, baseball gave him a routine. Unlike his athletic older brother, who decided to work, Danny Bautista kept playing baseball. By learning how to work, Bautista found a way to keep playing baseball. It was not an either/or decision for him.

"I woke up at four in the morning every day. I started working with my father when I was like ten years old. We would buy oranges and mangos. I sell them in the street. We'd make a little profit on that, and that's the way we'd make a living. My father really taught me how to be responsible. I came back to my house by nine in the morning. He came back by two, three in the afternoon. So there was, you know, a little time for going to the school. And I worked in the bakery to make a little money to go to the games Saturday and Sunday—and to buy some food, because we play in two games on both days. After the first game, you know, you're hungry. We also used to play in the street. But with no catcher. We used to play like, six on six, on a highway."

What about equipment? Bautista laughs. "A piece of wood, we cut in the tree and we made it like a bat." Really? You just shaved it off? You made your own bats? "Always, yeah. Whatever we can cut it." Some kids earned reputations for their expert carving ability. What about a ball and glove? "I never had a glove. I used my hands. Sometimes we'd use a milk carton—Parmalat. We used to use a ball made out of socks—real old socks. I would pick something in my house to put in the sock for a ball, and my friend can pick another one, the other friend can pick another one. And that way we made the baseball." The memories are fond, now that Bautista finds himself in a major-league clubhouse. "It was fun, you know. I'm really happy the way I've come through. It really made me keep on going harder."

A friend of the family told him not to bother. "He told me, 'Hey, the family you come from is so poor, don't even think about it. You got to go to work. Everybody got to work and make a living.' And he really broke my heart. He said, 'Hey look, Danny, it's just too much of a luxury and we don't have room for luxury here.' I don't say anything and I put my head down and keep working. I was boxing too."

Other family members, friends and neighbors, and scouts were more hopeful. "Because the way we were growing up, the main message is: *You can box. You can play baseball. You can do anything.* I was keeping going outside with my friends, just keeping playing, keeping playing. I talked to a lot of friends and they told me, 'Don't worry, man. You got too much talent. Keep on going. Keep playing."

For Bautista, the break came when a former major leaguer named Jesus de la Rosa observed him in a weekend game. De la Rosa played three games for the Houston Astros in 1975 and saw major-league talent in Bautista. "He talked to Ramon Pena, a scout from the Detroit Tigers. He told me, 'Hey, man, you're a good player. I think you're going to the big leagues one day.' But Pena doubted him because of his size—a skinny 150 pounds. "They come to my house and they tell me, 'Okay, you got one more chance.' They saw me. They pitched me like twenty-five balls and I get, like, twenty homers. I was fresh, you know. They told me to run sixty yards. I did it in 6.7 [seconds]. And then he's convinced and he said, 'Okay, I'm going to sign him.'"

Raw skills are never enough. Bautista struggles to learn to be patient at the plate. To get noticed, most Latin players need to show scouts power. As the old saying goes, you can't walk off the island. But at the highest level of baseball anywhere, patience is essential. "For me, the hardest thing to learn was patience. And learning how to relax, too. Because you want to do so much when you first come over here. You want to show so much."

Now that he has succeeded, Bautista is amused about his supposed lack of size. After all, Hank Aaron stood under six feet tall and weighed 180 pounds. "Well, they don't think that way anymore. They're looking for big boys."

◆ ◆ ◆

GETTING TO THE United States is just the beginning of the challenge for international athletes. Once they have been signed to big-league contracts, players face the terrifying task of living in an alien culture. Some of the shy players—like Vladimir Guerrero of the Montreal Expos—are so scared that they stay in their hotel rooms when they're not playing and order the same meals over and over because they only know the English for a few kinds of food.

Latin players come to the American game with great athletic ability but few of the skills that matter in the big leagues—cutting the corner of a base, hitting the cutoff man, backing up plays, running the rundown play with a minimum of throws. With few bilingual coaches or translators on the team's staff, many Latin players have a hard time understanding the pointers that coaches try to impart.

Luis Sojo, a utility infielder for the Yankees, has become the big brother to Latin players all over the major leagues. After trying out with all of the Venezuelan league's six teams and three major league teams, Sojo signed with the Toronto Blue Jays in 1986. He made it to the majors in 1990 and was soon traded to the California Angels. He has played for Seattle and Pittsburgh as well as the Yankees. He has become one of baseball's supersubs.

Before every game, as the teams stretch and take batting practice, Sojo plays the role of Leo Buscaglia, hugging players and taking younger players aside and creating a small cocoon where aliens can feel less alien. But he also finds himself stuck between the elements of Latin culture that give the game juice and those that place an extra burden on younger players.

As a veteran player, Sojo takes it upon himself to teach youngsters like Alfonso Soriano how to carry themselves and improve their game. He tries to create a small support structure among the Latin players so they don't get too isolated.

"The toughest part," says Sojo, "is when you have to go home after a game, because you don't want to leave the ballpark. You come to the United States for one reason, which is to play baseball. When you go home and watch TV and you can't understand anything, and even here where you can get every food that you can eat in Latin countries, you end up eating hamburgers and pizza and stuff like that. You don't want to leave the ballpark at all."

"They're trying to succeed in a different country, with a different culture and a different language, with no knowledge about how people feel about them," says Milton Jamail, who has interviewed five hundred Latin American baseball players and become friends with some of them. "It's like if you or I went to Russia with no language skills and tried to compete at the highest levels of business."

Latin players are intensely aware that their outward appearance could determine their reputation forever.

"If you look in spring training, they're always last in the instructional drills, because they're watching other kids to see how to behave," Jamail says. "You ask them how they're doing, and they'll just say okay. A kid will wear a pair of shoes that's too small because they don't want to complain. If they do, they're a complainer.... Some players will not make it because they're misunderstood, there's a coach along the way who's not sensitive to what they're trying to do and how they express themselves."

Alienation culturally can lead to alienation on the field. "Unfortunately for us, a lot of Latin players are emotional, they are very tough," says Sojo. "Sometimes they don't understand the situation that in this country things are different. They say, 'No, I want to do things my way,' but it doesn't work here. Latin baseball is more freestyle. And when you go to winter ball you see that. You see guys come to the game an hour before [games]. Sometimes they don't come to batting practice. And they don't take advice. I did that a lot in my country. I would call the coach and say, 'I'm not going to take BP [batting practice] today.' Here you can't do that, you have to be here to be with your teammates."

Coaches and other players watch the Latin players with a wary eye.

"They want to know what kind of person you are, what kind of attitude you have on the field," Sojo says. "And we have Latin players who do stupid things, and that's why you have every year players being released and new players coming in. Here you do things right. If you don't do them that way, you go home. I don't care how good you are. I still see Venezuelan players with a bad attitude and they get released and I say why, and they say, 'Well, I punched somebody' or 'I grabbed a glove from somebody else.' Why? You don't need that."

◆ ◆ ◆

AFTER SORIANO'S HOME RUN, the phone rings in the Diamondbacks' bullpen. Coach Glenn Sherlock answers. "Get ready," he shouts to Johnson. "You've got O'Neill." The Yankees' outfielder, a clutch World Series performer, was scheduled to bat four hitters later. "After one hitter, [Johnson] was good to go," Sherlock said. "I was amazed at how quickly he warmed up."

The phone in the Yankees' bullpen didn't have to ring. With the Yankees now in the lead, it was automatic that Mariano Rivera would come into the game in the eighth inning. During the regular season, Rivera almost never pitched more than one inning. But that was to keep him rested for the postseason. In the playoffs and World Series, Rivera has pitched two innings three times already. He's going to do it again tonight.

Schilling dispatches Brosius quickly—on a strike over the outside corner, a swinging strike at a high outside heater, and a swinging strike on a low splitter over the plate. David Justice, batting for pitcher Mike Stanton, works a 2–2 count before hitting a waist-high fastball into center field, past a waving Schilling and a diving Tony Womack. It's Schilling's first bad pitch—it has no real speed or movement, and it comes over the fat part of the plate. Schilling is finally tiring.

◆ ◆ ◆

As Bob Brenly walks to the mound in the eighth inning to remove Schilling, a light rain falls and the wind tosses hot dog wrappers and dirt around the field.

Schilling has thrown 103 pitches and he wants to throw more. But he is exhausted, even if he won't admit it.

As Schilling absorbs the reality—he had "guaranteed" a win before the game, but he's leaving the game in the eighth inning, losing 2–1—first baseman Mark Grace gives Schilling a love smack on the head. "I told him—verbatim—I said, 'Curt, I f— love you, dude,'" Mark Grace remembers. "I told him that right on the mound. I said, 'I f— love you.' That was an unbelievable effort on three days' rest—three days' rest, going about his 280th inning that year."

Brenly takes the ball from Schilling, telling him: "Hell of an effort, Hoss. We're going to Miguel on this guy here. Get a fresh arm in there. Hell of an effort, big man. I love you, brother. You're my hero. You're my hero. That ain't going to beat us. We're going to get that back and then some. That ain't going to beat us, big man."

Schilling looks around the field, wondering what happened to his masterpiece.

"He was certainly bummed out, you know, because now it's 2 to 1," says Grace. "But, you know, we were pumping him up. He just said, 'Don't let me down,' as he was walking back to the dugout. He's just trying to pump us right back up."

◆ ◆ ◆

With the Yankees now leading the game, 2–1, with a base runner and one out, Miguel Batista enters the game for Arizona. Batista was a starting pitcher all year for the Diamondbacks but Brenly has decided to use him as a reliever in the World Series. Batista has been all over baseball for ten years. He was scheduled to pitch in Game Four, but Schilling threw instead.

Batista always poses a risk on the mound. He throws the ball hard—his four-seam fastball zips along at 94 miles per hour—but he sometimes has trouble finding the plate. If he shows signs of control problems, Brenly will pull him right away. He might even pull him in the middle of an at bat.

Derek Jeter hits the first pitch, an inside pitch, down to Matt Williams, who is playing tight at third base. Williams snares the ball and throws to second base, where Counsell takes the ball. But Counsell double-clutches as he hops off the bag. With Justice going hard into second base, Counsell cannot turn a double play.

But Batista did his job. He was brought in to retire a single batter and then give way to Randy Johnson.

◆ ◆ ◆

RANDY JOHNSON, a lefty, enters the game with two outs in the eighth inning.

Like most pitchers, Johnson is ritualistic. He works on four days' rest and makes preparation for the game a precise ritual. On the day after a game, the Diamondbacks' left-hander does weight work for his legs and begins to think about the batters on the next team he'll face. The following day, Johnson focuses on his arm, doing weight work and playing some long-toss games of catch. On the third day, he works on his upper body and throws the game more as a pitcher, with special attention to his mechanics—motions, release points, landing on the mound. The day before the game, he focuses on mental preparation.

But tonight, Johnson did not have four days to prepare. "I had the focus, and obviously adrenaline takes over and you're able to do a lot of things that normally you probably wouldn't be able to do," Johnson says. "I probably wasn't throwing velocity-wise as hard as I was the day before. But that's understandable."

Like Clemens and Schilling, Johnson turns the contest between pitcher and batter into a game of psychological warfare.

"Your demeanor out there, your body language, can have a great effect on the opposition," he says. "If you show a lot of confidence, a warrior-type mentality out there, he's either going to step up and challenge that or not. And if he doesn't, then maybe you like to think you've got the upper hand." Another time, Johnson is more direct: "I'm not a nice guy. I'm a mean guy."

Derek Jeter has ideas about stealing a base. Johnson throws to first base to bring him back. Jeter is breaking toward second when Johnson throws the ball. Jeter U-turns back easily but Johnson has taken away his running game. Still hobbling from the third-inning ground ball and the fifth-inning force play, Jeter can't keep up start-stop-start movements with a strained hamstring.

Johnson walks around the mound, gathering his composure.

◆ ◆ ◆

WITH THE LEFT-HANDED Johnson in the game, Torre has replaced Paul O'Neill in the batting order with Chuck Knoblauch. O'Neill's career is now over.

For years, Knoblauch was the emblem of the Yankees' patience at the plate. Pitch after pitch, Knoblauch fouled the ball off, wearing down opposing pitchers, getting the dominant ones out of the game an inning earlier. Knoblauch further aggravated pitchers with elaborate rituals between pitches—adjusting his batting gloves, tapping his spikes with the bend of his bat, examining the bat held in front of him—before stepping in to the plate to take another ball or foul off a strike. Looking at him, nervous and twitching, you wonder how he can stay focused long enough to hit. *What's on his mind?*

That's a question the Yankees have been asking urgently for two years. Knoblauch has lost his ability to throw the ball from second base. "At first, it was close throws that Tino [Martinez] could get," says teammate Luis Sojo. "Now he doesn't know where the ball's going. Last year he still came to the ballpark happy. Now it's different. He's trying everything. It's not mechanical. It's up here." Sojo points to his head. "He's gone from one of the best to one of the worst. Knoblauch committed 13 errors in 149 games in 1998, 26 errors in 150 games in 1999, 15 errors in 82 games in 2000.

Knoblauch's throwing problem is part of a syndrome now known as Steve Blass disease. Blass, the hero of the 1971 World Series for the

Pittsburgh Pirates, suddenly lost his ability to throw the ball anywhere near the plate. This mysterious affliction, called the "yips" for no known reason, renders its victims unable to act instinctively. They think too much and lose the ability to let the body perform acts without thinking. To perform at elite levels, athletes can't think about what they're doing. They need to execute actions automatically.

As a broadcaster, Bob Brenly noticed a mechanical flaw in a 1999 playoff game between the Yankees and Red Sox. As he got ready to throw, Knoblauch looked at the ball instead of the target—almost guaranteeing that he would throw the ball wildly.

Distraction is lethal to an athlete. When thinking about the particular motions needed to perform an action, the athlete loses the ability to focus on the changing environment. Playing sports is like driving a car. If you have to think of the countless small actions needed to perform a simple task—pressing down the gas and brake pedals, turning the steering wheel, looking in the rearview mirror—you won't be able to concentrate on the traffic or street signs. Researchers at the University of Waterloo have confirmed this intuitive idea. The researchers asked hitters to both hit and recite some numbers that were read to them. The hitters who recited the numbers were impeded in their hitting. Not the most sophisticated experiment, but telling nonetheless.

Something psychological distracted Knoblauch so much that he would focus on the mechanics of the throw rather than get into the flow of the play. Theories abound. One theory was that Knoblauch's father's struggle with Alzheimer's disease crippled the son inside. Another theory was that Knoblauch couldn't handle the media glare of New York. A third theory was that Knoblauch was just a nervous guy—just look at his fidgeting at the plate—and that nervousness was bound to spill over into his fielding.

In spring training, manager Joe Torre gave Knoblauch a big show of confidence by announcing that he would be the Yankees' starting second baseman. Knoblauch got some psychological counseling and showed up for training a month early to practice throwing the ball. But nothing worked. Knoblauch couldn't even throw the ball well in exhibition games. Torre finally moved Knoblauch into an outfield platoon when he struggled in spring training games. The change seemed to work. Knoblauch's psychological hangup about throwing, somehow, was limited to playing infield.

As he steps to the plate, Knoblauch goes through his usual distracting routine of fidgeting and twitching. He tugs at his batting gloves and pulls at his pants. He twists his neck. He squints.

◆ ◆ ◆

KNOBLAUCH TAKES JOHNSON'S first pitch, a floater outside, for a ball. Kloblauch lines the next pitch right over the plate, down the left field line. It's a perfect swing, perfectly timed, with strong two-hand follow-through. But the ball falls foul by a foot. If Knoblauch hit the ball a few millimeters up the bat, it's a double and a two-run lead for the Yankees.

After another pickoff throw, Johnson throws a couple high hard ones outside the strike zone. So it's a 3–1 count. On an inside-out swing on a pitch just on the outside part of the plate, Knoblauch flies to right field. Knoblauch hits it just below the fat of his bat. It's Johnson's first great pitch—not a fastball but an off-speed pitch that fools the choosy Knoblauch.

Johnson is feeling his way in the game. Johnson's command in a game often mirrors his career: shaky at first, then dominant. Early in his career, with the Montreal Expos, Johnson has a hard time controlling his pitches, walking four, five, six batters a game, falling behind in the count—then forced to throw fastballs over the plate that hitters can hit hard. But over the years, as he gained control over his sprawling six-foot, ten-inch body, he became one of the dominant pitchers in modern history.

Whatever his fielding problems, Knoblauch still has the knack of forcing the pitcher to throw a lot of pitches. But tonight, Knoblauch's maddening patience probably helps Johnson.

Johnson acknowledges as much. "Throwing more pitches against Knoblauch was probably better just so I could get in the flow of the game and get a little looser and get the anxiety out of the way—and then be ready to go out there for the top of the ninth."

Chapter Twenty

MO

SINCE 1997, JOE TORRE has used Mariano Rivera to close down the opposition in the last inning or two of games the Yankees are winning. If Rivera can get those last outs, the game is effectively shortened to seven or eight innings.

Rivera might be the most dominant closer in baseball history. Since emerging as the setup man for John Wetteland in 1997, Rivera has pitched 358.33 innings, striking out 297 batters, walking just 92, with an earned-run average of 2.19. His earned-run average in World Series play, over fifty-one appearances, is 0.70—the lowest in history. During that span, Rivera has recorded twenty-four postseason saves; in nineteen of those games, Rivera pitched for more than one inning, defying a growing trend. He pitched eighty and two-thirds innings, striking out eighty-three batters and yielding twenty-one earned runs. In 2001, he earned fifty saves during the regular season, holding left-handed hitters to a .187 average and right-handed hitters to a .229 average.

Mike Lupica, a veteran columnist for the *New York Daily News,* calls Rivera "the greatest clutch athlete of all time."

What distinguishes Rivera is his demeanor. Over history, great relievers have been known best for their screwy or mad demeanors. Al Hrabosky was called the "Mad Hungarian" for his half-beard and disheveled appearance and his angry, stomping, glaring, spitting ways. Tug McGraw bopped to the mound with an intense gait, slamming his thighs with his glove. Sparky Lyle was known as much for his goofy off-the-field antics (like sitting on a birthday cake naked) as his mound performances. Dennis Eckersley was a windmill, throwing his pitches from a side angle and then rolling off the mound and pumping his fists and gleefully pointing to his strikeout victims.

Rivera is different. He embodies the ability to stay "pointed, dartlike, definite," to use Virginia Woolfe's words. "You can see his calm. He's not going to be rattled. He's a professional. He knows what he's doing," says longtime scout Billy Blitzer. "Mariano doesn't come in to intimidate you. He says, 'Here's what I got. Go beat me.'" After he took over the closer role from John Wetteland, Rivera told the *New York Times:* "He's stronger, but what I have is a strong mind.... If you have a strong mind in this game, you can beat anything."

Because his role is so well defined, Rivera has the luxury of preparing for games calmly and efficiently every night. Rivera watches the early innings of a game on a TV in the clubhouse. This gives him the opportunity to observe the tendencies of hitters that he might face in the eighth or ninth inning. He can also assess the umpire's strike zone. In the sixth or seventh inning, Rivera runs to the bullpen and stretches his rubbery body. If, and only if, the Yankees are leading by one, two, or three runs, Rivera starts to warm up. At Yankee Stadium, as he walks from the bullpen to the mound, the public-address system plays "Enter Sandman," a song by the heavy-metal group Metallica.

Rivera has failed only once in his long postseason career. He yielded a home run to the Cleveland Indians' Sandy Alomar Jr. in the first round of the playoffs in 1997 that helped the Indians get to the World Series. The Yankees led the best-of-five series two games to one and needed just four outs in a 2–1 game when Alomar lifted a fastball just beyond the reach of right fielder Paul O'Neill. The Indians won that game and the next to eliminate the Yankees. Unlike other pitchers who lost games in late innings—like the California Angels' Donnie Moore in the 1986 playoffs and the Philadelphia Phillies' Mitch Williams in the 1993 World Series—Rivera did not dwell on the loss. In fact, he reasoned that the home run confirmed his superiority. Had he not thrown the ball with such velocity, there's no way the ball would have made it out of the park.

◆ ◆ ◆

THE FOUNDATION OF Mariano Rivera's success can be found in Panama.

The son of a fisherman in Puerto Caimito, Rivera occasionally helped haul in the ocean crop. He played baseball with a cardboard glove, sometimes using rocks and coconuts for balls. Rivera was not always a pitcher, but he was always throwing something, like all the other kids.

Rivera's first love was soccer. He developed quickness, agility, and playfulness kicking a soccer ball. "You have to be really aggressive in the game, in football," he says. "You have to use your feet, so you have to be always moving left to right, side to side." But when he broke his ankle, he decided he couldn't play competitive soccer anymore. He transferred his passion to baseball. Rivera's continuing legacy as a soccer player is his flexibility and quickness—and the strength in his legs. Rivera does not have Roger Clemens's tree-trunk legs, but has long and elastic muscles that he uses to lift his lead leg and generate energy for his pitches. His pitching motion is so effortless—his calm demeanor betrays none of the grunting effort of a Clemens or a Schilling—that you sometimes do not realize just how much strength he generates when he rears into his motion.

Rivera signed with the Yankees as a free agent in 1990. He starred in the Rookie League in 1991—finishing the season with an 0.71 ERA in 52 innings—but the next year developed ligament problems in his pitching elbow. Dr. Frank Jobe recommended the radical but increasingly common Tommy John surgery to replace a damaged ligament. The Yankees instead asked Jobe to clean Rivera's elbow. Three years later, Rivera was throwing a straight fastball and little else and the Yankees were considering trading him.

The Yankees were negotiating a trade of Rivera to the Detroit Tigers when the reports of a zippier fastball came into Yankee Stadium. Minor league reports in 1995 revealed that the speed on his fastball jumped from 89 to 92 miles an hour to 95 or 96 an hour—"an act of God," Rivera now says. The Yankees held on to him.

"Gene Michael [the Yankees' scouting director] was calling me, saying, 'Did you see this guy?'" says Billy Blitzer, who scouts the two New York franchises for the Chicago Cubs and tracked Rivera in the minors. "The reports Michael was getting were that he was throwing the ball 94, 95 miles an hour. It happened out of nowhere." Rivera got his first shot at the Yankees in 1995 and won one of three decisions with an earned-run average of 10.20. A couple years later, Rivera added the cut fastball, a pitch that would become his specialty.

The Yankees still debated Rivera's role. When he became manager in 1996, Joe Torre knew Rivera had the devastating fastball to be an effective closer, but Torre hesitated to give him that role. He wondered aloud whether Rivera might be better off developing a changeup so that he would have a big enough repertoire to start games. Rivera worked as the setup man for closer John Wetteland for the 1996 World Championship team. He took over the closer role in 1997 and blew three of his first four save opportunities. Yankees' owner George Steinbrenner grumbled that his brain trust made a mistake letting Wetteland get away. Steinbrenner said he wasn't sure the team had an adequate closer on the staff.

But Rivera quickly established himself as the best closer in the game.

The cutter has defined Rivera's career as a closer. To throw the cutter, Rivera grips the ball with his index and middle fingers turned slightly to the left. He throws the ball like a fastball, but the grip and the snap give it late movement. A curveball bends along most of the trip from the pitcher's hand to the plate. But the cutter comes in harder, looking like a fastball even when the batter knows in his mind that it's no such thing. Because of the slight tilt to his release, the ball backspins on an odd angle. And then it falls down after the hitter has made his decision to swing—more often than not, burning into the hitter's hands or the thin part of the bat.

Rivera discovered the cutter when playing with different grips in the bullpen between starts. Like a mechanic tinkering with different parts—if he never made it as an athlete, Rivera says he might have been a mechanic—he is forever experimenting with grips and releases. "If the ball does something different, I try to do the same thing over and over, and if it's moving I try to put it in play," he says of his experiments. "If not, I move on." He will hold it softly and he'll grip it hard; he will release it with a snap down and then he'll let the ball squirt out in different ways. One day, playing catch with Ramiro Mendoza, "all of a sudden it was moving, it was moving-moving-moving, and one day, I put it in play and it worked."

Because he throws only one pitch, his control needs to be perfect. He cannot miss by more than an inch or two. When he's on—almost always—Rivera burns the ball into the batter's hands, then moves it in further, then comes up a bit, then down again, then—*surprise!*—outside, then in, and then in harder. Talking about one pitch that got "over the plate," he is asked how much he missed. "Maybe two, three inches," he says.

Something about his physical makeup, his tinkering ways, his body memory, his athleticism, his focus, makes the cutter *his* pitch—something that you can't just teach like a lesson in a workbook. Even though soccer was Rivera's passion as a youngster, he played all positions in baseball, giving his arm a deep sense of distances and speeds that other pitchers lack.

Buck Showalter was the Yankees' manager when Rivera struggled to find his niche. "Watching him for two years I couldn't figure out why the Yankees left him on the roster," he now admits. "He was this guy who came off [considering] Tommy John surgery and he played catch with Whitey Ford and Ron Guidry on the back field during spring training. Then we brought him up. We put him in a game against Chicago and he was going to spot start"—fill in whenever the Yankees needed an extra starter—"and pitch three or four innings for us and he went through the first two innings like a knife through butter. We turned around and said, 'Let's try one more, and then one more, and then....' If I had known then what I know now, we would have used him even more."

Rivera's early stats were not always impressive, but Showalter liked his focus. "The thing I liked about his minor-league numbers was his lack of walks, which I love—and his athleticism. He has great command of himself and his stuff. He has great presence. There's a certain presentation that all good relievers have."

When his career is over, Rivera plans to be an evangelical minister. He's part of a small band of Yankees who make God the centerpiece of their lives, giving the Almighty credit for wins and strikeouts and hits. Rivera says God sent him a clear message—"I am the one who has you here"—on July 16, 1999. God, says Rivera, gave him the extra miles per hour on his fastball just when he was about to be traded from the Yankees to the Tigers. And he has pledged his post-baseball life to serving the Lord.

◆ ◆ ◆

As he walks across the outfield toward the pitching mound, Rivera is a trim Buddha. His facial muscles are relaxed, his eyes calm, his mouth closed but not tight. Soriano's demeanor has been likened to an INS agent, who calmly, disinterestedly processes papers. But Rivera's demeanor is not a bureaucrat's alienation but the elite performer's attention to what matters and inattention to what doesn't.

Brain researchers have found that successful execution of any task—writing, teaching, golfing, pitching—requires turning off some parts of the brain and turning others on. Rivera can do that. All he notices when he pitches is the catcher's glove. He does not even notice the batter—unless the batter adjusts his stance to time Rivera's pitches better, in which case Rivera counters with an adjustment of his own. The batter is invisible except as a frame for Rivera's real focus of attention, which is where he wants to throw the ball to the catcher.

Rivera might not succeed as a starting pitcher—his repertoire is not big enough and his body not strong enough—but he has established the most impressive record of any closer in baseball history. He might be the best one-pitch pitcher in baseball history.

Rivera's cutter might be his only "out" pitch, but Rivera has developed his variations on that pitch. A four-seam pitch moves in on left-handed hitters, and a two-seam pitch moves in on right-handed hitters. Rivera's cutter drops as much as a foot while maintaining speeds of 95 miles per hour or more.

"He throws a 94-mile-an-hour cutter," says Mark Grace. "There's not a whole lot of people who can throw it because they either can't control it or they can't throw it as hard. He comes in to get three outs and that's the most important thing. He's tougher on left-handed hitters than righties but now he's developed a sinker that goes into right-handed hitters. What he does is come right after you. He throws strike after strike and it keeps coming on you. And you have to go get him or else you're going to be sitting in the dugout. He either throws you a strike or he throws a pitch that's tough to lay off because it looks like a fastball and then it's in on your hands."

Rivera is the king of the splintered bats. In the 2001 season, forty-four batters broke their bats against Rivera, about one or two per appearance. Hitters often use spare bats when facing Rivera because they don't want to lose their own wood. Even when they begin their swing early to meet the Rivera cutter, most hitters get around on the pitch late. Fielders position themselves accordingly for pop-ups and dribblers to the opposite side of the field.

"What sets Mariano apart is that he gets great movement and knows where it's going," says Mel Stottlemyre, the Yankees' pitching coach. "He's not going to come in and blow you away, but he has a plan and I don't think I've ever seen anybody throw as hard with that movement. Generally, the more velocity a pitcher attempts to generate, the more movement he loses, but Mariano has a live arm and has learned a lot about himself and how to make the ball move—and it's all late movement."

◆ ◆ ◆

ANOTHER FACE OF baseball's growing diversity, Luis Gonzalez, is the first player to face Rivera in the bottom of the eighth inning.

The crowd comes alive looking for a rally. Rivera stands on the mound, thin and emotionless, peering intently toward his target. The first pitch is up and in and Gonzalez takes it for a ball.

Gonzalez, the Diamondbacks' left fielder, is a son of Cuban exiles. Born and raised in Tampa, he speaks Spanish and English fluently. But he grew up comfortably. He walked two miles to school, not because he didn't have a choice but because he wanted the exercise. Every day, he drove with his friend Tino Martinez, parking the car two miles from school so they could get extra exercise walking and running.

Rivera throws a cutter up and inside for a ball, and then a fastball up in the strike zone before missing again inside. Gonzalez now enjoys a rare advantage in the count, 2–1. If the ball were just a little closer to the plate, Gonzalez might have gone for it. After missing on another inside cutter, he breaks the bat fouling off a cutter to the right side.

Even without any base runners, Rivera pitches from the stretch position, slowly bringing his hands to his waist and stopping before beginning his motion. Contrary to folklore, taking a full and uninterrupted motion is not what gives pitches power. It's the leg kick that does it, and even from the stretch, Rivera has plenty of leg kick. He keeps his hands close to his body as he brings the glove up with his leg, and then back down with his leg as he gets ready to launch the ball. As Rivera completes his motion, his right leg swings around. He throws the ball like he's throwing a football with a spiral, giving the ball its legendary movement.

The next pitch is almost in the same spot and Gonzalez swings over it. He's no match for Rivera.

Rivera is so focused on his own game that he doesn't notice anything else. "I am just paying attention to what I'm doing, I'm not paying attention to the batter," he says later. In this game, the finale of a long season, he is going to play to his own strengths rather than try to exploit the batter's weaknesses. It's an approach that manager Joe Torre endorses. "You can't get your mind all jammed with thoughts about what the other side's going to do. You have to keep yourself in the frame of mind to execute the way you need to execute. It's about you doing things the right way."

◆ ◆ ◆

MATT WILLIAMS, THE Diamondbacks' third baseman, is next up. He takes an open stance to see the ball better. After watching a fastball all the way into Jorge Posada's glove, Williams fouls off a cutter in on his hands. Williams tilts off-balance as he finishes his half-swing.

He tucks the bat under his armpit and walks around trying to think about what's coming next. He takes deep breaths. But he's still tentative, wary, looking to just get his bat on the ball. But he swings through a rising fastball up in the strike zone, by the letters. He is now Rivera's second straight strikeout victim.

Williams thought he could hit Rivera. "I had an at bat against him in New York. It was a good at bat. He threw me the cutters and I fouled a couple off, one a liner down the left field line. Another time I laid down a sacrifice bunt against him. I felt confident. But he elevated the ball on me three times, and the higher you get the ball, it's harder to lay off. It's easier to lay off a ball that's low because it looks farther away from you. Your natural reaction is to let it go because it doesn't look like a strike. He really elevated the ball on all three of us that inning. I was dead."

◆ ◆ ◆

WITH THE COUNT 1–0, Steve Finley lines an inside pitch to right field, just beyond the reach of Alfonso Soriano. Finley's open stance allows him to step away from the ball to extend his arms. This might be a solution to the Rivera riddle—position yourself back in the batter's box so you can use both your arms and body.

"Baseball's a game of adjustments," Finley says. "If you don't make adjustments then you're not going to last very long. If you're looking up in here and the ball goes out there, you're not going to hit it. But it's easier to make the adjustments when you have confidence in your body's ability to react to any pitch. If I'm looking in here and he throws one up here and you've got some stretch, you can still reach out there and foul it off. Whenever you're struggling, if you're having a tough time, if you're looking in there you're not even touching that pitch out there. But I'm able to make some adjustments. We call them emergency hacks."

◆ ◆ ◆

DANNY BAUTISTA STRIKES out on three pitches. He looks at a fastball over the plate for the first strike—Rivera is so intimidating that batters want to look at a pitch before swinging—and chases a cut fastball off the plate and a pitch up in the strike zone.

Bautista can only laugh when asked about hitting Rivera. "I mean, I was seeing the ball good and I was ready, my mind was really strong, and I say, 'Now, be ready for Rivera, you know. He comes after you.' That's what I told to myself. 'I've got to be ready and I'm gonna trust my swing.'"

Bautista tried to bail out on the pitch, to put more of the fat of the bat in the hitting zone, but Rivera was too much for him. "Well, you gotta stay inside on the ball and throw the bat where the ball is. I faced him in spring training and he got late movement and you got to be short with him, you got to have a shorter swing. If you got a long swing with Rivera, 95 percent of the time you going to be out."

Ultimately, Rivera beat him by messing with his mind. "It's a lot different watching on TV than when you face him for real. You see the ball and react. That's what I do with Rivera." But Rivera tricks Bautista's eyes by climbing the ladder. "He throws them high and higher and higher and they look like they're bigger because they're closer to your eyes. You swing late every time because it looks bigger."

A feeling of dread washes over the Diamondbacks' dugout and VIP boxes. The Yankees may not have dominated baseball this summer, but they know how to win. And with Mariano Rivera on the mound, the nine-inning game becomes the seven-inning game.

Is the game over?

Looks like it.

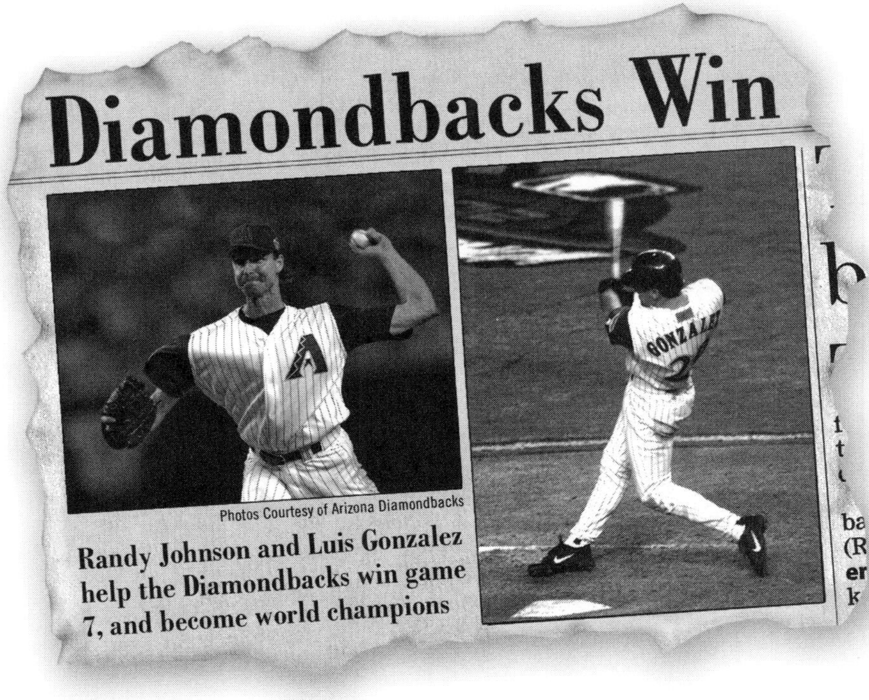

Diamondbacks Win

Photos Courtesy of Arizona Diamondbacks

Randy Johnson and Luis Gonzalez help the Diamondbacks win game 7, and become world champions

After pitching seven innings the night before,
Randy Johnson entered Game Seven with a chance
to win his third game of the World Series.
Slugger Luis Gonzalez did not need to use his
power to bring a championship to Arizona.

NINTH INNING

In which the game's tallest pitcher and most improbable power source—and some strange plays—produce one of the greatest comebacks in World Series history

CHAPTER TWENTY-ONE

THE BIG UNIT

JERRY COLANGELO, THE OWNER of the Arizona Diamondbacks, remembers the time he went to Randy Johnson's sprawling McMansion in a Phoenix suburb—a house with ten-foot-high doorways and Brobdignaggian furniture—to woo him to play for his team. The Diamondbacks had just completed their first year in the National League, winning sixty-five games and losing ninety-seven. Colangelo and the other team executives fretted at the decline in fan interest over the course of the year. The Diamondbacks decided to drop their long-term building plan and sign the best players available on the free agent market to create an instant winner.

Johnson was ready for Colangelo's pitch. He had just experienced his most difficult year since his early days with the Montreal Expos, when he struggled to throw the ball over the plate. In the first half of 1998, Johnson pitched like a conflicted man. He won nine and lost ten and gave up an average of 4.33 runs every nine innings. He battled the Mariners' front office over his contract, due to expire at the end of the year. He battled the Seattle media, who called him spoiled and overrated. And he battled his own demons. In the middle of the season, the

Mariners traded him to the Houston Astros. In a new setting, Johnson pitched as well as anyone has ever pitched. He won ten of eleven decisions, yielding just 1.28 earned runs a game.

Johnson felt vindicated but wanted to settle down and play for an organization where his prickly personality would not become an issue.

A year before, Colangelo had prepared the way for courting Johnson. Colangelo gave Johnson courtside season tickets to the Phoenix Suns, the National Basketball Association team that Colangelo also owned. For that favor, Johnson's agent promised him: "You'll be first in and last out when Randy is a free agent." When Colangelo came calling in November of 1998, Johnson expressed interest but balked.

"I understand Buck doesn't like long hair," Johnson said. Buck Showalter, then the manager of the Diamondbacks, had a reputation as a martinet, with strict rules for everything from dress to pregame drills. Showalter ran the team with the guidance of a detailed business plan for the organization. He reveled in setting strict standards for players up and down the organization, from the big-league club in Phoenix to the lowest minor-league team in Missoula, Montana.

The Diamondbacks' owner reassured Johnson. "Randy, if you had tattoos from the top of your head to the bottom of your toes and a big ring hanging out of your nose and the long hair, I'd say pass," Colangelo said. "But since it's only one out of three, it's okay." Johnson could keep the long hair.

◆ ◆ ◆

NOW RANDY JOHNSON is starting the ninth inning of the seventh game of the World Series.

When Bob Brenly summoned Johnson to get the last out of the eighth inning, it was the first time that a Pittsburgh starter had pitched in World Series games without a day of rest in more than four decades. In 1960, the Pirates' Bob Friend started against the Yankees in Game Six, and relieved in Game Seven. But Friend lasted only two innings in his start and failed to retire a batter in his relief appearance.

The Diamondbacks could not rely on their closer, Byung-Hyun Kim, to keep the game close. Kim tried and failed in Games Four and Five. If the game was on the line in Game Seven, manager Bob Brenly wanted to use someone else. Miguel Batista could throw against a batter or two, but Brenly was concerned about his ability to get into a rhythm in a short appearance.

So Johnson told Brenly that he would be available to pitch an inning or two.

Like any pitcher, Johnson is fussy and particular about his routine. He pitches every five days, using his four "off" days to prepare physically and mentally for the next start. "Everything is being prepared up until that fifth day. By the day of a start, I've done all my work in the weight room and the video room and my charts and who I'm going to be facing that day. When that fifth day comes, I come to the ballpark, I'm extremely focused, nobody talks to me. And I take it extremely serious because on that fifth day people are counting on me to go out and give an effort that they're expecting to see. I don't let anybody distract me. I'll dictate whether I'm going to smile, whether I'm going to laugh, whether I'm going to joke around with somebody on the day that I pitch."

On this day, Johnson would, in effect, compress that four-day routine into a few hours. He got his massage treatment from Russ Nua, then settled into the dugout to watch the game, then started stretching in the sixth inning. In the seventh inning, he ran out to the Diamondbacks' bullpen to warm up.

"I went down to the bullpen, and sat there. A lot of adrenaline was flowing. Then with the home run they took the lead, 2–1, and the phone rang, and myself and Miguel Batista got up. It's the World Series, all the aches and pains go out the window when there's so much riding on a game. I felt fine, but I think I was pretty much all adrenaline. It was a long year for me. I pitched a lot of innings, threw a lot of pitches over the course of the season, pitched the night before. I was probably mentally and physically beat. But it was one more game or one more inning, two more innings to pitch, and I was going to be able to do that."

Randy Johnson is not a guile pitcher—he's a power pitcher—but he had to operate on smarts in lieu of his every-fifth-day strength. "I had the focus. Velocity-wise, I probably wasn't throwing as hard as I was the day before, but that's understandable."

Relying on adrenaline can be dangerous because it's hard to control. When Johnson came into the game with two outs in the eighth inning, Chuck Knoblauch battled him. Usually, pitchers don't want to work so hard to get the first out. But in this case it was good for Johnson because it got him in his groove. If Knoblauch popped out on the first pitch, Johnson might still be looking for his groove in the ninth inning.

But he has it now.

"When you're in a zone, nothing else around you affects you," he says. "You don't hear anybody else, everything's kind of a blur. It's almost like special effects in a movie. Everything around is a blur. It's just you and the catcher and the hitter and that's the kind of tunnel vision you have to have. Late in the flow of the game, as a power pitcher, the fastball's there and you're making your pitches and you're executing everything. It's like a volcano. That's the best way I can put it. You have something building and eventually in the ninth inning it blows."

◆ ◆ ◆

THE SCORE REMAINS 2–1 Yankees as their center fielder, Bernie Williams, faces Randy Johnson in the top of the ninth inning.

Randy Johnson's great advantage as a pitcher is his height. He's six feet, ten inches, which makes him the tallest player in baseball history. He releases the ball close to eight feet from the ground, with a sidearmed slingshot motion that makes it difficult for hitters to pick up the ball—and gives the ball extreme angles as it comes into the plate.

The late Durwood Merrill, who umpired hundreds of games behind home plate, once remarked: "At six-ten, the Big Unit has a mighty big advantage with those long legs and that long stride. He looks like a big hairy half-tarantula as he goes into the windup. Instead of throwing the ball from sixty feet and six inches, he sometimes seems looks like he's delivering from fifty feet and five inches. Johnson's arm is thirty-eight inches long, which means he's actually delivering the ball three feet behind a left-handed batter. The amazing part is that the ball winds up on the outside part of the plate, causing the left-handed hitter to lean so far forward that he's almost falling on his nose."

Scott Bradley, Johnson's former battery mate with the Seattle Mariners, marvels at the natural advantage of the higher release point. "All the angles change when you're hitting against a tall pitcher," says Bradley, who has become the head coach of the Princeton team. "Batters aren't used to seeing the ball released seven and a half feet off the ground. When I first caught Randy, I used to turn my glove over on a low strike, thinking the ball was going to be in the dirt, and then get handcuffed when the ball came in on the knees. Batters took that pitch all the time. The downward angle was so steep it fooled their eyes."

◆ ◆ ◆

WILLIAMS, A SWITCH-HITTER batting right-handed, looks hopeless against Johnson's heat and sidearm slants. He takes the first pitch for a ball up in the strike zone, then takes a strike that starts from a place so far out of the strike zone that no batter would even consider taking the bat off his shoulder, but then the ball veers into the zone for a called strike one. After fouling off the next pitch, Williams flies to short center field for the first out.

◆ ◆ ◆

JOHNSON'S SIZE AND volatility worried the scouts who watched Johnson in high school and college. Mets' scout Joe McIlvane filed this report after a visit to Livermore High School on the east side of San Francisco Bay in 1982: "Timid due to awkwardness [but] plenty of room to fill out. No concept yet, just a thrower. Johnson is like a box of Cracker Jacks, there's a surprise inside. Our only problem is whether we will like the surprise. He's a boom or bust. Long way to go yet. Has no pitching mechanics. With his long arms could eventually bury all left-handed hitters. *A real gamble.*"

Bob Poole, who scouted Johnson for the Philadelphia Phillies, remembers Johnson's risky makeup: "He was wild, had no command, but there was no doubt he could throw the baseball," he says. "There was no doubt this was something special." He struck out 121 batters in sixty-six and a third innings as a high school senior in 1982, but won just four of eight games with an earned-run average of 3.11.

Height has posed an endless challenge to Johnson since he played at Livermore High School. Even dressing was a challenge back then. To get a wearable pair of knickers, Johnson had to take the bottoms of the legs from one pair and sew them on to another.

Johnson reminded Rod Dedeaux, his coach at the University of Southern California, of "a guy falling out of a window, his arms and legs going in all directions." Johnson spent three years at USC under Dedeaux, one of the legendary coaches in college sports. Dedeaux has worked with some of the best collegiate players in history—Tom Seaver, Mark McGwire, Dave Kingman, Fred Lynn, and fifty others who went on to the big leagues—and he went to work on Johnson.

Johnson's handicap in controlling that big awkward body is that virtually no one else has been in the same situation. He had no giant role models, no founts of advice on doing it the right way.

To throw the ball well, the pitcher needs to coordinate his body in one motion. Leaning back on the back foot, lifting the front foot, bringing the hips and torso around, rearing back, whipping the arm forward, following through to absorb the shock—somehow everything needs to come together in a single fluid motion. Such coordination is difficult for even the most compact players. But it's especially demanding for tall pitchers like Johnson.

"He had flaws in his delivery. He wanted to work on everything he didn't do well—he wanted to hit, he wanted to improve his fielding, not just a pitching motion."

Dedeaux broke down with Johnson's delivery, piece by piece. One time he would work on his leg lift, and another time he tried to improve the way he cocked his arm, and another time he would try to land on the mound better. Every mechanical improvement made the rest of the motion better. Landing better, for example, improved his control, gave his pitches better location and movement, and took strain off his arm.

Johnson was "very coachable," Dedeaux says. He remembers being very impressed when Johnson grinded his way through a cold and rainy game in high school. "He really had the guts and desire to throw the way he did. You got to love the game to work hard on a blustery day like that."

Drafted by the Montreal Expos in the second round of the 1985 amateur draft, Johnson took years to control his delivery. After two years in the minor leagues, he won his only three decisions with the Expos in September 1988. He lost four straight games the next year and was traded to Seattle, where he won seven and lost nine. In 1990, he pitched a no-hitter against Detroit and made the All-Star team. But control was always a problem. He led the league in walks with 120 in 1990, 152 in 1991, and 144 in 1992.

During the 1992 season, Hall of Fame pitcher Nolan Ryan and Houston Astros pitching coach Tom House, one of baseball's leading scholars of pitching mechanics, noticed that Johnson was landing on his heel rather than the ball of his feet. That caused his body to slide over toward third base instead of coming straight toward home plate.

"That was critical," Johnson recalls. "They helped me with my mechanics, and that made a big difference. Before, I was landing all over. You land wrong, you're going to be inconsistent with your release point. You're landing here one time, you land over there another time, your pitches are going to be hard to control. After working on that during the off-season and side sessions and during the game, I got consistent and got more confident and then started utilizing my ability. Everything became more fluid. Having to be precise with your mechanics—being a power pitcher, that's much more critical.

Landing on the mound the right way was just part of the challenge of Johnson's height. Before throwing the ball, Johnson needed to control his arms and limbs, which had the tendency to fly away from his body. Without a compact delivery, Johnson put extra strain on his back and arms—and had poor control.

"The challenge is being consistent, being as tall as I am as a pitcher," Johnson says quietly in the corner of the Diamondbacks' clubhouse. "I don't think I was ever holding back. It was extremely frustrating at a younger age because I knew what I was capable of doing...There'd be bits of brilliance, but I wasn't consistent. I'd go out and pitch well one game and come back five days later and be inconsistent; you'd wonder if it was the same pitcher."

Over the years, Johnson has developed such pinpoint control that he can fool hitters on pitch after pitch. Mark Connor, the Diamondbacks pitching coach, says: "Randy can start you off within the strike zone and you'll never see another strike after that. And you can't hit it. His slider gives the appearance of being a strike and ends up being a ball, and hitters are swinging at it. We've seen guys fall down trying to hit his slider and then lock up trying to hit a 100-mile-an-hour fastball on their hands."

◆ ◆ ◆

JOHNSON'S NEXT VICTIM is Tino Martinez. With one out, the Yankees' first baseman takes a slider that misses on the inside of the plate for a ball. Martinez then watches, like a helpless spectator, as Johnson throws an impossible pitch on the outside corner. No way Martinez could ever hit the ball for more than a dribbler down the third base line. The arc of the ball is extreme. Johnson's height and the long sweep of his arm across from his left side creates one of the widest arcs imaginable.

A hitter gets fewer clues about what pitch Johnson is throwing. Batters guess whether a ball is a fastball, splitter, or changeup based on the motion of the arm and the follow-through. Curveballs and changeups usually have a slower arm motion and follow-through, so batters know to hold their swing for a split-second. The most successful pitchers—like Greg Maddux of the Atlanta Braves—throw different pitches with indistinguishable motions and arm speeds so batters have no idea what kind of pitch is coming. Johnson's motion varies according to pitch, but the batter has less time to discern the difference because of his closer release point.

Pitching is like snapping a whip. Whips exert the greatest force when snapped from far away. The longer the arc, the greater the force at the end of the arc. Throwing with a long arm, Johnson exerts a much stronger whip-like motion—and also puts much less stress on his arm. Unlike Schilling and Clemens, Johnson is lean. His long arms are strong and muscled, but supple and flexible.

At the end of Johnson's whip are probably the longest fingers in the game. Those fingers hold the ball deep into his hands. His ability to conceal the ball takes away any hint of his pitch selection. He snaps the ball out of nowhere.

In contrast to drop-and-drive pitchers like Roger Clemens and Curt Schilling, Johnson gets his power from his core more than thick legs. His back and abdominal muscles allow Johnson to maintain his center of gravity and to withstand the whiplash of his large body and limbs.

"Your core is very critical," Johnson says. "Swinging a bat, throwing a baseball, that's where you get roughly 50 to 60 percent of your torque—your spine. I learned all that way back in '96 after I had back surgery. I started doing exercises to strengthen my back, core exercises. You throw a ball, well, you're throwing a ball through your abdominals. They're tightening as you throw; it's a natural reflex for your body to do that. When you're in the weight room doing sit-ups and core exercises, the easier it's going to be for you to do those things. The goal is to distribute all this energy evenly throughout your body, so not one area of your body's being over-labored. It's critical in your arms. If you got weak core, weak legs, [and a] strong arm, eventually your arm will not be so strong after awhile because all the force will be going to your arm."

As he approaches the age of forty, Johnson throws more pitches than anyone else in the game—sometimes 110, 120, 130, even 140—and he throws harder, with a bigger bite in the ball, as the game progresses.

If he has a two- or three-run lead, Johnson admits that he can lose his focus in the middle innings. That's when he summons anger like a method actor. "I'm very much a self-motivated person, but sometimes you can be on cruise control and next thing you know now you're losing the ballgame because you weren't focused."

◆ ◆ ◆

TINO MARTINEZ FOULS off the next pitch, a little higher in the strike zone, and then grounds the next pitch on the outside of the plate to shortstop Tony Womack for an easy play at first base. Womack takes his time and Martinez moves well down the line. If Womack struggled clutching the ball, Martinez might have been safe. But Womack makes the play easily.

Two outs.

◆ ◆ ◆

BEING THE TALLEST player in baseball history poses not just physical challenges, but also psychological challenges. As he was growing up in California, Johnson endured endless taunts about his height and strange looks. Johnson burned, and often lost himself in confusion and anger, when opponents openly gawked and laughed and called him Big Bird. For years, the ridicule worked against Johnson. But once he gained physical control of his body, he turned the anger to his advantage.

Johnson's face has been described as a Picasso—thin and angular, with a sharp nose, strong lines down the nose and along the mouth to the chin, with tufts of whiskers under his lip, down past his sideburns, here and there on his scarred face. With his patchy facial hair and his glare, Johnson gives the appearance of a war-weary Confederate soldier.

Johnson always knew, growing up, that he was an outsider. He called himself a freak. "Being six-seven or six-eight [feet tall] when I was growing up, I felt different," he recalls. "Everybody kind of looked at me. I felt really skinny and out of place, always different. I was shy and very quiet.... It was something that was hard growing up. I'll be walking down a mall and if people stare like I'm some kind of freak."

Coach Dedeaux remembers Johnson absorbing merciless taunts of opponents during his college career. "He handled it like a gentleman," Dedeaux remembers. "But I think he decided to take on this image, the idea that he could be a terror out there on the mound. He took advantage of that." When Johnson played at USC, Dedeaux made a point of standing on the front slope of the mound so that Johnson would loom over him, terrorizing hitters waiting for their turns at the plate. "Make them know he's a giant," Dedeaux now says, chuckling.

Dedeaux says Johnson's later decision to wear long, stringy hair and a nasty glare gave him a way to overcome the taunts by confirming them: *You think I'm strange looking? A freak? Look at this.*

The hurt and the anger never went away completely. As he has matured into one of the best left-handed pitchers in baseball history, though, the anger has become a resource that Johnson summons when he needs to refocus his attention and gather his energy.

"It usually happens late in the game, seventh, eighth inning. I've gotten up to this point, we're still winning the ballgame. Not too many hitters can elevate their game to another level, so [in the] eighth or ninth inning the hitters sure won't expect that from the pitcher. My biggest attribute is being able to turn it up even one more notch later in the game. It's almost [having] a bit of a rage or feeding frenzy out there.

We've gotten this far, now I'm going to shut the door, and do whatever it takes to get through those next three outs...You worked so hard to get to that point. Don't have a mental collapse. That rage gets me to that next level."

Anger can be distracting, but it can also focus attention and create a new store of energy. "It's my game day, and all my preparation coming to a head, and I just get good results that way. I don't want to be passive out there. When I go out there, there's a little bit of fire in me."

It took years for Johnson to convert his anger into a positive force. "As a young player I'd let my emotions get the best of me, get rattled out there. You need to keep the focus. Anybody can get that extra adrenaline, but you have to keep focused and utilize it to your advantage. The one thing that I think I'm able to do over my career—pitch with rage, and now I'm able to control it. It's a controlled rage, if you will. I almost feel like: 'Don't cross my line.'"

◆ ◆ ◆

JORGE POSADA, THE third batter in the top of the ninth inning, gets the next sample of Johnson's power and control.

Posada swings and misses at the first pitch, which gets in the inside of the plate. He leans on his back foot so he can transfer his weight forward decisively. But he's off balance when the ball sizzles in. Blinking, Posada adjusts, shakes his head.

His mind cleared, Posada swings at the next pitch on the outer part of the plate, fouling the ball the other way. He also fouls off the next pitch, just over the knees on the inner part of the plate. The ball dribbles away just to the left of the third base line.

Posada has been hanging tough, but he looks hopeless on the next pitch, a nasty curve on the low inside part of the plate—probably too low and too inside, but something Posada had to whale at anyway. Posada strikes out swinging.

Johnson is just hitting his stride. He's ready to pitch two or three innings if he has to.

◆ ◆ ◆

THE LEGACY OF Randy Johnson will continue long after he retires.

Johnson's success has prompted baseball people to seek out more tall players. Scouts and front-office people now understand that power comes not just from powerful legs, but also from leverage. Major league teams have ordered their scouts to find tall pitchers to take on the game's horde of muscle-bound hitters. Scouts have taken to recruiting college basketball players and traveling as far as China to find long and lean athletes. A Stats Inc. survey of 1,532 pitchers in the game from 1990 to 2000 revealed that 214 pitchers stood at least six feet, five inches, twice as many as those who stood under six feet.

Kevin Towers, the general manager of the San Diego Padres, justifies the shift: "The taller guys are the guys whom the scouts project that their fastball's going to get faster. They've got a larger frame where they can fill out and gain strength. With a smaller pitcher, there's not much projection involved; you can't figure he'll get much more power." Jim Beattie, an executive with the Montreal Expos, adds: "With the bigger guys, we're more patient. The thinking is, we can't teach velocity, but we can teach the breaking ball."

In the last decade, baseball has seen more flamethrowers than any previous period of baseball history. Throwing the ball 100 miles per hour was once considered an oddity, but about a dozen contemporary pitchers have done it—including Roger Clemens and Randy Johnson.

Just how fast will pitchers throw in the future is a matter of speculation. Marvin Chien and John Keefe of the University of Denver have calculated that if certain muscles could be strengthened by 20.8 percent and limb velocity could be increased by 25 percent—which they say is possible—a six-foot, three-inch, 210-pound pitcher could conceivably throw as fast as 135 miles an hour. A seven-foot pitcher weighing 295 pounds could throw 150 miles an hour.

Most experts consider such speeds a fantasy. Pitch speeds today top out at around 102 or 103 miles per hour. That's probably fast enough for most hitters.

Chapter Twenty-Two

BREAKS OF THE GAME

IN THEIR LONG HISTORY of World Series play, the Yankees have won 109 of 110 games that they led after eight innings. And now, with Mariano Rivera pitching in the bottom of the ninth inning, after an overpowering three-strikeout performance in the eighth inning, it seems a foregone conclusion that the Yankees will win this game and the World Series.

The Diamondbacks have never seen anyone like Rivera before. "We saw a couple pitchers during the course of the season who relied a lot on a cut fastball, but there was nobody that had a cutter like Rivera's," said Bob Brenly. On pitch after pitch, the cutter burns into the hitter's hands, even when he's expecting it. The pitch is never a surprise, but the sting is always something of a surprise. Part of the reason is Rivera's motion. "His delivery was so smooth that the ball just seemed to explode out of his hand," Brenly says. "For a guy who seemingly wasn't working very hard on the mound, he was throwing extremely hard, with a lot of late movement on that cutter."

Even though Rivera is starting his second inning of work—which he almost never does during the regular season, but frequently does in the postseason—he is rested. He has not pitched for two days. The teams had an off-day after Game Five, and Game Six was a blowout not requiring Rivera's services. Pitching for two innings should not tax his strength. Manager Joe Torre used Rivera for two innings four times in seventy-one appearances during the regular season in 2001 and four more times in the playoffs and World Series. Rivera was unhittable in the eighth inning—retiring three of four batters on a total of fourteen pitches, with three strikeouts against the heart of the Diamondback lineup.

The Diamondbacks' owner, Jerry Colangelo, is not feeling good about his team's chances. "I was with my wife, hoping and praying that something good would happen. And with each event that unfolded, you know, your energy just goes down, you lose something. But you're excited. I was a little down going into the ninth. It was my wife that was keeping me up."

But the Diamondbacks have a strategy to beat the unbeatable Rivera.

Mike Rizzo, the team's director of scouting, noticed what everybody notices when they watch Rivera—that his cutter veers hard into the hands of left-handed hitters. With the late movement of Rivera's cutter, lefties almost always get jammed. To compensate for Rivera's killer pitches on the hands, the Diamondbacks adopted a one-time-only plan: violate the most basic rule taught to hitters from their days in Little League and *step into the bucket.*

Hitting gurus of all stripes teach batters that it's death to step away from the plate—into an invisible "bucket"—because they take their eyes off the ball and lose the power that comes from shifting their hips into the ball. But the Diamondbacks decided that they needed to step away from the plate to avoid getting jammed by Rivera.

Rizzo explains the strategy. "When Rivera comes in, he throws almost exclusively the cut fastball. To succeed [against Rivera], left-handed hitters have to throw their hips open and make sure they get their hands out and fly open with their bodies."

Left-handed hitters coming up in the inning—Mark Grace and Tony Womack for sure, and Craig Counsell and Luis Gonzalez if the Diamondbacks can get anyone on base—plan to test Rizzo's theory.

"You have to understand that his pitch is going to end up in on your knuckles, if you don't make some kind of an adjustment," Brenly says.

"Some guys who normally would try to hit the ball to the big part of the park, they were throwing that bat head out there, trying to make sure that they got the good part of the bat on the ball, rather than get jammed in on the fists."

Get the ball into play with some wood, and you have a chance. That's not going to happen against Rivera with a full swing.

"That's part of baseball, making adjustments," Brenly says. "Our guys were very good at it all year long, and it came to a head in the last inning of Game Seven in the World Series. Every guy that went to the plate had a game plan in mind of how they were going to do battle against this guy."

◆ ◆ ◆

THE LEFT-HANDED Mark Grace is the first Diamondback to step to the plate. Grace took practice swings on the on-deck circle with Greg Colbrunn, a veteran reserve player who was getting ready to pinch hit for Damian Miller. "Should I be taking a strike, or what do you think?" Grace asks Colbrunn. "Hell no, go up there and take it into the seats," Colbrunn says.

No chance. "If you try to hit home runs off him, you're playing right into his hands," Grace says. "He's going to eat you alive. The thing you've got to do with a guy like him, you can't try to do too much. You just have to take what he gives. If he makes a mistake, then you might be able to do some damage. But he doesn't make many mistakes. It's 96, 97 miles an hour, cutting that much"—he holds his hands a foot apart—"and just bullying you."

Grace's goal is simple—put wood on ball. "My attitude is, by hook or by crook, I've got to get on base. If I don't get on base, we probably don't win the World Series. If I get on base, we can bunt. We can move a runner up. We can put the pressure on the Yankees. If I make an out, and the next guy gets on, that takes away the bunt. If I've got to stick my head in front of one, I will. You'll get over a concussion in month or so. So that was my attitude."

The thirty-seven-year-old Grace has the discipline—and, even as a senior citizen, the bat speed—to watch a pitch longer than most hitters. And he doesn't chase bad pitches.

"Gracie was always just so controlled," Brenly says. "He never really hit for a lot of power, although I think he could have. He had a very controlled swing, and he could control not only the entire strike zone but pitches off the strike zone, away, up, down, in. He could always get a bat on the ball, get a piece of the ball. Just a great contract hitter, with a tremendous eye for the strike zone, very rarely swung at a bad pitch. If you didn't throw him a strike, he'd take his walk.... And he never overextended. He never got out of what he was physically capable of doing."

Rivera retired Grace earlier in the series. Grace knows what he's going to see, but that doesn't make it any easier. "He's got one pitch, and that's the fastball, and some will cut and some won't. But you know there's no tricks to him. That's what makes him so incredible. He's got one pitch. He doesn't have an off-speed pitch. Yet he still dominates, as much as anybody."

Taking a slightly open stance, Grace looks at the first pitch up and inside—a perfect pitch by Rivera, tempting but unhittable. Grace takes a short swing on the next pitch—a cutter, inside, naturally—and hits it into short center field for a leadoff single. As he swings, his feet are both facing Rivera. His arms are extended completely. "You can't try to pull that ball. I mean, it's like a 97-mile-an-hour slider. It's a joke. So you've just got to keep your hands in front of you, let the ball hit the bat. I've always been able to do that kind of stuff."

The ball jumps a foot beyond Rivera's reach, then beyond the reach of shortstop Derek Jeter and second baseman Alfonso Soriano. Bernie Williams fields it in center field after three bounces.

"When you stay inside, that barrel will stay through the strike zone for a while, longer than if you're trying to pull it," says Grace. "And, you know, it was a good pitch by him—and to be quite frank, it was a good piece of hitting by me." He pauses. "It felt great because I got a lot of momentum going in our dugout and kind of put some idea that, you know what, maybe this guy's not invincible. You know, 'If Gracie can hit him, we can probably hit him.'

"It was as clean as any other hit I got. It didn't vibrate. I got it on the barrel. We broke a lot of bats that day. But mine wasn't one of them."

Seconds after Grace reaches first base, Bob Brenly sends Dave Delucci in to run for him. "I realized, my season's over," Grace says. "This dream season is over. Come on, guys, let's go. Let's do it."

The crowd comes alive.

◆ ◆ ◆

BUT BUNTING AGAINST Rivera is hard. Rivera's pitches come in tight on the hands—sizzling toward the upper part of the strike zone—and are not easy to hit on the ground. It would be hard for Damian Miller, the next batter, to get a bunt down.

But Bob Brenly doesn't care about statistical analyses of the bunt, which say it's a loser. His decision to use the sacrifice bunt is automatic. No hesitation. Rather than using Colbrunn to pinch-hit, Brenly decides to keep catcher Miller in the game and have him bunt.

The bunt play offers an opportunity to unsettle the defense. The first and third basemen run toward the plate as the pitcher moves into his windup. That leaves a lot of room on the outer part of the infield for the hitter to tap the ball. It also sharpens the angles for the infielders on a hard-hit ball. Other infielders must re-deploy themselves, too. The second baseman has to cover first base. He has to take a throw at first base, but he's not used to stretching for the ball. The sacrifice also alters the pitcher's plan. A pitcher who ordinarily throws the ball down and away has to pitch up and inside to induce the hitter to pop up the bunt.

Once the hitter puts the bunt down, anything can happen.

Miller fouls off the first pitch off the third base line. Before the next pitch, Rivera throws to first base to keep Delucci close to the bag. Rivera might be able to force Delucci at second base on a bunt if he can prevent him from taking a long lead.

On the next pitch, Miller pulls away from the plate to put the fat part of his bat on the ball. The ball runs in on him, but he bunts it on the ground.

The ball bounces twice toward Rivera, in front of the pitcher's mound. Rivera fields the ball cleanly, turns toward second base. He decides to throw to second for a force play.

In 455 games in the major leagues, Rivera has made just one error. The Panamanian uses his agility as a soccer player to pounce on the ball. He shags balls in the outfield during batting practice and makes an effort to work on grounders—soft ones and hard ones—in infield drills. Rivera is one of the best fielding pitchers in the game.

But Rivera throws the ball away from shortstop Derek Jeter, who is covering second base. Rivera fumbles, slightly, with his footing, and never gets a good grip on the ball. When he releases the ball, it rolls off his hands too late. Rivera doesn't snap the ball. Broadcaster Tim McCarver tells his Fox TV viewers that Rivera is so used to throwing cutters with movement that he can't throw the ball straight to second base. Rivera disagrees, insists that he's made that same play countless times. "I didn't have a good grip on the ball," Rivera says. "If I make a good throw, he's out by far. It just got away from me."

The hobbling Jeter, taking the ball at second base, compounds Rivera's mistake. Waiting for the ball, Jeter tries to stretch to catch the ball for the force play. With one leg reaching back to the bag as he tries to avoid the sliding Delucci, Jeter can't stretch far enough to make the catch. Jeter could come off the bag and tag the base runner, but he's decided to take the throw like a first baseman. Jeter's back foot is on the far side of the bag, requiring him to stretch an extra inch or two.

Delucci tucks his left leg under his body and extends his right leg, shearing Jeter's extended leg. Both players' legs get tangled together. The ball skips off Jeter's glove and bounces into center field. Bernie Williams races from center field and grabs the ball ten feet away on one bounce.

Delucci is safe. The Diamondbacks now have runners on first and second with no outs.

"The bunt play is going to be close if you go to second for a force," Jeter says. "You're going to be playing like a first baseman. The ball ran away and I reached for the ball but I couldn't get it. Then Delucci got me—he cut me on the foot. But it was the World Series. I'm not going to come out of the game."

Bob Brenly has gotten lucky with his decision to have Miller bunt. "I'm a feel manager," he says. This time, his gut feeling worked.

◆ ◆ ◆

THE COMPLEXION OF the game is now completely different.

As Delucci bounces up from his slide, Jeter struggles to get up. He wobbles on his hands and knees. Trainer Gene Monahan runs out of the dugout to look at the shortstop, who earlier strained his ankle on a grounder up the middle. Jeter has faked injuries before—he is a master of decoys to lull the opposing team into complacency. But this time it's real. He has twisted his body throughout the game. Now the twists are hobbling the shortstop.

Should the Diamondbacks bunt again? Bob Brenly does not hesitate to say yes. Jay Bell stands at the plate to pinch hit for Johnson. Bell had eight sacrifice bunts in 2001. In his prime years with the Pittsburgh Pirates, he had thirty-nine sacrifices in 1990 and thirty in 1991.

Rivera's first pitch to Bell veers in toward the inside part of the plate. It's a straight fastball over the plate—probably the best pitch a hitter will ever see from Rivera. It's a hitter's pitch. But Bell is bunting, not swinging away. He taps the ball back to Rivera, just to the third base side of the three-foot-wide dirt path between home and the mound. Rivera's pitch burns in so hard that Bell has to move his bat forward to hit the ball—not the best technique for deadening the ball on a bunt. Bell hits it harder than he would like.

Rivera moves quickly to get to the ball, using both hands to field it. He moves fast, knowing he can get the lead runner at third base and maybe even start a double play. Rivera grabs the ball deliberately. He gets a good grip. He sets and throws to third, stepping forward with a complete motion. He grimaces as he throws. With complete concentration, he guides the ball to third base. But he puts a snap on the ball, too. Perfect throw.

As third baseman Scott Brosius takes the ball, Delucci slides, headfirst, into the bag. He is out by ten feet. If he had gone in feet-first, he might have tripped up Brosius, but he didn't.

Brosius steps politely over the sliding Delucci and walks deliberately toward the center of the diamond. Bell, a slow runner, is only about halfway down the first base line when Brosius tags third base. Tino Martinez waits at first for a throw, but it never comes. On the last play of his major league career, Brosius plays conservatively. There will be no double play.

Greg Colbrunn, waiting on deck to hit, is surprised. "I couldn't believe it. He had the double play. At that point, I knew we had a chance."

"I was surprised, too," says Luis Sojo, a utility infielder for the Yankees. "He had plenty of time. He could make the play."

Posada, watching the play near the plate, says it was a simple matter of not being mentally alert. "We didn't prepare," Posada says. "You get the guy out at third base and you know who the runner is—Bell, and he's not a speedy runner. You got to be able to get the runner. You don't want to make an error, but you got to get the runner at first base. It's too loud for anyone to say anything to Brosius. It's got to come with instincts."

Bob Brenly, the Diamondbacks' manager, can afford to be more diplomatic: "In game-deciding situations, you're always taught to make sure you get the out. Don't try to make a miraculous play. Just make a routine play. And in Brosius's mind, he overestimated how fast Jay was. He did have enough time to make that relay throw across the infield. But his experience in the game told him to take the out, don't try to make the miracle play. You throw the ball away at first base, and all kinds of bad things can happen."

Now, instead of being one out away from a win, the Yankees are two outs away. They have given the Diamondbacks that most precious commodity, an out.

◆ ◆ ◆

When Damian Miller reaches second base on the play, Bob Brenly calls on Midre Cummings to run the bases.

Cummings has played reserve roles for eight years in the major leagues, with Pittsburgh, Philadelphia, Boston (twice), and Minnesota, before coming to Arizona this year. In Cummings, a native of the Virgin Islands, scouts once saw a rare combination of speed and power. He won a starting outfield job with the Phillies in 1997 and starred—hitting .303 in sixty-three games—but got released in spring training the next year. He's never won another full-time job. His role now is to run the bases.

◆ ◆ ◆

WITH NO OUTS and runners on first and second, the Diamondbacks' shortstop, Tony Womack, tries to get a run home. Womack takes the first pitch for a ball. Rivera was trying to tempt him and get ahead in the count. The ball sinks as it moves inside and low. Posada jerks his glove inside to make the catch, so far inside that he cannot "frame" the pitch over the plate. The next pitch is high and inside for another ball. It's 2–0.

Womack faced Rivera once before in the World Series, in the tenth inning of Game Five in New York. Womack grounded out to second base. He broke his bat on—what else?—a cut fastball. Now, for Womack, that groundout is a data point. It tells him something about how hard Rivera throws, how he can get around on the ball, how he just needs to get in front of the ball a fraction of a second sooner. If Rivera gets the ball over the plate, Womack has a chance to hit it hard.

Rivera faces the common dilemma of a pitcher behind in the count. Does he continue to jam the hitter inside, or change the pattern? If Womack steps back from the plate, he might be able to hit the inside pitch. Rivera moves the next pitch over the plate, a little high, but Rivera gets the call from Rippley. Now the count is 2–1. Then Womack fouls off a searing fastball on the outside of the plate. The count is even, 2–2.

Rivera now enjoys the advantage in the battle. He's moving the ball around the plate the way he needs to.

Rivera decides to go back to familiar territory, the inside of the plate. Womack is ready. He stands back in the box. The ball moves in on Womack, but he's far enough back in the box to get the fat of the bat on the ball. Womack lets the ball hit the bat, rather than rotating his body hard to hit it. And Rivera's pitch, while biting, is not as hard as it usually is. The pitch comes in at 94 or 95 miles per hour instead of 97.

That slight difference helps Womack get around on the pitch. Womack uses a short swing, letting go of the bat with his top hand immediately after contact. Womack hits the ball hard to left field. Jorge Posada has positioned his glove on the inside part of the plate, but Rivera throws the ball a couple inches closer to the plate. "I got the pitch inside," Rivera remembers. "Just not inside enough."

Womack was looking inside. He had already seen two good inside pitches.

"That was a broken bat," Rivera says later. "I got into his kitchen and he got his bat out. He hit the ball on the line."

The ball bounces two feet inside the right-field line. Shane Spencer lopes over to pick up the ball right on the right-field line. Spencer steps into the ball, ready for a good long throw, but he doesn't have the time to catch the speedy Cummings rounding third base for home or even Womack going to second base with a double. Bell is a slow runner, but he was running on the pitch and he makes it to third easily.

The score is now tied, two runs apiece.

Diamondbacks' owner Jerry Colangelo doesn't know what to make of the unfolding play. He jumps up, looks, starts to cheer, stops. His eyes dart around different parts of the field—the outfield, then the plate, then the base paths—before he is confident enough to exult.

◆ ◆ ◆

WITH WOMACK'S DOUBLE, the game has taken its biggest shift, statistically speaking.

The Diamondbacks' chances of winning increase from 35.4 to 84.3 percent, according to one analysis. Mathematician Doug Drinen has determined a team's chance to win a game in every conceivable situation. Drinen, a lifelong baseball fan who teaches at the University of the South in Sewanee, Tennessee, calculates the changing odds for every at bat over the course of the game. Here are some of the twists and turns of the game so far:

Inning	Event	Change in odds
Top of first	Batting leadoff, the Yankees' Derek Jeter strikes out	Yankees' odds of winning decline from 50 percent to 47.8 percent
Home second	With one out, the Diamondbacks' Mark Grace singles, putting runners on first and second	Diamondbacks' odds improve from 55.4 to 59.2 percent
Home sixth	With no outs, Danny Bautista's double scores Steve Finley with the game's first run	Diamondbacks' odds improve from 62.9 to 71.3 percent
Top of sixth	With one out, the Yankees' Tino Martinez ties the game, 1–1, with a single	Yankees' odds improve from 43.4 to 56.2 percent
Top of eighth	Leading off, the Yankees' Alfonso Soriano homers to give the Yankees a 2–1 lead	Yankees' odds improve from 50 to 73.6 percent
Home eighth	With two outs, the Diamondbacks' Danny Bautista strikes out to end the inning	Diamondbacks' odds decline from 24.2 to 17.3 percent
Home ninth	With one out, Tony Womack's double ties the score, 2–2	Diamondbacks' odds improve from 35.4 to 84.3 percent

The average baseball game has upwards of four hundred observable events, and countless twitches and nods, decisions, and plays not made. Every one of those events can change the complexion of the game. Statistics provide a general hint about how much.

Tony Womack's double has turned the 2001 World Series upside down.

◆ ◆ ◆

As THE ADVANTAGE in World Series games veers back and forth between the Yankees and Diamondbacks, the on-field reporters for Fox TV and ESPN run back and forth behind the stands, between the two dugouts. They want to be in the winning dugout when the game ends to get interviews. But the balance of power has shifted so quickly that the reporters do not know where to be. In the last two games in New York, when the Yankees staged ninth-inning rallies, they rushed madly from the visiting to the home dugout.

Now, they are standing in the Yankees' dugout watching the game collapse for the champions, wondering whether they should somehow make their way to the Diamondbacks' bench. But if they do, who's to say the Yankees will not stage another late comeback?

"The distance between the dugouts, under the stands, is greater at the BOB than at Yankee Stadium," says Charley Steiner, the reporter for ESPN. "Are we going to going back to the Arizona side? No, we decide to stay in the Yankees' dugout. If the Diamondbacks win, we're going to have to rush past the Yankees as they come into the dugout."

◆ ◆ ◆

THE SLIGHT CRAIG COUNSELL comes to the plate. The Yankees move the infielders and outfielders in. The infielders are playing on the inner lip of the infield dirt, with the base runners behind them, hoping for a possible play at the plate. The left-handed-hitting second baseman doesn't have a lot of power.

The second baseman is the only Diamondbacks player who has played for a World Series champion. He scored the winning run for the 1997 Florida Marlins team that beat the Cleveland Indians in the eleventh inning of Game Seven. Counsell was a man without a team in 2000 when he agreed to play in the minor leagues for the Diamondbacks' AAA affiliate in Tucson. He got a chance to play regularly in 2001 when injuries put Matt Williams and Tony Womack on the disabled list. When baseball resumed play after September 11, Bob Brenly benched Jay Bell at second base in favor of Counsell.

◆ ◆ ◆

LUIS GONZALEZ fantasizes as he stands in the on-deck circle watching Counsell, a left-handed hitter, at the plate. He imagines what it will be like to celebrate if Counsell gets the hit to win the game. He can see himself getting in the middle of the celebration pictures.

"I'm just trying to take everything in. This guy [Counsell], he's going to win the World Series right here. Where do I want to be, in the pictures and all? You know, I'm a fan, too. And you watch the Super Bowls and the World Series of the past and the NBA Finals, and you still get goose bumps, things like that, when you watch it."

Counsell hits the first pitch, a cutter moving in on his fists—vintage Rivera—foul the opposite way. Counsell got a good swing at the ball, extending his arms, but the ball veered in toward the bat handle and Counsell hit over the ball. The ball squirted toward third base. Rivera was sharp—and was now ahead in the count, 0–1.

Rivera stays inside on the next pitch. Counsell leans his body back, wagging his bat behind him, but keeps his fists in the hitting zone. The pitch hits Counsell's right wrist. Counsell skips happily to first base.

Now the bases are loaded for the Diamondbacks' best hitter, Luis Gonzalez.

Did Counsell take the pitch for the team? Did he do less than he could to get out of the way of the pitch? On the replay, it looks like he put his hands into the pitch as he leans his lanky body back. He says no.

"I don't think anyone wants to get hit by a pitch. You have the opportunity to win the World Series. I've had some big hits in big games before, so I can do it. Even Don Baylor would tell you the same thing." Right now, Baylor is baseball's all-time leader in getting hit by pitches; he did it 267 times.

"I wasn't trying to get hit," Counsell says. "It was the same situation in 1997." That's when Counsell got a crucial hit in the Florida Marlins' winning rally late in the seventh game of the World Series. "With a man on third, I thought, 'Okay, now I'm going to be aggressive.' It's not a time to be patient. You're against Rivera, who comes in on you, and you don't think about getting too close to the plate."

Mark Grace, bouncing around the Arizona dugout, is giddy. "Now, hell, we've got our best offensive player in the box, against their best pitcher," he says. "Something's going to happen here."

Curt Schilling sits still in the dugout. "I wouldn't move on the bench," he says later. "I wanted to get up and watch for the whole inning, but I was playing the luck seat."

The pitcher who takes a more rational approach to the game than anyone else, it seems, is superstitious.

Whatever it takes.

Chapter Twenty-Three

END GAME

On the eve of the World Series, the Diamondbacks' owner, Jerry Colangelo, had a fantasy.

A reporter asked whether he would predict a Diamondbacks' victory over the Yankees.

"I said, no, but I'll tell you what I want. I want this Series to go seven games. I want to win it in front of our home crowd in the ninth inning, with the score tied, the bases loaded, two outs, and Gonzo at the plate. So as it was unfolding, I knew."

Now Luis Gonzalez steps up to the plate with the bases loaded and the score tied 2–2.

Waiting to hit, Gonzalez imagines the scene like a fan.

"Just walking up, there are so many things going through your mind," Gonzalez remembers. "I mean, I was thinking, here I am, thirty-plus years old. It's been an awesome season for me. Hit all the home runs. Here I am in a dream situation. You know, if I get the hit, story-book season. If I don't get the hit, I let everybody down. I've got things going through my mind. What's my family thinking now? You know,

I'm standing and looking around. I mean, you've got fifty-thousand-plus people on their feet. You know the whole world is watching this game. It's Game Seven. It's not Game One or Two, where the audience is so-so. Somebody's leaving a champion, and the other team is going home. It's strange, and you don't know how you're going to react. Never been in that situation before."

Gonzalez has become a power hitter in recent years, but now was a good time to revert to his slap-hitting ways. If he could get the ball past the infield, the Diamondbacks would become world champions.

Before the game, Posada talked with Clemens and other pitchers about how to get Gonzalez. "We talked about Gonzalez a lot," Posada says. "Obviously, by the seventh game of the World Series we had seen him quite a few at bats already and I thought that Gonzalez was not getting to pitches on the inside, and I told them that before the game. Especially a good fastball like Clemens had."

Gonzalez saw Rivera in the eighth inning. No other hitter hit against Rivera more than once in a game all year.

Seeing Rivera's pitches earlier in the game—and feeling them bore into his hands—gives Gonzalez a unique advantage. Batters learn over the course of a game, improving their hitting as they see a pitcher for a second or third time. Crunching the numbers on 1.69 million at bats between 1984 and 1995, David W. Smith found that batters hit .259 in the first at bat, .268 on the second, .272 on the third, and .276 on the fourth.

Gonzalez decides to make one adjustment this turn at the plate. He chokes up. He did not choke up, not once, all year. He didn't choke up in the eighth inning. He was going for a home run. "He struck me out last time on cutters, and you know he's going to do a cutter again," says Gonzalez. "So you know what? In my dream, I hit a home run. In reality, all I've got to do now is put the ball in play."

The Yankees' infielders met on the mound to talk strategy. Everyone shows up—Rivera and catcher Jorge Posada, corner infielders Scott Brosius and Tino Martinez, shortstop Derek Jeter and second baseman Alfonso Soriano.

Here's an idea: maybe the Yankees should play the infield back and the outfield in, since long fly balls would be sacrifice flies and extra-base hits don't matter anyway, with the winning run on third base. Another option is to play the corner infielders in and let the second baseman and shortstop play back. That's what the Yankees did with the score tied at two runs apiece and the bases loaded in the ninth inning of Game Five. It worked. Alfonso Soriano nabbed a scorching liner up the middle to save one or two runs from scoring.

But the Yankees worry about a ground ball moving slowly through the wet infield grass at Bank One Ballpark, allowing Bell to score from third base.

"We talked about different ways to play it," Posada says. "We thought of bringing in just the two corner infielders. If the ball's hit hard up the middle we could go for a double play. But we finally decided to play all the infielders and outfielders in. Mariano's such a good pitcher and gets a lot of jam shots, so we decided to play the infield in. It's a gamble you take. It could work, or it might not. You think he's going to either strike them out or hit the ball where we can field it."

Jeter thinks the decision is easy. "There's not much of a conversation to have on that play. You can't play back because not too many people are going to hit the ball hard enough against Mo. If you play back and you get a ground ball, you're not going to be able to get the runner. Mo jams most left-handers and in order to turn a double play it's got to be a hard-hit ground ball. The only thing that might happen if you play back is you catch that ball, and you get one out and then you go and get another out. But you're not going to get a double play on a ground ball, so to keep the game tied on a grounder you have to play the infield in."

When he's not striking out batters, Rivera usually gets groundouts. During the 2001 season, hitters grounded out 102 times against Rivera and popped up 53 times. In his postseason career, the count is 59 to 36; in 2001, it's 25 to 9. But Gonzalez tends to hit the ball into the air. In addition to his 57 homers, he hit 36 doubles and 7 triples in 2001. He grounded out 135 times and popped-up 194 times.

So it's a ground ball pitcher against a fly ball hitter. It's almost a matter of chance whether Rivera would get Gonzalez to hit the ball on the ground or in the air.

Shane Spencer, who has been brought in from a deep right-field position to play just behind the infield, knows the risks of playing everyone in. "Here I am playing thirty, forty feet from the infield dirt. You're taking a chance. But the chances of Gonzalez squaring a ball up against Rivera are not that good."

"I probably would have done the same thing," says Mark Grace. "If you play it back and he hits a broken-bat ground ball, you can't turn two and the winning run's going to score and people are going to ask, 'Hey, how come you didn't play him in?' So you're damned if you do, and you're damned if you don't."

Still, Tim McCarver wonders about the decision. "Left-handers get a lot of broken-bat hits into the shallow part of the outfield," McCarver tells his TV audience. "That's the danger of bringing the infield in with a guy like Rivera on the mound."

Gonzalez talked to himself as the Yankees met on the mound. "When they decided to bring the infield in, I was just hoping to get something—just loop anything out there," he says. "But the way [Rivera] throws with the cutter in, I think they were thinking if I hit a weak ground ball, that run's going to score, and they wouldn't be able to turn a double play." But they can get the runner at home on a soft grounder if they play the infield in.

Mike Rizzo's scouting report is on Gonzalez's mind when he faces Rivera. "Yeah! Step in the bucket!" says Gonzalez. "You know what he's going to throw. It's not like he's going to trick you up there with something different. You've still got to go up there and hit it. That's what is so good about baseball. You can know what the pitcher's going to throw and all kinds of things, but it's still the human element of the game is in going out there and performing and trying to get the job done."

Gonzalez fouls back the first pitch. He hits the pitch on the inside part of the strike zone, back behind the plate. Gonzalez's timing is off. He is too late and he cuts under the ball. He steps back and breathes heavily.

◆ ◆ ◆

PRODUCERS FOR FOX TV use all the tricks of Hollywood—cross-cutting shots that jump from the dugout to the field, never more than a few seconds for any one shot, close-ups that show the burning eyes and the sweat and the pores of the skin—to gin up the tension.

The producers sitting in a truck outside the stadium bark orders: *Get Rivera! Cut to Jeter! Cut to Torre! Back to Mo! Get Grace again!*

In the last half-inning, from the time the broadcast returned from a commercial break to the game's final moment, Fox shows 263 pictures, an average of 2.27 seconds for each image. The camera cuts quickly, back and forth, to images of Mariano Rivera, Joe Torre, Bob Brenly, Mark Grace, Jerry Colangelo, Curt Schilling, Randy Johnson, Paul O'Neill, Steve Finley, Craig Counsell, Yankees' general manager Brian Cashman, Derek Jeter's father Charles, nail-biting fans, the increasingly raucous Arizona dugouts, and the pom-pom waving crowd. That is two or three times the number of "cinematic techniques" per minute that a typical Hollywood movie or TV show uses.

The images jump so fast that the broadcasters have a hard time keeping up. Long after Delucci is shown replacing Grace on first base and a new hitter comes to the plate, broadcaster Joe Buck tells the audience about the move.

◆ ◆ ◆

Just as Rivera gets ready to throw the next pitch, Diamondbacks' manager Bob Brenly experiences a mild panic attack.

"That ninth inning happened so quickly, and it seemed like we used so many players," Brenly recalls. "I turned to Bob Melvin, the bench coach, and I said, 'God, do we have everything covered?' My concern was, who are we going to send out there defensively if this game stays tied?" Grace is out of the game. So is Miller. So is Johnson. Who, he wonders, would pitch, play first base, and catch? Colbrunn—who stood on deck on three separate occasions this inning, patiently waiting for a chance to pinch-hit, forever caught in a batter's purgatory—could play first base. Rod Barajas could catch. Forty-year-old Mike Morgan could pitch. Morgan has been warming up in the bullpen with Byung-Hyun Kim, but Brenly didn't want Kim. Not after Kim blew two games in New York.

In that moment of doubt, Brenly turns away from the action on the field, and almost misses the final play of the game.

But Brenly looks back to the field in time.

◆ ◆ ◆

MARIANO RIVERA, IN that trancelike state that accompanies all his pitches, gets ready to throw the ball. He has a strike on Gonzalez—a good start. He looks down, spits, and moves into his motion from the stretch position.

Gonzalez waits on the next pitch, like he knows what's coming.

The ball veers in about belt-high on the inside of the plate. Gonzalez, this one time, abandons his open-then-closed stance. He keeps his body open, facing the pitcher, as Rivera throws a fastball in on the hands. It's an almost-perfect pitch from Rivera.

Gonzalez hits the ball right under the label—"Right over my thumbs," he says. "My hands were stinging."

The bat produces a *thunk*, not a *crack*. That's usually bad news for the batter. It means he didn't hit the ball well.

The infielders know what's happening. They stand still, stuck in their drawn-in positions.

In the owner's box, Jerry Colangelo watches the ball float into the outfield: "It was like time was frozen. When he hit the ball, it just looked like the ball was suspended and it was not ever going to come down. And I found myself screaming: 'Get down! Get down! Get down!'"

Jay Bell knows what is happening and races home from third base, clapping his hands, moving in a herky-jerky way, exuberant, screaming.

The stadium is silent, at least for that moment in time, for Colangelo and the rest of the Diamondbacks. "I looked over at Jay, at third, and it looked like he was running in slow motion, all the way, until he hit home plate," says Colangelo. "And then, in my mind, it was like an explosion."

Mark Grace, watching from the dugout, experiences an overwhelming burst of emotion—"A feeling that I've never felt before, including the birth of my children. Happiness, relief, joy, accomplishment. It made it all worth it—those years that I lost in Chicago, the years in the minor leagues, when you're making seven hundred bucks a month, living with six other guys in a shit-hole in Peoria, Illinois, and Pittsfield, Massachusetts."

Jeter stands helpless on the infield grass. The ball glides over the left side of second base, just beyond the infield dirt, and falls softly, like a beach ball, onto the damp outfield grass.

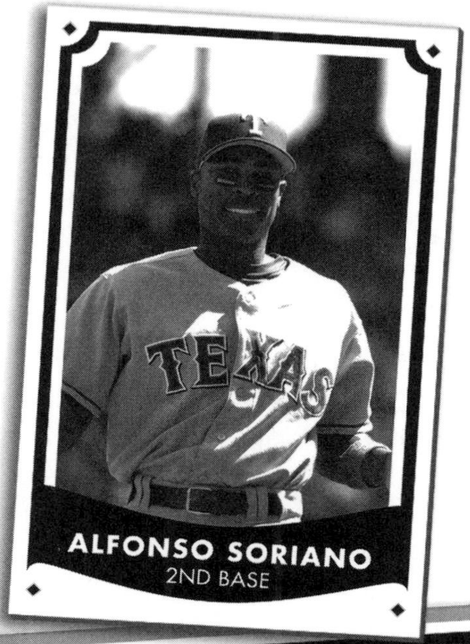

Many of the top players in the 2001 World Series —including Curt Schilling and Alfonso Soriano— moved on to starring roles with other teams. In 2004, Schilling helped the Boston Red Sox win their first World Series championship in eighty-six years, while Soriano starred for the Texas Rangers.

Photos by Isabel Chenoweth

POSTGAME

In which the champions celebrate their victory, the vanquished make plans to restore their empire, and one player quietly thanks God for the game's saving grace

Chapter Twenty-Four

ECSTASY AND AGONY

With his soft hit—a hit that broke his bat, a hit that would have been a harmless pop fly to shortstop Derek Jeter if the Yankees' infielders had played in their normal positions—Luis Gonzalez jerks both of his arms into the air in celebration.

The players, coaches, trainers, and hangers-on in the Diamondbacks' dugout spill onto the field. Grounds crew members push a large stage onto the outfield. Reporters for Fox TV skitter about, looking for players to interview—Luis Gonzalez, Mark Grace, Tony Womack. Soon, the Bank One Ballpark's sound system booms the classic anthem of triumph, Queen's "We Are the Champions."

"There's just absolutely no way to prepare for the emotions that come out at a moment like that," says Bob Brenly, the Diamondbacks' manager. "You always wonder what will it be like, what would I do, but there's no way you can anticipate or choreograph what's going to happen. While we were all out there on the field, I saw grown men crying their eyes out. Mike Morgan kissed me. The emotions I saw on the field that night from those veteran players who had ridden the buses and taken the cortisone shots and had the surgeries, and the good years and the bad years...now they all had something that they could hang their hat on and be proud of, and it didn't matter what happened from that point on."

No player enjoyed the status of champion more than Luis Gonzalez. The ultimate fan as well as the hero of the Diamondbacks' World Series stirring rally, Gonzalez knows that this experience will be with him always.

"The biggest thrill for me is when...somebody's wearing your jersey, or somebody comes up to you and says, 'I still remember 2001, the World Series, where I was at when you got that hit.' And to me, that's priceless. They can't take that away from you." Years later, Gonzalez still reveled in his game-winning hit. "I probably hit it right under the label—right over my thumbs, really," Gonzalez later remembered. "My teammates made fun of me. They said I was jumping up and down, not from joy but from my hand stinging from where I hit the ball."

Yankees' executives took a philosophical approach to the loss. Losing a great World Series didn't hurt so much in light of 9/11 and the team's healing role in New York after the attacks. Rick Cerrone, the Yankees' top PR man and a lifelong Beatles' fan, found solace in the words of Paul McCartney. "There was something about 2001 that seemed predestined, something that was greater than any of us," Cerrone says. "Even Boston rooted for us after 9/11. The plays in the ninth inning of Game Seven were unlike us, but I still thought we were going to win. But it doesn't work that way. I remember when Linda McCartney died, Paul said, 'No one gets away with a perfect life.'"

The Yankees returned to Yankee Stadium, one by one, to clean out their lockers and say good-bye for the winter. Mariano Rivera decided he was glad he gave up the game-winning hit to Luis Gonzalez.

Rivera noted that Enrique Wilson, a utility infielder for the Yankees, was planning to take American Airlines Flight 587 to his home in the Dominican Republic on November 12. Wilson changed his plans when the Yankees lost the Series and canceled their victory parade down the Canyon of Heroes in New York. The flight that Wilson had planned to take crashed in Queens, New York, killing all 264 people on board.

When baseball came back to life in the spring of 2002, the Diamondbacks and Yankees remained dominant. Some of the players who took the field for the Yankees and Diamondbacks were different, but both teams continued to win.

The Yankees continued to dominate baseball in the next four years, winning an average of 100 games a year (the next best team, the Atlanta Braves, averaged 97 wins over that span). The Yankees won another four consecutive American League East division titles in 2002, 2003, 2004, and 2005. The Yankees could not be expected to win forever, but they planned to try. Owner George Steinbrenner spent record sums on salaries to get the game's premier players in pinstripes. The Yankees' payroll ran over $200 million in 2005, at least twice as big as even close competitors and four times as big as many small-market teams. The Yankees obtained baseball's greatest sluggers—Jason Giambi, Alex Rodriguez, Gary Sheffield. The Yankees only lost one major offensive player. To get Rodriguez, arguably the best player in baseball, the Yankees traded Alfonso Soriano to the Texas Rangers. Soriano became an all-star, but A-Rod did better, winning his second Most Valuable Player award in three years in 2005. Before the 2005 season the Yankees obtained Randy Johnson.

The Yankees seemed to lust over every premier player in the game. The front-page headline in the satiric newspaper *The Onion* said it all: "Yankees Ensure 2003 Pennant by Signing Every Player in Baseball." The spoof article quoted Steinbrenner: "We'd like to welcome the entire roster of Major League Baseball into the Yankees' family. With these acquisitions, we are in position to finally nab that elusive twenty-seventh World Series title."

The Yankees set a team attendance record of 4,090,000 in 2005, with an average of 50,500 fans a game—the best in all of baseball. An average of almost 40,000 fans flocked to every Yankee road game. After years of lobbying the state and city governments for a new stadium on the west side of Manhattan, the Yankees announced plans in 2005 to build a new stadium in the Bronx near the current Yankee Stadium.

Despite their superiority during the regular season, the Yankees returned to the World Series in only 2003, when they lost to the Florida Marlins. They suffered the greatest humiliation in postseason history in 2004. After winning the first three games of the best-of-seven American League Championship Series, the Yankees lost the next four games and the pennant to their bitter rivals, the Boston Red Sox. The Red Sox went on to win the World Series, ending a period of eighty-six years without a championship. One of the stars of the Red Sox triumph was Curt Schilling, who got fifty-five stitches on his right ankle to prevent a loose tendon from snapping off. The Red Sox gave out their glittering World Series rings in a 2005 ceremony at Fenway Park with the Yankees looking on (to their credit, clapping).

The Diamondbacks won 98 games and the 2002 National League's Western Division title, with Randy Johnson and Curt Schilling enjoying even more sparkling seasons on the mound. But with both Johnson and Schilling injured for much of 2003, the Diamondbacks fell into third place. Then the bottom fell out. In 2004, the Diamondbacks lost a team-record 101 games.

By the 2005 season, the only players remaining from the 2001 championship team were Luis Gonzalez and Craig Counsell. Johnson and Schilling were gone. So was Steve Finley, whose grand slam home run in the final game of the 2004 season helped the Los Angeles Dodgers win the National League's Western Division title. So were Mark Grace and Matt Williams, who retired. So was Damian Miller, the steady catcher who went on to manage the pitching staffs of the Chicago Cubs, Oakland Athletics, and Milwaukee Brewers. So was Tony Womack, who moved on to the St. Louis Cardinals and then the Yankees. Byung-Hyun Kim played for the Boston Red Sox. Danny Bautista retired before the 2005 season.

When a team falls apart, the manager gets fired. Bob Brenly lost his job as Diamondbacks' manager in 2004 when the team struggled to a 29–50 record in the first half of the season. Over his three and a half years piloting the team, the Diamondbacks had an overall record of 303–262. Brenly became a broadcaster with the Chicago Cubs in 2005.

Things got so bad for the Diamondbacks in 2004 that they actually fired the head of their ownership group, Jerry Colangelo. The team was taken over by Jeffrey Moorad, who made his millions as an agent for players.

The gig was up for the Diamondbacks and their managing partner, who played his own version of the Joe Hardy role in *Damn Yankees*, buying a band of talented veteran players on a play-now-pay-later plan. The difference is that Jerry Colengelo did not negotiate an escape clause for his bargain.

But he still has his World Series ring.

New York Yankees

PITCHERS

NO.	PLAYER	B	T	HT.	WT.	BORN	CITY
22	Roger Clemens	R	R	6-4	238	Aug 4, 1962	Dayton, OH
26	Orlando Hernandez	R	R	6-3	190	Oct 11, 1969	Villa Clara, Cuba
41	Sterling Hitchcock	L	L	6-0	205	Apr 29, 1971	Fayetteville, NC
55	Ramiro Mendoza	R	R	6-2	175	Jun 15, 1972	Los Santos, Panama
35	Mike Mussina	R	R	6-2	185	Dec 8, 1968	Williamsport, PA
46	Andy Pettitte	L	L	6-5	225	Jun 15, 1972	Baton Rouge, LA
42	Mariano Rivera	R	R	6-2	185	Nov 29, 1969	Panama City, Panama
29	Mike Stanton	L	L	6-1	215	Jun 2, 1967	Houston, TX
45	Jay Witasick	R	R	6-4	235	Aug 28, 1972	Baltimore, MD
39	Mark Wohlers	R	R	6-4	207	Jan 23, 1970	Holyoke, MA

CATCHERS

NO.	PLAYER	B	T	HT.	WT.	BORN	CITY
43	Todd Greene	R	R	5-10	206	May 8, 1971	Augusta, GA
20	Jorge Posada	B	R	6-2	200	Aug 17, 1971	Santurce, PR

INFIELDERS

NO.	PLAYER	B	T	HT.	WT.	BORN	CITY
12	Clay Bellinger	R	R	6-3	195	Nov 8, 1968	Oneonta, NY
18	Scott Brosius	R	R	6-1	202	Aug 15, 1966	Hillsboro, OR
2	Derek Jeter	R	R	6-3	195	Jun 26, 1974	Pequannock, NJ
24	Tino Martinez	L	R	6-2	210	Dec 7, 1967	Tampa, FL
19	Luis Sojo	R	R	5-11	185	Jan 3, 1966	Caracas, Venezuela
33	Alfonso Soriano	R	R	6-1	180	Jan 7, 1978	San Pedro de Macoris, DR
25	Randy Velarde	R	R	6-0	200	Nov 24, 1962	Midland, TX
14	Enrique Wilson	B	R	5-11	180	Jul 27, 1975	Santo Domingo, DR

OUTFIELDERS

NO.	PLAYER	B	T	HT.	WT.	BORN	CITY
28	David Justice	L	L	6-3	200	Apr 14, 1966	Cincinnati, OH
11	Chuck Knoblauch	R	R	5-9	170	July 7, 1968	Houston, TX
21	Paul O'Neill	L	L	6-4	215	Feb 25, 1963	Columbus, OH
47	Shane Spencer	R	R	5-11	225	Feb 20, 1972	Key West, FL
51	Bernie Williams	B	R	6-2	205	Sept 13, 1968	San Juan, PR

Manager: Joe Torre
General Manager: Brian Cashman

Arizona Diamondbacks

PITCHERS

NO.	PLAYER	B	T	HT.	WT.	BORN	CITY
34	Brian Anderson	B	L	6-1	183	Apr 26, 1972	Portsmouth, VA
43	Miguel Batista	R	R	6-2	195	Feb 19, 1971	Santo Domingo, DR
54	Troy Browhawn	L	L	6-1	190	Jan 14, 1973	Cambridge, MD
51	Randy Johnson	R	L	6-10	232	Sept 10, 1963	Walnut Creek, CA
49	Byung-Hyun Kim	R	R	5-11	177	Jan 21, 1979	Kwangsan-Ku Songjunsdon, South Korea
32	Albie Lopez	R	R	6-2	240	Aug 18, 1971	Mesa, AZ
36	Mike Morgan	R	R	6-2	226	Oct 8, 1959	Tulare, CA
38	Curt Schilling	R	R	6-4	231	Nov 14, 1966	Anchorage, AL
22	Greg Swindell	L	L	6-3	230	Jan 2, 1965	Fort Worth, TX
40	Bobby Witt	R	R	6-2	205	May 11, 1964	Arlington, VA

CATCHERS

NO.	PLAYER	B	T	HT.	WT.	BORN	CITY
48	Rod Barajas	R	R	6-2	220	Sept 5, 1975	Ontario, CA
26	Damian Miller	R	R	6-2	212	Oct 13, 1969	La Crosse, WI

INFIELDERS

NO.	PLAYER	B	T	HT.	WT.	BORN	CITY
33	Jay Bell	R	R	6-0	184	Dec 11, 1965	Eglin A.F.B., FL
28	Greg Colbrunn	R	R	6-0	212	Jul 26, 1969	Fintana, CA
4	Craig Counsell	R	R	6-0	175	Aug 21, 1970	South Bend, IN
44	Erubiel Durazo	L	L	6-3	225	Jan 23, 1974	Hermosillo, Mexico
17	Mark Grace	L	L	6-2	200	Jun 28, 1964	Winston-Salem, NC
9	Matt Williams	R	R	6-2	219	Nov 28, 1965	Bishop, CA
6	Tony Womack	L	R	5-9	170	Sept 25, 1969	Danville, VA

OUTFIELDERS

NO.	PLAYER	B	T	HT.	WT.	BORN	CITY
29	Danny Bautista	R	R	5-11	170	May 24, 1972	Santo Domingo, DR
13	Midre Cummings	L	R	6-0	195	Oct 14, 1971	Saint Croix, VI
25	Dave Delucci	L	L	5-10	198	Oct 31, 1973	Baton Rouge, LA
12	Steve Finley	L	L	6-2	180	Mar 12, 1965	Union City, TN
20	Luis Gonzalez	L	R	6-2	195	Sept 2, 1967	Tampa, FL
16	Reggie Sanders	R	R	6-1	205	Dec 1, 1967	Forence, SC

Manager: Bob Brenly
General Manager: Joe Garagiola Jr.

INDEX

Aaron, Hank (Henry), 79, 143, 153, 218, 231
Adrenaline, 121, 133, 235, 255, 256
Alomar, Sandy, Jr., 240
American Sports Medicine Institute, 113–116, 183, 224
Andrews, James, 113
Anger, 52, 191–193, 197, 261-263
Arizona Diamondbacks, 11, 17, 57, 61, 62, 64, 65, 73, 89, 139, 145, 148, 154, 169, 209, 253, 254, 266
Arm strength and injuries, 4, 42, 50, 84, 86, 87, 110, 112, 115
    effects of early career, 18, 113, 158
    mechanics, 115, 129, 158, 182, 183, 197, 235, 237, 242, 243, 257–259
Athletic Desire Index, 196
Baker, Dusty, 75, 77, 80, 81
Bank One Ballpark, 29, 59, 60, 160, 168, 208, 276, 281, 289
Baseball Prospectus, 10, 164, 166
Baserunning, 9, 10, 165, 173, 202
    aggressiveness, 10, 98, 99
    importance, 9, 10, 165
Batista, Miguel, 203, 209, 223, 234, 235, 255
Bautista, Danny, 8, 17, 28, 30, 46, 55, 57, 102, 110–112, 119, 156, 161, 163, 164, 167–175, 203, 223, 229, 230, 248, 275, 292
Bell, Jay, 61, 62, 135, 146, 170, 174, 184, 271, 272, 276, 281, 284, 295
Blitzer, Billy, 35, 193, 240, 242
Bonds, Barry, 21, 22, 79, 88, 135, 136
Brain and physical actions, 2, 18, 19, 52, 73, 77, 80, 83, 84, 100, 149, 186, 219, 242, 244
Brenly, Bob, 5, 25, 57, 65, 70, 72, 96, 127, 137, 144–149, 163–166, 169, 170, 175, 188, 203, 209, 234, 235, 239, 254, 255, 265–271, 273, 276, 283, 290, 292, 293
Brosius, Scott, 70, 82, 171, 172, 209, 233, 271, 272, 280
Caminiti, Ken, 22
Carew, Rod, 134
Carroll, Will, 158
Catching, 4, 9, 45–58, 183, 192, 222, 273
    calling pitches, 45, 46, 48, 51, 96
    framing pitches, 49, 50
    importance of experience, 44–46, 48
    relationship with pitchers, 45–47, 51, 52, 96
    umpires, 50, 55, 56
Cerrone, Richard, 290
Chapman, Kenneth, 144
Chien, Marvin, 264
Christensen, Donald, 196
Clemens, Roger, 11, 12, 46, 53, 55–58, 62, 70, 71, 73, 82, 89, 94, 95, 98, 100, 101, 103, 104, 107–122, 136–139, 156,159–161, 164–169, 179, 182, 197, 210, 235, 241, 260, 264, 280
Colangelo, Jerry, 283, 284
Colbrunn, Craig, 19, 146, 267, 269, 272, 283
Coleman, Gene, 94
Complete games, 127, 167, 203, 211, 212
Corzatt, Richard, 174
Counsell, Craig, 8, 9, 11, 12, 70–73, 98, 135, 137, 138, 145
Csikszentmihalyi, Mihaly, 28
Cummings, Midre, 272, 274
Cutoff plays, 8–10, 35, 36, 41, 43, 63, 135, 171, 231
    replay plays, 36, 53, 131, 277
Damn Yankees, 62, 292
Dedeaux, Rod, 258, 262
Defense Independent Pitching Statistics (DIPS), 155, 178, 180
Defensive positioning, 9, 11, 17, 34, 36, 37, 39–44, 48, 49, 81, 96, 98, 139, 147, 148, 154, 155, 167, 177, 180, 198, 200, 245
Delucci, Dave, 269–271, 283
Denbo, Gary, 129
DePodesta, Paul, 197
DeRenne, Coop, 81
Diamond Mind Baseball, 180
Dominican Republic, 42, 43, 163, 218, 223, 224, 226, 229, 290
Downs, Rick, 195
Draft, amateur, 224, 258
Drinen, Doug, 157, 274
Eskersley, Dennis, 212, 240
Events that affect odds of winning, 275
Expected Future Runs, 165
Feet, 20, 81, 85, 117, 241, 258, 259, 263, 268
Fielding statistics, 25, 27, 34, 37–40, 155
Fielding, 24, 27, 28, 38, 98, 237, 238, 258
    Diamondbacks' excellence, 26, 27, 30, 97
    importance, 37, 89
    (See also infield, outfield, catcher, relays and cutoff)
Finley, Steve, 8, 17–20, 23–32, 24, 89, 133, 145, 159–161, 163–167, 169, 172, 195, 204, 247, 275, 283, 292
Flow, 28, 138, 237, 238

Foreign players, 218, 219, 223–225
Friend, Bob, 254
Gambling, 7–12, 64
 2001 World Series odds, 64, 65, 275
Game of inspection, 167
Game preparation, 45, 93, 94, 96, 98, 101, 145, 147, 235, 240, 255, 263
Gerardi, Joe, 46
Giambi, Jeremy, 35, 36
Gladwell, Malcolm, 84
Gonzalez, Luis, 11, 12, 19, 28, 30, 67, 70, 72, 135, 138, 145, 159, 245, 245, 266, 276, 277, 279–282, 284, 289, 290, 292
Grace, Mark, 26, 43, 44, 52, 56, 57, 61, 65, 70, 97, 98, 101, 102, 119, 120, 131, 13, 145, 146, 166, 175, 197, 202, 205, 222, 234, 245, 266–269, 275, 277, 282–284, 289, 292
Green, Dallas, 144
Grinding, 194
 Tino Martinez at-bat in fifth inning, 128, 129, 136, 137, 139
Guerrero, Vladimir, 231
Gustafson, Cliff, 109, 121
Gwynn, Tony, 78, 99, 120
Hang time, 30, 31
Henderson, Rickey, 165, 175
Hernandez, Orlando, 47, 223
Hershiser, Orel, 181
Heus, Edythe, 19, 21, 29, 31, 32
Hirschbeck, Mark, 53, 56
Hit zones, 222, 248
Hitting mechanics, 8, 70, 77, 82–89, 129, 182, 183, 197, 201, 277
Hitting, 42, 69–73, 244
 stances, 75, 77–79, 83, 88
 linear versus rotational, 75, 78, 79, 83, 85, 87, 88, 117
 One-Hand Fred, 75, 77, 79, 80, 82, 134
Holtzman, Jerome, 211
Home runs, 22, 29, 51, 75, 76, 88, 94, 129, 130, 131, 134, 135, 153, 155, 160, 170, 173, 176, 178, 179, 192–194, 202, 208, 213, 220–222, 233, 240, 241, 255, 267, 279, 280, 292
House, Tom, 195, 259
Human Performance Technologies, 83
Infield defense, 6, 7, 32, 33, 41, 45, 71, 148, 177, 269, 276
Injuries, 18, 23, 24, 25, 62, 108–109, 110, 111, 113, 115, 116, 118, 158, 173–175, 211, 271, 276, 292
Inner- and other-directed personalities, 200
Internationalization, 225
Jamail, Milton, 227, 232
James, Bill, 39, 113, 143, 144, 148, 211
Japan, 78, 218, 219, 223
Jeter, Derek, 2–6, 8, 14, 17, 34–37, 40, 41, 55, 57, 62, 63, 95, 97, 100, 102, 109, 112, 120, 127, 129, 138, 139, 171, 172, 193, 194, 197–200, 202, 203, 213, 220, 235, 236, 270, 271, 280, 281, 283, 284, 289, 294
 debate over fielding, 34–41
Johnson, Randy, 48, 51–53, 61, 100, 101, 105, 110, 117, 128, 133, 145, 148, 157, 176, 178, 179, 180, 195, 197, 208, 233, 235, 236, 238, 253–264, 271, 283, 292, 295
Kane, Steven, 174
Karl, Scott, 178, 179
Kasparov, Garry, 149
Keefe, John, 264
Kehoskie, Joe, 225
Kim, Byung-Hyun, 105, 116, 129, 209, 223, 254, 283, 294, 297
Knoblauch, Chuck, 135, 220, 236–238, 256, 294
La Russa, Tony, 109, 142, 212
Laban, Rudolf, 28
Larsen, Don, 142–143
Lau, Charley, 78, 79, 85
Lewis, Michael, 197
Linear style of hitting (see “Hitting”)
Luck, 149, 180
Maddox, Elliott, 202
Maddux, Greg, 56, 77, 95, 132, 179, 260
Managers, 94, 108, 109, 136, 139, 144, 145, 147–149, 163, 165, 166, 181, 193, 197–199, 201, 202, 207, 208, 211, 212, 242, 246, 254, 264, 270, 272, 292
 field strategy, 148, 163
 fit of managers and teams, 143, 144
 longevity of managers, 144, 292
 style of managing, 144, 147, 254, 272
Mandelbaum, Michael, 135
Martinez, Pedro, 102, 108, 137, 226
Martinez, Tino, 12, 24, 28, 35, 55, 63, 73, 82, 95, 128, 129, 136, 137, 139, 161, 203, 213, 246, 260, 261, 271, 275, 280
Mattingly, Don, 129
McCarver, Tim, 9, 10, 34, 35, 55, 136, 147, 172, 173, 174, 175, 192, 193
McCracken, Voros , 179, 180
McIlvane, Joe, 257
Melvin, Bob, 164, 283
Mendoza, Ramiro, 161, 208, 243
Michael, Gene, 242
Miller, Damian, 4, 48, 52, 57, 122, 175, 203, 221, 267, 269, 272, 292
Miller, Matt, 197
Minaya, Omar, 224
Moore, Donnie, 240–241
Morgan, Mike, 146, 147, 203, 209, 283, 289
Muller, Richard, 170
Murray, Tricia, 110

Muscles, 112, 115, 200, 213, 218, 222, 241, 244, 260, 264
numbers, 2, 18, 20
small and large, 18–21
slow- and fast-twitch, 30, 83, 86, 87, 236, 238
heavy-weights training, 18–22, 109, 145, 199, 235, 261
imbalanced training, 18–20
Music and athletic performance, 77
Mussina, Mike, 63, 192
Nelson, Jeff, 208, 210, 212
Nervousness, 24, 71, 204, 205, 236, 237
New York Yankees, 10, 11, 35, 62–65, 99, 127, 130, 143, 147, 148, 154, 163, 172, 173, 181, 194, 200–204, 207–208, 220, 224, 225, 236, 238, 239–243, 248, 265–267, 272, 275, 276, 279–281, 289–292
Niekro, Phil, 180
Nomo, Hideo, 147, 219, 225
Nua, Russell, 127, 145, 255
O'Neill, Paul, 7–9, 11, 55, 63, 99, 102, 157, 192–195, 198, 202, 233, 236, 283
family, 194, 198
intensity, 102, 192, 193, 198
One-Hand Fred, 75, 77, 79, 80, 82, 134
OPS (on-base plus slugging percentage), 110, 155, 167, 170
Orza, Gene, 225
Outfield defense, 7, 9, 24, 37, 38
Pace of events in baseball, 45, 53
Palmer, Pete, 165
Panama, 223, 241, 270
Pappas, Arthur, 158
Pettitte, Andy, 108, 112
Phoenix, Ariz., 253, 254
growth of baseball, 61
sprawl, 60
Physics of baseball, 171
Pierre, Juan, 134
Piniella, Lou, 193
Pinker, Steven, 186
Pitch counts, 110–111, 137, 203
Pitch location, 47, 183
Pitches, aerodynamics of, 103–104
cut-fastball, 2, 182, 242–247, 265–268, 270, 273, 277, 280, 282
split-fastball, 2, 3, 5, 12, 18, 46, 48, 53, 57, 73, 82, 100, 101, 103, 109, 117, 119, 120, 129, 130, 132, 135, 156, 160, 161, 168, 182, 203, 210, 220–222, 233, 260
Pitching motion, 3, 103–104, 110, 113–119, 183, 241, 258
Pitching strategy, 95
brushback pitches, 8, 53, 57, 58, 127, 130, 156, 168, 208, 210, 221, 273, 277
getting ahead of hitters, 47, 183
location of pitches (see "Pitch location")
mixing pitches, 98, 137, 161
pitch counts, 110, 137, 203
power pitching, 23, 27, 77, 89, 107, 112, 116, 121, 132, 209, 255, 256, 259
waste pitches, 101, 210
Podres, Johnny, 95, 98
Poole, Bob, 257
Posada, Jorge, 12, 28, 35, 36, 46–49, 52, 55, 57, 58, 63, 70, 71, 73, 82, 97, 111, 112, 122, 133, 135–137, 159, 169, 176, 197, 204, 213, 246, 263, 272, 273, 280, 281
Positional advantage, 224
Positioning, 17, 36, 37, 49, 96, 147, 155, 198
Psychology of competition, 45, 193, 195, 196, 200
anger, 52, 191–193, 197, 261–263
impact of veterans, 63, 146, 148, 193, 204
importance of desire, 61, 93, 193, 196, 197, 198, 201, 258
relative importance of psychological and physical abilities, 93, 133, 135, 195, 196, 235, 237, 238, 261
Purcell, Edward, 171
Pythagorean formula for wins, 148
QuesTec Umpire Information System, 183
Randomness, 149, 170, 171, 178–180
Records, 21, 76, 136, 137, 244, 291, 292
Relief pitching, 116, 129, 148, 177, 209, 211, 212, 254
evolution, 21, 144
closer, 27, 30, 62, 207, 208, 210–212, 239, 240, 242, 244, 254
saves, 176, 177, 239
setup man, 208, 210, 239, 242
Richman, Arthur, 141–143
Riesman, David, 200
Ripken, Cal, 99, 153
Rippley, Steve, 6, 17, 53, 54, 55, 131, 136, 208, 273
Rivera, Mariano, 79, 105, 129, 147, 148, 179, 194, 197, 207, 208, 210, 212, 223, 233, 239, 240–248, 265, 267–271, 273, 274, 277, 280–284, 290
Rizzo, Mike, 266, 282
Robinson, Jackie, 225
Root, Wayne Allyn, 64, 65
Rose, Pete, 69, 93, 119, 155, 175
Rotational style of hitting (see "Hitting")
Ruth, Babe, 62, 75, 77, 79, 141, 173, 194, 202
Ryan, Nolan, 109, 157, 158, 259
Sabermetrics, 154
Sacrifice bunt, 149, 163, 164, 247, 269
Sanders, Reggie, 43, 163, 169
Save statistic, 177
Schilling, Curt, 3–6, 7, 12, 17, 26, 29, 51, 53,

55, 57, 58, 61, 65, 70, 77, 93–100, 102, 103, 105, 122, 127–129, 136, 137, 139, 145, 155, 179, 197, 202, 203, 209, 210, 217, 260, 278, 283, 292
Schmidt, Mike, 79, 81
Scouting, 96, 98, 119, 135, 147, 154, 163, 193, 223–225, 230, 231, 240, 242, 257, 264, 266, 272, 282
Selig, Bud, 208, 209
September 11, 276
Sherlock, Glenn, 233
Showalter, Buck, 60, 142, 144–146, 181, 182, 243, 254
Sinins, Lee, 158
Size, 40, 230, 231, 257
Sliding, 36, 139, 171–175, 259, 270, 271
Smith, Ronald, 196
Society for American Baseball Research (SABR), 154, 173
Sojo, Luis, 139, 223, 231–233, 236, 272
Soriano, Alfonso, 35, 42, 43, 70, 95, 137–139, 155, 156, 175, 209, 210, 217–223, 232, 233, 244, 247, 268, 280, 281, 291
Sounds of hits, 25, 26, 132
Southwick, Larry, 144
Spahn, Warren, 158, 180
Specialization, 197, 208, 211, 212
  designated hitter, 65, 213
  pinch runners, 211
  relief pitching, (see "Relief pitching")
Spencer, Shane, 17, 18, 25–32, 35, 47, 100, 128, 137, 169, 194, 204, 205, 274, 281
Spray charts, 168
Stadium effects, 29, 149, 173, 176
Stanton, Mike, 192, 208, 210, 212, 213, 233
Statistics, 10, 29, 37, 38, 40, 45, 54, 64, 76, 130, 145, 147–149, 153–157, 159, 164–167, 170, 176–179, 181–185, 193, 198, 202, 207, 211, 243, 269, 274, 275
  difficulties gathering good data, 181–183
  futuristic innovations, 183, 185
  growing use, 10, 147, 149, 155, 176, 186, 193, 269
  tallies, 39, 155
  rates, 41, 83, 85, 86, 113, 117, 155, 165, 66, 176
  modern statistical measures, 29, 39, 40, 148, 155, 170, 176–178, 211
Stats Inc., IV, 39, 76, 110, 131, 168, 264
Stealing bases, 9, 50, 147, 149, 154,155, 165–157, 213, 236
Steinbrenner, George, 63, 141, 142, 146, 242, 291
Steiner, Charley, 139, 198, 276
Stengel, Casey, 143
Steroids, 22, 23, 153
Steve Blass Disease, 236, 237
Stottlemyre, Mel, 48, 62, 63, 245
Strategy, 21, 37, 45, 52, 77, 93, 96, 99, 111, 147, 148, 155, 163–165, 173, 176, 177, 217, 266, 280
Streaks and slumps, 170, 171, 191, 199
Tendu, 130, 156, 159, 182, 185
Thin slicing, 84
Tieg, Donald, 83
Tippett, Tom, 180
Torre, Joe, 47, 48, 63, 108, 109, 133, 137, 141–143, 146–149, 161, 198–202, 207–210, 212, 220, 236, 237, 239, 242, 246, 266, 283
Towers, Kevin, 264
Training, 18–25, 31, 32, 61, 71, 80, 84, 87, 93, 94, 107, 129, 132, 135, 137, 138, 144, 145, 182, 183, 185, 200, 205, 220, 224, 232, 237, 243, 248, 272, 289
Triples, 6, 9, 27, 29, 30, 32, 36, 99, 157, 160, 173, 175, 176, 192, 281
Turocy, Theodore, 167
TV broadcast, 63, 182
Umpires, 9, 17, 47, 49, 50, 52–57, 108, 109, 120, 131, 183, 192, 199, 208, 213, 240, 256
  controversial calls, 47, 52–57, 183, 191, 192
  setting tempo of game, 53
  strike zones, 6, 47, 53, 54, 240
  working with catchers (see "Catchers")
Venezuela, 223, 231, 233
Wetteland, John, 208, 212, 239, 240, 242
White, Ken, 64, 87
Williams, Bernie, 12, 19, 103, 112, 119, 134, 135, 169, 171, 200–204
Williams, Matt, 9, 11, 12, 33, 36, 41, 61, 62, 75, 76, 80, 82, 97, 139, 144, 145, 172, 184, 197, 205, 222, 235, 246, 276, 292
Williams, Ted, 76, 78, 79, 85, 93, 153
Wilson, Enrique, 290
Win probability, change in, 40, 64, 148, 164, 177
Win Shares, 39–41
Womack, Tony, 8, 9, 31, 55, 70, 137, 142, 192, 198, 240, 241, 276, 290, 291
World Cup, 218
Yankee Stadium, 65, 128, 137, 142, 192, 198, 240, 241, 276, 290, 291
Yesalis, Charles, 22
Zen, 64, 170, 201
Zheng, Nigel, 115, 224
Zimmer, Don, 193